Mantoloking, New Jersey

Santiago de Cuba

Southampton, New York

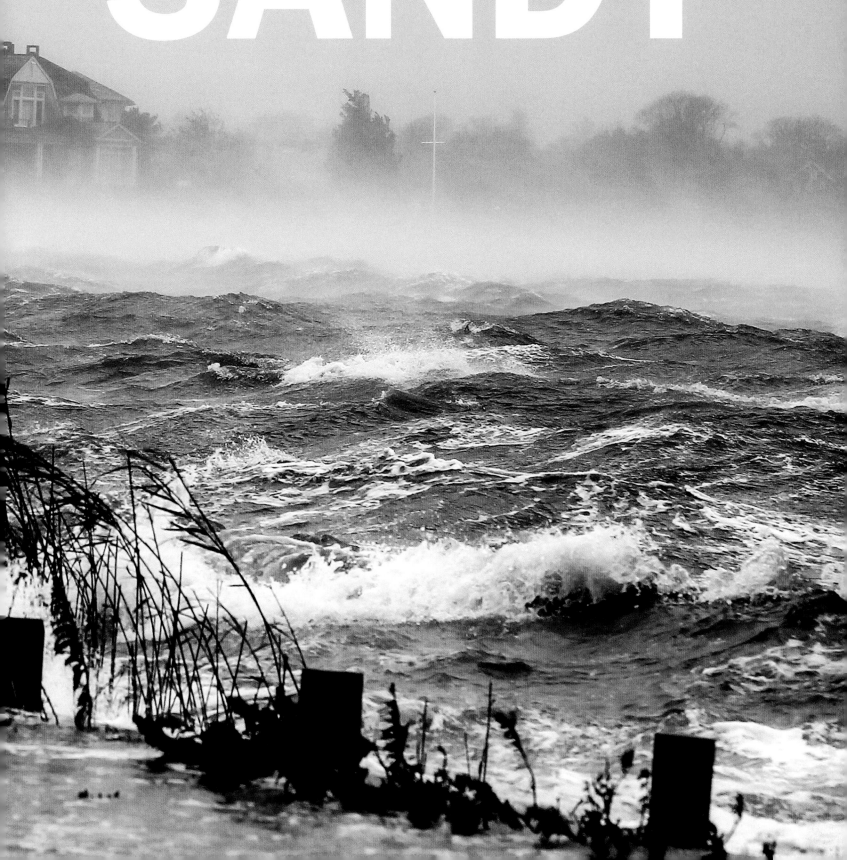

SURVIVING
SANDY

Breezy Point, Queens, New York

Reuters/Lucas Jackson

SURVIVING SANDY

THE SUPERSTORM THAT RESHAPED OUR LIVES

SURVIVING SANDY
THE SUPERSTORM THAT RESHAPED OUR LIVES

Published 2013

Compiled by a committee of Parents & Friends of Pascack Valley Learning Center

Copyright © 2013 Ambient Funding
P.O. Box 395, Tallman, NY 10982-0395

This book is a documentary of the effect of an unprecedented natural phenomenon known as Superstorm Sandy, and the life-altering effect of its widespread destruction.

The publishers wished to assemble a real-life panorama of human experience, from challenges at the highest levels of government to the terrifying experiences of our shore-dwelling neighbors who braved a night of unspeakable trauma and weeks and months of struggle to recover and rebuild.

The book describes how earlier warnings were not taken seriously enough, nor were warnings that immediately preceded the path of the hurricane. Yet no warning could prepare America's East Coast for the horrifying events of October 29-30, 2012.

We do not know when another storm like Sandy may come our way, but we do know that those who survived its raging will definitely take weather more seriously in the future. We trust this book will serve as a silent tutor of preparation, responsibility, courage and hope.

Publisher | Ambient Funding Corporation
Book Design and Production | fourcolorplanet.com
Contributing Writer | Mia Toschi
Copy Editor | Barbara Moroch
Printed and Bound | Craft Print International Ltd

ISBN: 978-0-615-84317-9

www.survivingsandybook.org

A portion of the proceeds from this volume will be donated to organizations providing relief to victims and assisting in the rebuilding.

AP/John Minchillo

ENDPAPER

October 30, 2012
A birdseye view of the devastation
to the shoreline and homes in
Mantoloking, New Jersey.

FLYLEAF SPREAD

October 26, 2012
People wander through debris-strewn
streets after Hurricane Sandy battered
Santiago de Cuba. The Cuban government said that 11 people had been
killed when the storm hurtled across
the island. Most died due to falling
trees and collapsing buildings in the
Santiago de Cuba and neighboring
Guantanamo provinces.

HALF TITLE SPREAD

October 29, 2012
Water driven onto a roadway by
Superstorm Sandy breaks over a safety
barrier in Southampton, New York.

TITLE SPREAD

December 27, 2012
Clouds roll over destroyed
homes, almost two months after
Superstorm Sandy devastated the
Breezy Point region of the
Queens borough of New York.

THIS SPREAD

October 29, 2012
Sea water floods the Ground Zero
construction site in New York. Sandy
forced the shutdown of mass transit,
schools and financial markets,
sending coastal residents fleeing,
and threatening a dangerous mix of
high winds and torrential rain.

PUBLISHER'S NOTE

he students, faculty, directors, and parents and friends of the Pascack Valley Learning Center in Airmont, New York, wish to convey their gratitude to all who gave so much to create this amazing publication called Surviving Sandy. After countless hours of volunteer work by students, parents, and friends of the school – collecting stories, doing research, and assembling pictures – this premium documentary has been published by Pascack Valley Learning Center's charitable fundraising arm: Ambient Funding. A portion of the proceeds from the sale of this work will be donated to the charities supporting the ongoing recovery and rebuilding operations.

It is at once a scholarly work, and a gripping narrative – a compendium of contributions from men and women, boys and girls, government officials and private citizens; those who received, and those who gave so generously and unselfishly. Words fail us in thanking those who contributed to Surviving Sandy.

This book weaves a rich fabric of personal experiences – both triumph and tragedy. It has been contributed to by so many – those who spoke and those who listened, those who sought and those who were found. We are assured it will be read and appreciated by all.

"Courage is resistance to fear, mastery of fear, not absence of fear."
— Mark Twain

THE CASINO PIER: Once so tall, now so small. The amusement pier in Seaside Heights, New Jersey before (BELOW) and after Sandy's wrath.

"Do not underestimate this storm ...
They are talking about surges we have not seen before,"
Gov. Cuomo warned at a morning briefing on Oct. 29, 2012.

FOREWORD

October 28, 2012 Standing on the beach overlooking the Atlantic Ocean as sand blows at his feet, Charles McAleer of Berlin, Maryland, surveys the storm effects from Hurricane Sandy, which has yet to arrive in the region.

Sandy, the Superstorm that roared up the East Coast of America and barreled ashore on the coasts of New York and New Jersey, was unprecedented in its mass and severity. Over the span of a few hours, millions of dollars of damage were done, scores of people lost their lives, and land and lives were reshaped forever.

In the face of this challenge, Americans did what they do best; they helped one another. From the valiant first-responders who risked their lives to save others, to the dedicated public servants who worked for days with little rest, to the charity organizations who provided food and shelter, Superstorm Sandy, although devastating, brought to light once again the resilience and faith of our great nation.

Following this devastation, students, faculty, parents, and friends of the Pascack Valley Learning Center sought an opportunity to raise funds for charities supporting the recovery and rebuilding operations.

A bake sale, originally intended to raise funds for the school was unselfishly converted, by the students, into a fundraiser and clothing drive for the Sandy victims. A check for $2,800 and clothing and other items valued at over $4,000 were donated to those suffering privation.

One of Sterling's sister schools in Australia had raised substantial funds there for the organizations connected with search and rescue missions during the "Black Friday" Victoria bush fires in 2009, and the Queensland floods in 2010.

Pascack Valley Learning Center saw the opportunity for a similar charitable outreach by publishing a book documenting the Superstorm and the challenges faced by government agencies and private citizens alike in preparing for, surviving, and recovering from the havoc it caused.

This book documents in a unique way the trials of those days, from scholarly reviews of the weather patterns that contributed to this meteorological monster, to poignant tales of personal rescue and survival. This book will serve to inform and warn generations to come that nature must be taken seriously.

CONT

October 30, 2012 As Sandy moves inland, waves pound a lighthouse on the shores of Lake Erie, near Cleveland, Ohio. High winds spinning off the edge of Superstorm Sandy took a vicious swipe at northeast Ohio early Tuesday, uprooting trees, cutting power to hundreds of thousands, closing schools and flooding parts of major commuter arteries that run along Lake Erie.

AP/Tony Dejak

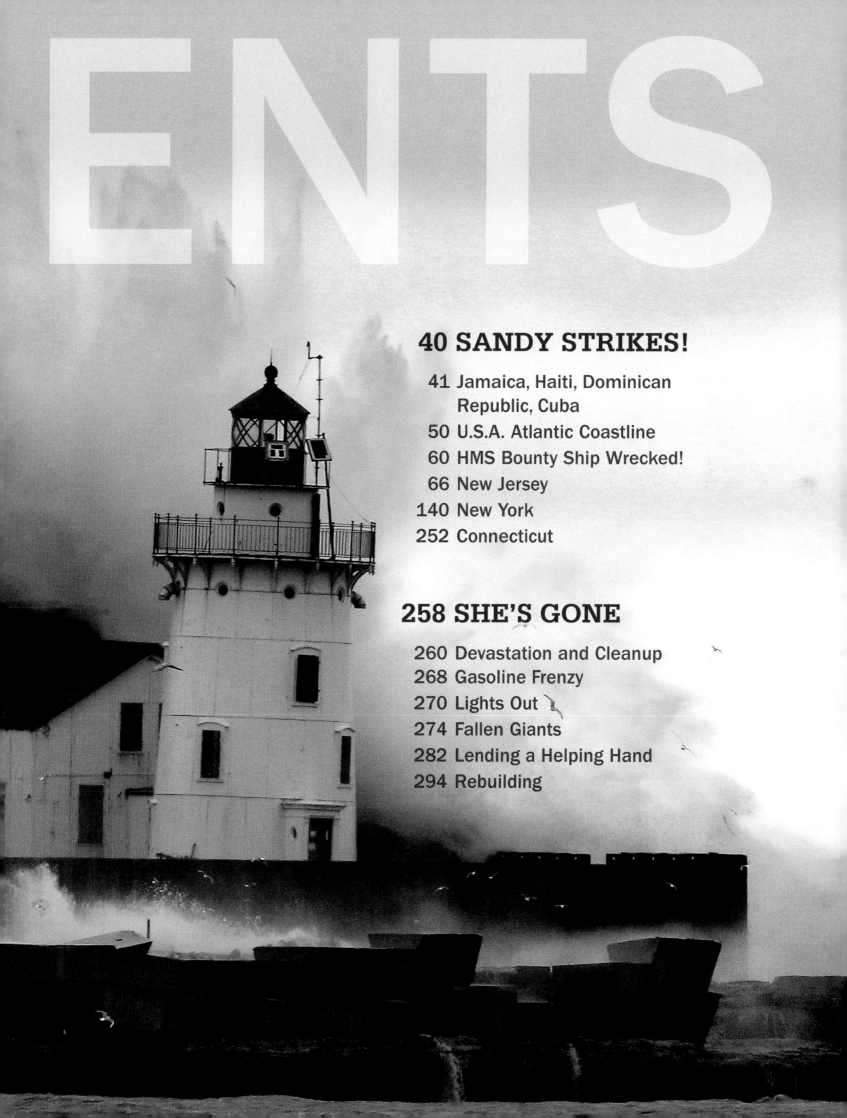

ENTS

SANDY
IS BORN

Sandy was born a tropical depression the morning of October 22 in the Caribbean Sea, just north of the Isthmus of Panama. After turning south late on the 22nd, it started on its northward path on the 23rd, crossing Jamaica on October 24th as a Category 1 Hurricane, proceeding across eastern Cuba on October 25th as a Category 2 Hurricane, and then dropping back to Category 1 late on the 25th. By this time, heading due north through the Bahamas Islands, Sandy was being viewed by meteorologists as a possible but remote threat to the northeastern seaboard of the United States. By the morning of October 27, Sandy began a turn to the northeast, a typical track of most Atlantic Basin hurricanes as they reach more northerly latitudes (30-35 degrees north). In spite of this turn, the threat to the NE Coast became more real as various conditions in the atmosphere began to develop that would alter Sandy's path. On Monday morning, October 29th, these conditions caused Hurricane Sandy to make a left turn, putting it on a path perpendicular to the coast, where it made landfall about 8pm just south of Atlantic City, New Jersey.

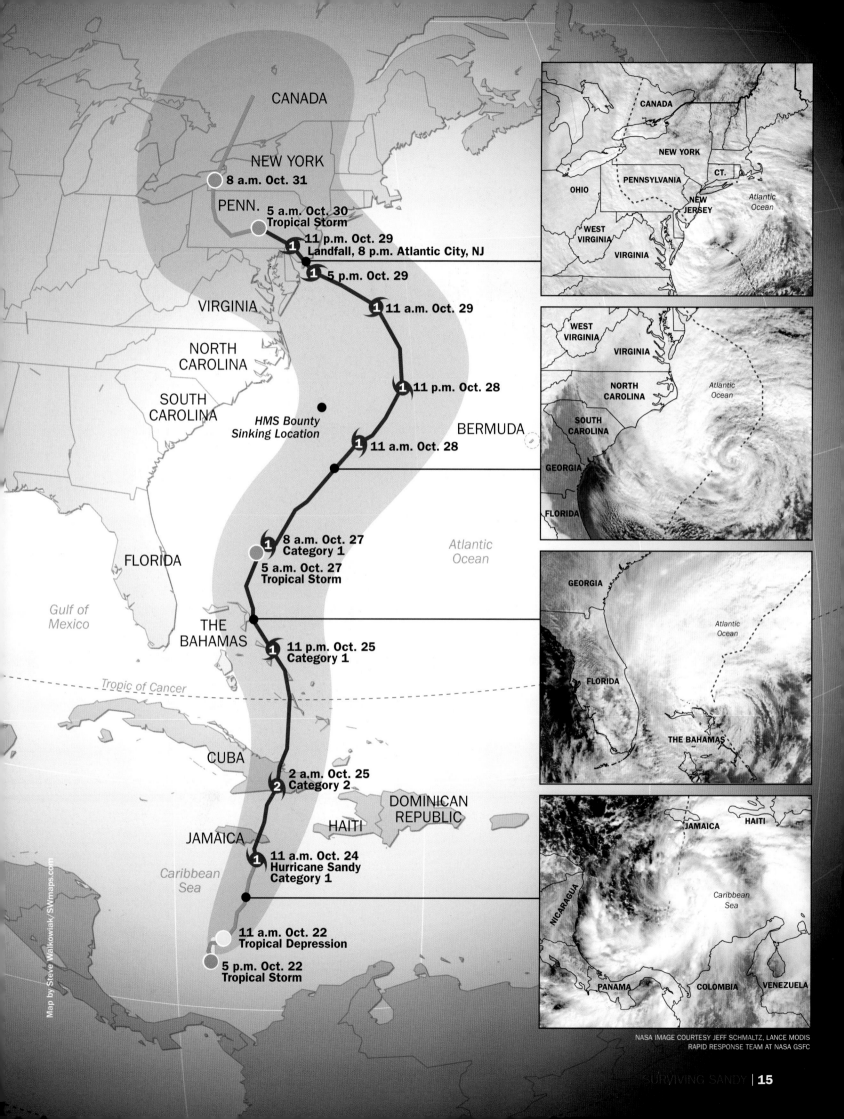

CANADA

NEW YORK
8 a.m. Oct. 31

PENN.
5 a.m. Oct. 30
Tropical Storm

11 p.m. Oct. 29
Landfall, 8 p.m. Atlantic City, NJ

5 p.m. Oct. 29

11 a.m. Oct. 29

VIRGINIA

NORTH
CAROLINA

11 p.m. Oct. 28

SOUTH
CAROLINA

HMS Bounty
Sinking Location

11 a.m. Oct. 28

BERMUDA

FLORIDA

8 a.m. Oct. 27
Category 1

5 a.m. Oct. 27
Tropical Storm

Atlantic
Ocean

Gulf of
Mexico

THE
BAHAMAS

11 p.m. Oct. 25
Category 1

Tropic of Cancer

CUBA

2 a.m. Oct. 25
Category 2

DOMINICAN
REPUBLIC

HAITI

JAMAICA

11 a.m. Oct. 24
Hurricane Sandy
Category 1

Caribbean
Sea

11 a.m. Oct. 22
Tropical Depression

5 p.m. Oct. 22
Tropical Storm

Map by Steve Walkowiak/SWmaps.com

CANADA

NEW YORK

OHIO

PENNSYLVANIA

NEW
JERSEY

CT.

Atlantic
Ocean

WEST
VIRGINIA

VIRGINIA

WEST
VIRGINIA

VIRGINIA

NORTH
CAROLINA

Atlantic
Ocean

SOUTH
CAROLINA

GEORGIA

FLORIDA

GEORGIA

FLORIDA

Atlantic
Ocean

THE BAHAMAS

JAMAICA

HAITI

NICARAGUA

PANAMA

COLOMBIA

VENEZUELA

Caribbean
Sea

NASA IMAGE COURTESY JEFF SCHMALTZ, LANCE MODIS
RAPID RESPONSE TEAM AT NASA GSFC

SURVIVING SANDY | 15

HURRICANES

THE MOST POWERFUL AND DEVASTATING STORMS ON EARTH

JETSTREAM

WARM WATER

H

TRADE WINDS

PRIME INGREDIENTS FOR TROPICAL DEVELOPMENT

AccuWeather.com

AccuWeather

The word **"hurricane"** is derived from the Spanish word, huracan. In turn, the word huracan probably came from Hunraken, the Mayan storm god, or Hurakan, the Quiche god of thunder and lightning, or any of a number of other Caribbean Indian terms for evil spirits or big winds. Although the word was originally used to describe any localized tropical cyclone in the West Indies, it now classifies the powerful tropical cyclones that develop in the North Atlantic Ocean, the Gulf of Mexico, the Caribbean Sea, or the eastern North Pacific Ocean, east of the International Dateline and north of the equator. "Tropical cyclone" is a generic term for low-pressure systems with a defined wind circulation, born over tropical, or sometimes subtrop-

ical waters. About every four to five days, a tropical wave of low pressure moves along with westerly winds. Some of these waves develop into tropical depressions, tropical storms, and hurricanes. In developing tropical cyclones, strong thunderstorms occur. Air pressure drops at the surface of these storms. This low pressure attracts warm moist air from the ocean's surface. The Coriolis force causes the resulting low-level winds to spiral in a counter-clockwise direction around the center of the low in the Northern Hemisphere. (Winds swirl clockwise in the Southern Hemisphere.) Typically, an "eye" forms when the tropical cyclone reaches hurricane strength, but an eye is not necessary for a tropical cyclone to become a hurricane.

(ABOVE) Marshall Moss, VP-Forecasting (standing left), and Henry Margusity, Severe Weather Expert (standing center), discuss Hurricane Sandy's track with fellow meteorologists at the Accu-Weather Forecast Center. (RIGHT) **October 29, 2012** Branch Chief of the Hurricane Specialists Unit James Franklin looks at monitors showing Hurricane Sandy at the National Hurricane Center.

THE SAFFIR-SIMPSON HURRICANE SCALE

This scale was developed in the early 1970s by Herbert Saffir, a consulting engineer in Coral Gables, Florida, and Dr. Robert Simpson, then director of the National Hurricane Center. The scale is based primarily on wind speeds and includes estimates of barometric pressure and storm surge associated with each of the five categories. It is used to give an estimate of the potential property damage and flooding expected along the coast from a hurricane landfall.

CATEGORY	SUSTAINED WINDS	TYPES OF DAMAGE DUE TO HURRICANE WINDS
1	74-95 mph 64-82 kt 119-153 km/h	**Very dangerous winds will produce some damage:** Well-constructed frame homes could have damage to roof, shingles, vinyl siding and gutters. Large branches of trees will snap and shallowly rooted trees may be toppled. Extensive damage to power lines and poles likely will result in power outages that could last a few to several days.
2	96-110 mph 83-95 kt 154-177 km/h	**Extremely dangerous winds will cause extensive damage:** Well-constructed frame homes could sustain major roof and siding damage. Many shallowly rooted trees will be snapped or uprooted and block numerous roads. Near-total power loss is expected with outages that could last from several days to weeks.
3 MAJOR	111-129 mph 96-112 kt 178-208 km/h	**Devastating damage will occur:** Well-built framed homes may incur major damage or removal of roof decking and gable ends. Many trees will be snapped or uprooted, blocking numerous roads. Electricity and water will be unavailable for several days to weeks after the storm passes.
4 MAJOR	130-156 mph 113-136 kt 209-251 km/h	**Catastrophic damage will occur:** Well-built framed homes can sustain severe damage with loss of most of the roof structure and/or some exterior walls. Most trees will be snapped or uprooted and power poles downed. Fallen trees and power poles will isolate residential areas. Power outages will last weeks to possibly months. Most of the area will be uninhabitable for weeks or months.
5 MAJOR	157 mph or higher 137 kt or higher 252 km/h or higher	**Catastrophic damage will occur:** A high percentage of framed homes will be destroyed, with total roof failure and wall collapse. Fallen trees and power poles will isolate residential areas. Power outages will last for weeks to possibly months. Most of the area will be uninhabitable for weeks or months.

Information from the Weather Channel Storm Encyclopedia and the National Hurricane Center

HOW SANDY MEASURES UP

COMPARING THE WINDS OF SANDY AND KATRINA

The scenes of devastation and wreckage that Hurricanes Sandy (2012) and Katrina (2005) left behind were tragically similar. Both storms flooded major cities, cut electric power to millions, and tore apart densely populated coastlines. But from a meteorological perspective the storms were very different. Katrina was a textbook tropical cyclone, with a compact, symmetrical wind field that whipped around a circular low-pressure center. Like most tropical cyclones, Katrina was a warm-core storm that drew its energy from the warm waters of the tropical Atlantic Ocean. Sandy had similar characteristics while it was blowing through the tropics. But as the storm moved northward, it merged with a weather system arriving from the west and started transitioning into an extra-tropical cyclone. The names sound similar, however there are fundamental differences between the two types of storms. While tropical cyclones draw their energy from warm ocean waters, extra-tropical cyclones are fueled by sharp temperature contrasts between masses of warm and cool air. Extra-tropical cyclones also tend to be asymmetric, with broad wind and cloud fields shaped more like commas than circles. So when tropical cyclones become extra-tropical, their wind and cloud fields expand dramatically. Their strongest winds generally weaken during this process, but occasionally a transitioning storm retains hurricane force winds, as was the case with Sandy. A pair of wind maps illustrate some of the differences. A map of Sandy's winds produced with data from a radar scatterometer on the Indian Space Research Organization's (ISRO) Oceansat-2, showed the strength and direction of Sandy's ocean surface winds on October 28, 2012. A map of Hurricane Katrina's winds was made from similar data acquired on August 28, 2005, by a radar scatterometer on NASA's retired Quick-SCAT satellite.

SANDY'S WINDS PRODUCED WITH DATA FROM A RADAR SCATTEROMETER ON OCEANSAT-2

HURRICANE KATRINA'S WINDS WERE PRODUCED FROM DATA ACQUIRED ON AUGUST 28, 2005, BY NASA'S RETIRED QUICKSCAT SATELLITE.

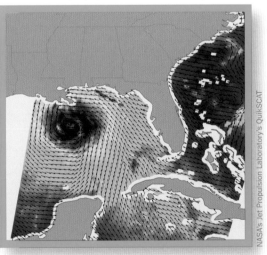

Indian Space Research Organization OceanSat-2 missions.

NASA's Jet Propulsion Laboratory's QuikSCAT

Wind speeds above 65 kilometers (40 miles) per hour are yellow; above 80 kph (50 mph) are orange; and above 95 kph (60 mph) are dark red.

Data courtesy of the Jet Propulsion Laboratory's QuikSCAT and the Indian Space Research Organization OceanSat-2 missions. Jenni Evans, Bryan Stiles, Brian McNoldy, and Alexander Fore contributed to this feature. Adam Voiland, NASA's Earth Observatory. Courtesy of nasa.gov

Hurricane Sandy was a late storm in the hurricane season; Storms that form in this period are typically larger in size (but lower in wind speed) due to the greater temperature difference between the air (which is cooler) and the Gulf Stream waters (still quite warm) which the storm followed up the coast. While it was only a Category 1 storm at landfall, the sheer size of Sandy created an IKE equivalent to more than two of the 16 Kiloton (67 Terajoules) atom bombs dropped on Hiroshima. In addition, the destructive power of the storm surge was the equivalent to an EF3 tornado and the colliding of waves with other waves when Sandy turned to the northwest registered approximately 2-3 on seismographs as far away as Seattle.

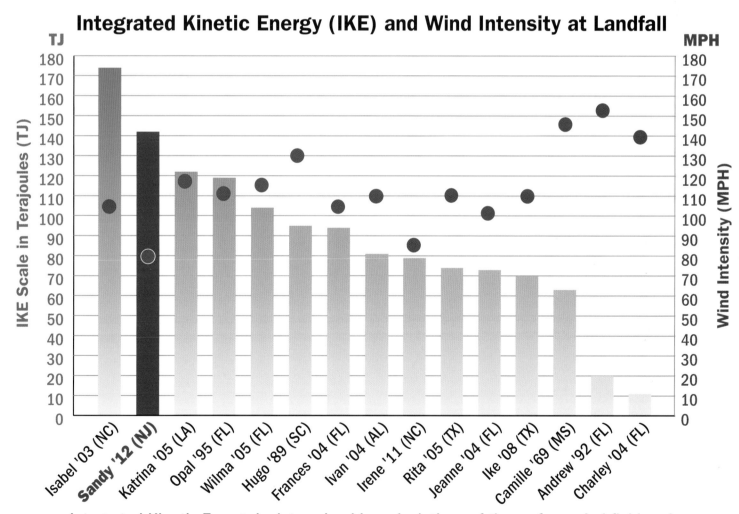

Integrated Kinetic Energy (IKE) and Wind Intensity at Landfall

Integrated Kinetic Energy is determined by calculations of the surface wind field and the wind's effect on the storm surge and waves and their destructive potential.

SUPERSTORM

HURRICANE SANDY
October 28, 2012
The Geostationary Operational Environmental Satellite 13 captured this natural-color image of the superstorm at 1:45 pm Eastern Daylight Time (17:45 Universal Time).

NASA Earth Observatory image by Robert Simmon with data courtesy of the NASA/NOAA GOES Project Science team.

COLD FRONT

PATH OF SANDY

EYE OF SANDY

WARM OCEAN

WARM OCEAN

WARM OCEAN

SANDY!

H
GREENLAND HIGH

L
SECONDARY LOW

SANDY, A STORM THAT UNCHARAC- TERISTICALLY STRENGTHENED AS IT MOVED NORTHWARD, WAS QUICKLY MORPHING INTO A SUPERSTORM.

With Sandy moving toward the Eastern Seaboard and Halloween approaching, predictions became more certain that this was indeed going to be a monster. Media outlets were quick to attach other appellations to this storm such as FRANKENSTORM, BLIZZACANE, and NOREASTERCANE.

How did Sandy become a superstorm?

Key ingredients combined to create this "perfect" storm:

> Gulf Stream water temperatures were 5° above normal
> A "Nor'easter" was absorbed into the storm, further strengthening Sandy
> Landfall occurred at the astronomical high tide
> A strong high pressure system set up south of Green- land, blocking northward progression of the storm
> Sandy was caught in a "negative tilt" of the jetstream, pulling it toward the coast of New Jersey
> A stalled cold front over the Appalachians contributed to significant temperature differences in the storm

With historic low pressure of 940 millibars, winds reaching 90 mph and a forward speed between 25 and 28 mph, this storm literally slammed into the New Jersey coast. The New Jersey coastline, running northeast to southwest, as well as the south-facing coast of Long Island, created the perfect set-up for maximum storm surge. Storm surge heights were as high as 10' above normal high tide levels where the storm's eye made landfall and to the northeast of the eye all the way up through central Long Island. These heights were accen- tuated at harbors, inlets and river mouths by the funnel- ing effect of the adjacent land masses. New York Harbor, including Lower Manhattan, Staten Island, Brooklyn and portions of metro New Jersey, also saw unbelievable surges. The eastern end of Long Island and the far south coast of New Jersey largely escaped the worst of the surge simply because they fell outside the range of the main surge area.

The storm surge itself was historic due to a near perfect combination of factors; Namely, extremely low central pressure causing a dome of water to rise under the storm (much like the moon's pull on the oceans), landfall occurring at the time of astronomical full-moon high tide, and rapid forward movement of the storm itself. This, combined with a very strong northeasterly wind which pushed the water up onshore, resulted in devastating storm surge flooding.

A TURN FOR THE WORST

WHAT CAUSED SANDY TO TURN INTO THE COASTLINE?

Firstly, an abnormally strong high pressure system set up just south of Greenland resulting in a blocking high pressure air mass which occurred as Sandy moved north. High pressure systems have a clockwise wind rotation circulating out from the center. This creates a blocking effect and hinders the forward motion of low pressure systems such as Sandy that are travelling northeast. Contrary to highs, low pressure systems have a counterclockwise wind rotation that circulates into the center. Another low pressure system blocked movement to the east and out to sea. Secondly, the lack of any effect from the Pacific Ocean due to neutral El-Nino/La-Nina conditions which usually force the jet stream (high altitude steering winds) to the north allowed the jet stream to dip down lower in the U.S. At the time of Hurricane Sandy, the jet stream dipped down bringing a cold front which stalled across the Appalachians west of the coast. If this cold front had continued out into the Atlantic it would no doubt have pushed Sandy offshore. Super high winds embedded in the jet stream (a band of strong west-to-east winds in the upper atmosphere) pushed the "trough" of the jetstream into what is known as a negative tilt, wrapping it under and around Sandy and effectively pulling it towards the northwest and into the coast.

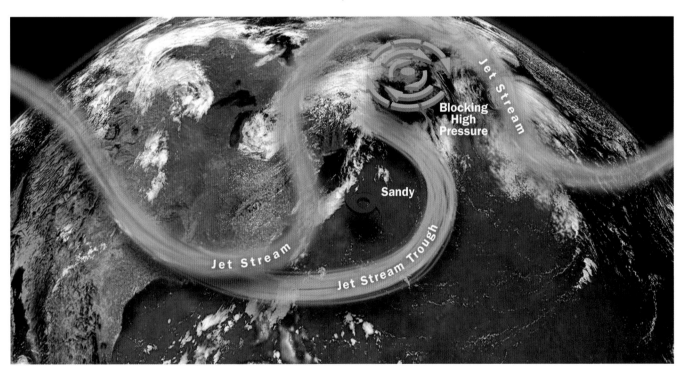

Map showing the Greenland High and the negative tilt of the Jet Stream (high level steering winds) that drew Sandy northwest to the coast

IMPACT OF HURRICANE SANDY

Data as of Friday, Nov. 2, 2012

- Killed **98**
- Refineries shut **3**
- Pipelines/ ports shut **14**
- Current outages **4.4 mln**
- People living at Red Cross shelters **8,357**
- Areas declared in state of major disaster by FEMA

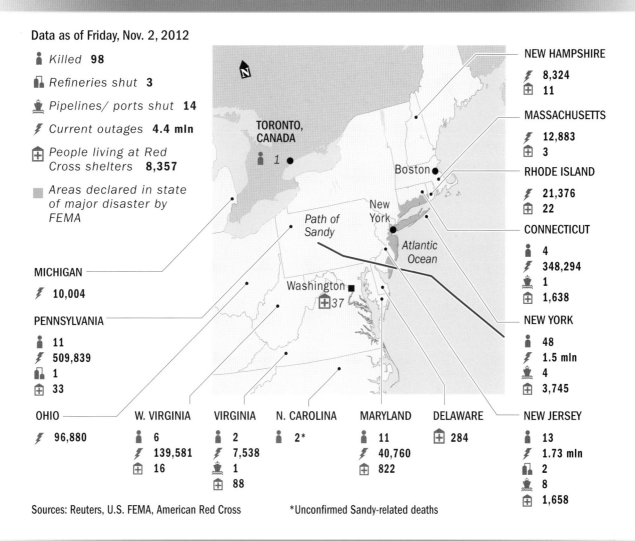

TORONTO, CANADA — 1

Path of Sandy

New York

Boston

Atlantic Ocean

Washington — 37

MICHIGAN
- 10,004

PENNSYLVANIA
- 11
- 509,839
- 1
- 33

OHIO
- 96,880

W. VIRGINIA
- 6
- 139,581
- 16

VIRGINIA
- 2
- 7,538
- 1
- 88

N. CAROLINA
- 2*

MARYLAND
- 11
- 40,760
- 822

DELAWARE
- 284

NEW HAMPSHIRE
- 8,324
- 11

MASSACHUSETTS
- 12,883
- 3

RHODE ISLAND
- 21,376
- 22

CONNECTICUT
- 4
- 348,294
- 1
- 1,638

NEW YORK
- 48
- 1.5 mln
- 4
- 3,745

NEW JERSEY
- 13
- 1.73 mln
- 2
- 8
- 1,658

Sources: Reuters, U.S. FEMA, American Red Cross   *Unconfirmed Sandy-related deaths

HURRICANE SANDY—BY THE NUMBERS

IMPACTS	WINDS	RAIN	SNOW	RECORD PRESSURE	WAVES/SURGE
7.5 million without Power	Eatons Neck, NY 94 mph	Andrews AFB, MD 15.3" (unconfirmed)	Redhouse, MD 29"	Atlantic City, NJ 948.3mb (28.00"Hg)	**TOP WAVES**
Over 100 killed	Montclair, NJ 88 mph	Easton, MD 12.55"	Clayton, WV 33.0"	Philadelphia, PA 953mb (28.23"Hg)	39.67 feet 500 miles southeast of Atlantic City, NJ
Many towns destroyed	Westerly, RI 86 mph	Wildwood Crest, NJ 11.67"	Champion, PA 13"	Harrisburg, PA 963mb (28.46"Hg)	32.5 feet just outside New York Harbor entrance
Jersey Coast changed	Madison, CT 85 mph	Virginia Beach, VA 9.57"	Haywood County, NC 24"	Scranton, PA 971mb (28.69"Hg)	21.7 feet lower Lake Michigan
Thousands of trees down	Cuttyhunk, MA 83 mph	Milford, DE 9.55"	Norton, VA 24"	Trenton, NJ 958mb (28.31"Hg)	**TOP STORM SURGES**
Massive coastal flooding	Allentown, PA 81 mph	Maysville, WV 7.75"	Mt. Leconte, TN 34"	Baltimore, MD 965mb (28.49"Hg)	The Battery, NY ~9 feet above normal
	Highland Beach, MD 79 mph		Payne Gap, KY 14"	Harrisburg, PA 964mb (28.46"Hg)	Kings Point, NY ~12.5 feet above normal
	Chester Gap, VA 79 mph		Bellefontaine, OH 3.5"		New Haven, CT ~9 feet above normal

(TOP GRAPHIC) Reference from Reuters/G. Cabrera, 11/2/2012

NE L

MARKS

October 28, 2012 A Grand Central Station display board broadcasts the closure of the commuter rail and subway service in New York as the MTA gets ready for Hurricane Sandy.

Timothy A. Clary/AFP/Getty Images

THE EAST COAST BRACES FOR SANDY

INFORMATION

ATTENTION CUSTOMERS
DUE TO THE PENDING STORM
METRO-NORTH RR WILL SHUT DOWN
SERVICE AT 7PM TONIGHT
YOU ARE ADVISED TO LEAVE
BEFORE 7PM TO GET TO YOUR HOMES

ELECTIONS

(BELOW) **October 28, 2012** President Barack Obama at a Hurricane Sandy briefing at the Federal Emergency Management Agency (FEMA) headquarters in Washington, DC.

DAYS BEFORE THE PRESIDENTIAL ELECTION, OBAMA AND ROMNEY SCRAMBLE TO BALANCE HURRICANE RESPONSE WITH CAMPAIGN EFFORTS.

President Barack Obama spent months prior to the arrival of Sandy balancing the responsibilities of the Presidency and campaigning for re-election. With the approach of Hurricane Sandy looming, and realizing that any slip-ups in preparation would fall squarely on his shoulders, President Obama altered his schedule and scrapped campaign events in the days leading up to the storm. He returned to Washington to monitor Sandy's developments and deploy aid to the devastated areas. "My first priority has to be making sure that everything is in place," Obama told campaign employees. With just days before the elections, Obama's response would be a significant factor in swaying undecided voters. Any mistakes would portray him as placing politics before the public, but a swift response would highlight Obama's leadership and increase his chances for re-election. After Sandy charged up the Eastern Seaboard, Obama sprang into action. He flew to the devastated areas and personally comforted the victims earning him the title Comforter-In-Chief. He delivered encouraging words to first responders and ordered FEMA to "cut red tape" to expedite aid, receiving praise from all parties. Independent NYC Mayor Bloomberg endorsed Obama and Chris Christie (R-Gov.) publicly referred to Obama's response as "outstanding," "incredibly supportive" and deserving "great credit."

October 29, 2012 U.S. President Barack Obama makes a statement in the White House briefing room in Washington, DC following an update on Hurricane Sandy.

(ABOVE) Reuters/Jonathan Ernst, (LEFT) Brendan Hoffman/Getty Images

(ABOVE AND RIGHT) Justin Sullivan/Getty Images

With the Superstorm nearing landfall on the East Coast, Republican challenger Mitt Romney was also confronted with the challenge of balancing his campaign efforts and hurricane response participation. The race was a dead heat and little time remained to sway undecided voters. Romney decided to cancel three campaign stops in Virginia, and instead join running mate Paul Ryan at his events. This gave him flexibility and the opportunity to leave the campaign trail and aid the response forces in a moment's notice. After Sandy's fury was unleashed, Romney held a Storm Relief Event in swing-state Ohio, which was originally scheduled to be a campaign rally. The time was pushed up four hours and the tone of the occasion was altered to focus on recovery rather than confronting Obama. Many political analysts claim that Romney's response was weak, and dashed his chances for election. He drew criticism from fellow Republican Chris Christie, the popular governor of hard hit New Jersey, mainly fueled by the failure to call him and express empathy and support. Romney would later credit the hurricane for Obama's re-election stating that, "Sandy made Obama look presidential and understanding," a view shared by many.

October 30, 2012 (TOP) During a Kettering Storm Relief event in Kettering, Ohio, former Massachusetts governor and Republican presidential candidate Mitt Romney assists in loading a truck with relief provisions that will be transported to storm damaged areas in New Jersey. (ABOVE RIGHT) **October 29, 2012** Mitt Romney during a pensive moment, looking out the window of his campaign plane en route to Moline, Illinois.

NEW JERSEY PREPARES

October 27, 2012
The Mae West Hotel in Cape May, New Jersey, is boarded up by Bob Grabenstetter, Paul Young and Mike Kern as they prepare for Hurricane Sandy's arrival.

October 28, 2012 (OPPOSITE, TOP TO BOTTOM) Across from One World Trade Center, workers sandbag the outside of the Exchange Place PATH station, which is situated in a susceptible part of New Jersey; A sand barrier is created on the Cape May beach to help prevent storm surge from the impending Hurricane Sandy; The Trump Casino announces its closing as Hurricane Sandy barrels toward Atlantic City.

William Thomas Cain/Getty Images

AS SANDY DASHES TOWARD THE NEW JERSEY COAST, HOW WILL RESIDENTS RESPOND?

As Hurricane Sandy hurtled towards the Eastern Seaboard, New Jersey Governor Chris Christie declared a State of Emergency on the morning of Saturday, October 27th. The residents of New Jersey were rapidly preparing in anticipation of the arrival of Category 1 Sandy, predicted to make landfall on Monday, October 29th. The predictions were dire, warning of unprecedented flooding due to a high tide coupled with a record-breaking storm surge, and heavy rainfall likely to last for more than 20 hours. Residents boarded up their homes and prepared to evacuate. Government workers mounded sand high on the beaches with huge loaders, attempting to block the storm surge from pushing inland. Even the famous Atlantic City casinos closed their doors. Would this be enough? Officials were doing their best to impress the severity of the storm on New Jersey residents, and the Governor pleaded with people to heed the mandatory evacuation orders issued for the public's safety. Once the storm hit, there was no guarantee that rescuers could reach the residents if their safety was in jeopardy. A chief concern was the Raritan Bay area, and mandatory evacuations were in place for residents of the bay's southern coast before Sandy arrived. The majority of school districts (350 of the 590 total) were ordered to close for Monday, many of which stayed shut for the remainder of the week. The New Jersey mass transit system was suspended. When Superstorm Sandy finally arrived on Monday evening, it became clear that any precautions that had been taken were undeniably essential.

October 27, 2012 (ABOVE) Edward Dickson, Director of the New Jersey Office of Homeland Security and Preparedness, left, and Governor Chris Christie, right, take note as Robert M. Hanna, President of the N.J. Board of Public Utilities, speaks to a gathering in North Wildwood, as they set out preparation strategies.

NEW YORK PREPARES

October 28, 2012 Benny the dog observes as his master Fred of Long Beach, NY, fills sandbags in preparation for Hurricane Sandy's approach.

(BELOW LEFT TO RIGHT) A lower Manhattan Starbucks has water bags outside the door to protect it; People flock to a Rockaway Beach hardware store to prepare as Hurricane Sandy approaches the Queens borough neighborhood.

October 27, 2012 During a press conference, Mayor Michael Bloomberg updates New York City residents on preparations made for the arrival of Hurricane Sandy.

(TOP TO BOTTOM) Edward Reed/NYC Mayors Office/Getty Images, Don Emmert/AFP/Getty Images, AP/Craig Ruttle, (FAR RIGHT)Scott Eelis/Bloomberg/Getty Images

COLLECTIVE VIGILANCE WAS KEY TO WEATHERING THE STORM IN THE BIG APPLE.

With Sandy rushing towards them, the residents of New York prepared to protect themselves from the immense storm. New York was well in the danger zone of Superstorm Sandy as she headed up the East Coast, and New Yorkers were warned that the storm was severe. The NYC Coastal Storm Plan was in place and city officials sought to take every precaution possible. Sandbags surrounded buildings and lines backed up at stores as residents rushed to get essentials and equipment to hunker down. Mayor Michael Bloomberg urged employers in New York City to allow employees who were not involved in shelter or first response to get home quickly for their safety. Mandatory evacuations were issued for residents in the coastal towns, and schools in New York City were ordered to be closed on Monday and Tuesday. The water levels were expected to remain at dangerously high levels for over 24 hours, forcing many roads to close. Manhattan residents were very vigilant as they anticipated that the Hudson and East Rivers could meet at high tide.

October 29, 2012 (ABOVE) Flights are cancelled one after the other at New York City's La Guardia airport. (ABOVE LEFT) A Stelter's Marine worker on City Island cleans the bottom of a boat that is being hauled out of the water before Sandy's arrival. (LEFT) A maintenance worker in lower Manhattan covers a sidewalk grate at the 2 Broadway building while a child takes the opportunity to use it as a temporary new play structure.

NEW YORK MTA PREPARES

October 26, 2012 Metropolitan Transit Authority (MTA) workers lay down plywood over subway grates at the Staten Island Ferry Terminal to prevent flooding in New York. (BELOW, LEFT TO RIGHT) Entrance to Bowling Green Station in New York is boarded with plywood and sandbags. October 28, 2012 An MTA employee tapes off the turnstiles to bar access to the New York City subway.

(TOP) Peter Foley/Bloomberg/Getty Images.
(BOTTOM LEFT TO RIGHT) MTA Photo, Reuters/Carlo Allegri

LONG KNOWN FOR KEEPING NEW YORK CITY MOVING, THE MTA SHUTS IT ALL DOWN FOR HURRICANE SANDY.

The Metropolitan Transportation **Authority** runs the subways, buses, commuter railroads, bridges and tunnels that keep the New York City metropolitan area moving – but the MTA prepared for Sandy by shutting it all down. At the direction of Governor Andrew Cuomo, MTA crews parked all their subway cars and commuter trains on high ground, protected low-lying infrastructure with sandbags and plywood, parked buses in protected depots and shut down tunnels under the East River.

MTA experts had studied the potential for a devastating hurricane for years. Experts had warned that rising sea levels could leave tunnels under the East River and train yards near the coastline vulnerable to flooding. The MTA had started planning for long-term adaptations, and had taken steps to protect some subway openings. But New York had never faced a storm like Sandy.

Subways and commuter trains stopped running at 7 p.m. Sunday, October 28, to give crews time to store safely all their operating equipment, then get themselves to safety. The Hugh L. Carey and Queens-Midtown tunnels shut down Monday afternoon. On a normal weekday, the MTA carries 8.5 million passengers on its mass transit network and almost 800,000 vehicles at its seven bridges and two tunnels. But as Sandy bore down, New York's transportation network shut down.

October 29, 2012 (LEFT COLUMN, TOP AND MIDDLE) MTA New York City Transit prepares for flooding at the Lenox Terminal @ 148th Street; Riverdale station of Metro-North sign informing that railroad service is suspended in preparation for Hurricane Sandy in New York City. (BELOW LEFT TO RIGHT) At the direction of Governor Andrew M. Cuomo, MTA Bridges and Tunnels closed the Hugh L. Carey Tunnel (formerly the Brooklyn-Battery Tunnel) at 2 p.m.

MTA PREPARES

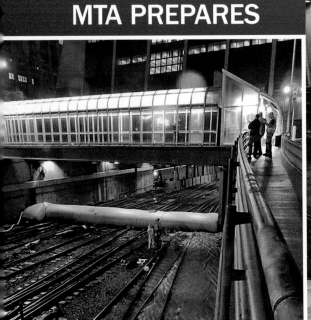

RAILROADS PREPARE

As public transportation shut down in advance of Sandy, the busiest commuter railroads in America shut down as well. On the eastern edge of New York state, Long Island Railroad crews removed hundreds of crossing gates to keep them safe in the wind. Far north in Poughkeepsie, Metro-North Railroad moved locomotives and train cars to high ground.

The preparations for the storm were most visible in the New York City train stations that see more than a million people on an average day, were locked up tight for Sandy. At Penn Station, where more than 640,000 customers from the LIRR, NJ Transit and Amtrak fill the corridors every day, all were silent.

At Grand Central Terminal, where 750,000 people pass through its century-old portal into its breathtaking central hall every day, the emptiness was eerie. A skeleton crew of Metropolitan Transportation Authority police and Metro-North workers kept watch over the grand old terminal, ready to weather the storm.

(ABOVE AND BELOW) Long Island Railroad crews, anticipating the worst, work into the night to set up a dam in an attempt to keep the water out of the Westside Yard.

October 28, 2012 (ABOVE) LIRR Concourse at Penn Station closed as Superstorm Sandy approached New York.

November 1, 2012 (LEFT) A timetable board displays continued cancellations at Penn Station as MTA resumed limited service in New York.

October 28, 2012 (ABOVE) The MTA Police watch as the last people are cleared out of New York's Grand Central Station, part of their shutdown of the City's entire transit system as of 7 p.m.

October 29, 2012 (RIGHT) Superstorm Sandy brings the normally bustling Grand Central Station to a close.

NYSE PREPARES

October 29, 2012 Sandbags form a protective barrier around the New York Stock Exchange before the arrival of Hurricane Sandy in New York City.

(OPPOSITE, TOP) Sandbags await removal at a Lower Manhattan Financial District building near Ground Zero, two days after Hurricane Sandy struck New York City.

Peter Foley/Bloomberg/Getty Images

THE POWER OF HURRICANE SANDY TRUMPED THE POWER OF WALL STREET

New York's Stock Exchange, the financial engine of the world located on Wall Street in lower Manhattan, geared up for Hurricane Sandy. The predictions were extreme, forecasting record-breaking storm surges which placed the Stock Exchange in a precarious position. The location is surrounded by water on three sides less than half a mile away. Although the Stock Exchange rarely stops for weather, as Sandy neared landfall its trading floor was empty. Sandbags surrounded the building to minimize water damage, and generators were fueled and tested ready to restore power in a moment's notice. Will this be enough? After the wrath of Sandy had passed, the New York Stock Exchange was forced to keep its doors shut for two consecutive days. This was the first time since 1888 that the Exchange had been closed for that period of time due to a natural disaster. The Stock Exchange was fully capable of opening; however due to the widespread damage they didn't have any employees available to man the trading floor. Trading resumed on Wednesday, October 31st, restoring a sense of normalcy for many economists around the world.

October 29, 2012 (BELOW) The floor of the New York Stock Exchange is empty of traders, a rare phenomenon; trading is seldom closed for weather. All major U.S. stock and options exchanges remained shut down as Hurricane Sandy approached the East Coast.

CONNECTICUT PREPARES

THE COMMUNITY COMES TOGETHER TO MINIMIZE SANDY'S IMPENDING DANGER AND DESTRUCTION.

Connecticut is a strategically located state on the Eastern Seaboard. It also sat directly in the path of Superstorm Sandy in October, 2012. Preparation for Hurricane Sandy started well before the storm arrived on the evening of Monday the 29th. Sand was piled high on the beaches to barricade homes from the storm surge predicted to overwhelm the coastal residents. At 1 P.M. on October 29, Governor Malloy ordered highways be closed to all non-emergency vehicles. Residents all across the state soon realized that they needed to band together to take as many precautions as possible. President Obama announced Connecticut was given approval for the Pre-Landfall Emergency Declaration giving the governor access to 61,000 National Guard troops. The residents of Connecticut were left with a terrifying feeling as the storm approached on Monday. As they waited for the unprecedented, Connecticut had done everything they could to prepare for this immense storm.

October 28, 2012 (LEFT, TOP TO BOTTOM) Officer Dewitt Smith distributes mandatory evacuation notices to residents before Hurricane Sandy's arrival in Bridgeport, Connecticut; Brian Walsh and Julie Noonay load trash bags with sand to prepare for Hurricane Sandy in Stratford; West Shore Fire Department personnel stand outside the West Haven firehouse surrounded by sandbags as they await the arrival of Hurricane Sandy and the large volume of water it will bring.

(BELOW) Ed Morrisey boards up a friend's house in Milford, anticipating Hurricane Sandy's appearance.

Photos by Reuters/Michelle McLoughlin

October 28, 2012 Defensive berms are constructed by earth movers on Compo Beach as the first signs of Hurricane Sandy loom in Westport, CT. (BELOW) A woman walks past a boarded-up building on the beach in Fairfield.

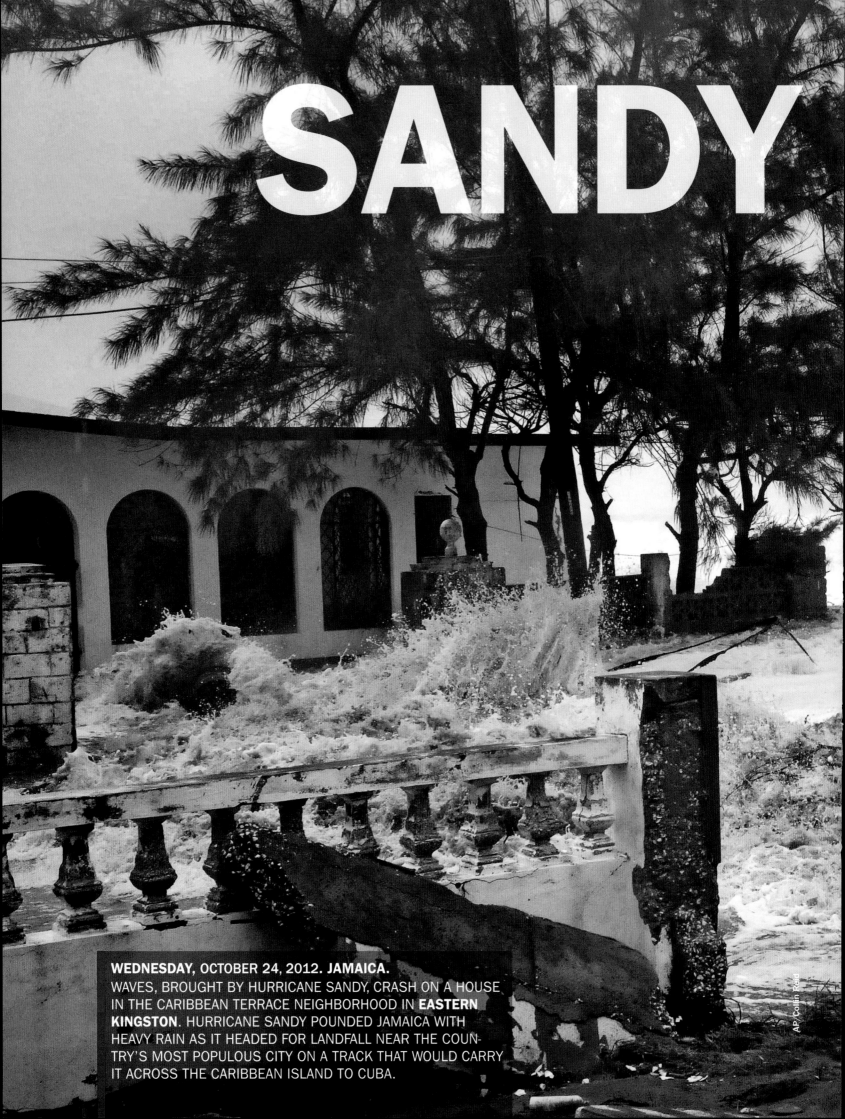

SANDY

WEDNESDAY, OCTOBER 24, 2012. **JAMAICA.**
WAVES, BROUGHT BY HURRICANE SANDY, CRASH ON A HOUSE
IN THE CARIBBEAN TERRACE NEIGHBORHOOD IN **EASTERN
KINGSTON**. HURRICANE SANDY POUNDED JAMAICA WITH
HEAVY RAIN AS IT HEADED FOR LANDFALL NEAR THE COUN-
TRY'S MOST POPULOUS CITY ON A TRACK THAT WOULD CARRY
IT ACROSS THE CARIBBEAN ISLAND TO CUBA.

STRIKES!

HURRICANE SANDY'S FIRST DEADLY STOP: JAMAICA

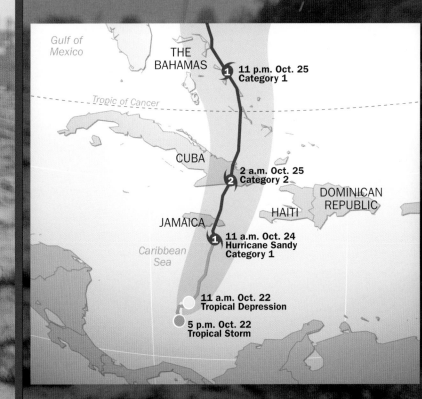

Gulf of
Mexico

THE
BAHAMAS
1 11 p.m. Oct. 25
Category 1

Tropic of Cancer

CUBA
2 2 a.m. Oct. 25
Category 2

DOMINICAN
REPUBLIC

HAITI

JAMAICA
1 11 a.m. Oct. 24
Hurricane Sandy
Category 1

Caribbean
Sea

11 a.m. Oct. 22
Tropical Depression

5 p.m. Oct. 22
Tropical Storm

THURSDAY, OCTOBER 25, 2012. HAITI
HAITIAN MEN WALK ACROSS A BRIDGE OVER RUSHING FLOOD
WATERS CAUSED BY HURRICANE SANDY IN **PORT-AU-PRINCE**.
HURRICANE SANDY BARRELED TOWARD THE BAHAMAS
THURSDAY AS A POWERFUL CATEGORY 2 STORM AFTER BAT-
TERING JAMAICA, HAITI AND CUBA. ALTHOUGH FORECASTERS
PREDICTED THE STORM WOULD WEAKEN, SANDY REMAINED
A HURRICANE AS IT PASSED THROUGH THE CARIBBEAN.

SANDY'S DEADLY WRATH LEAVES
MORE THAN 50 DEAD IN HAITI

YET ANOTHER BLOW TO HAITI FROM HURRICANE SANDY

THURSDAY, OCTOBER 25 2012. HAITI
RESIDENTS WADE THROUGH A FLOODED STREET CAUSED BY HEAVY RAINS
FROM HURRICANE SANDY IN **PORT-AU-PRINCE**.

(OPPOSITE) A WOMAN REMOVES MUDDY WATER OUT OF HER HOME IN
LA PLAINE, AFTER HEAVY RAINS FROM HURRICANE SANDY. THE STORM
DAMAGED MANY VITAL CROPS ON THE ISLAND. TWO-THIRDS OF HAITI'S
PEOPLE FACED HUNGER AND MALNOURISHMENT AS PROBLEMS
CONTINUED FOR MONTHS AFTER THE STORM.

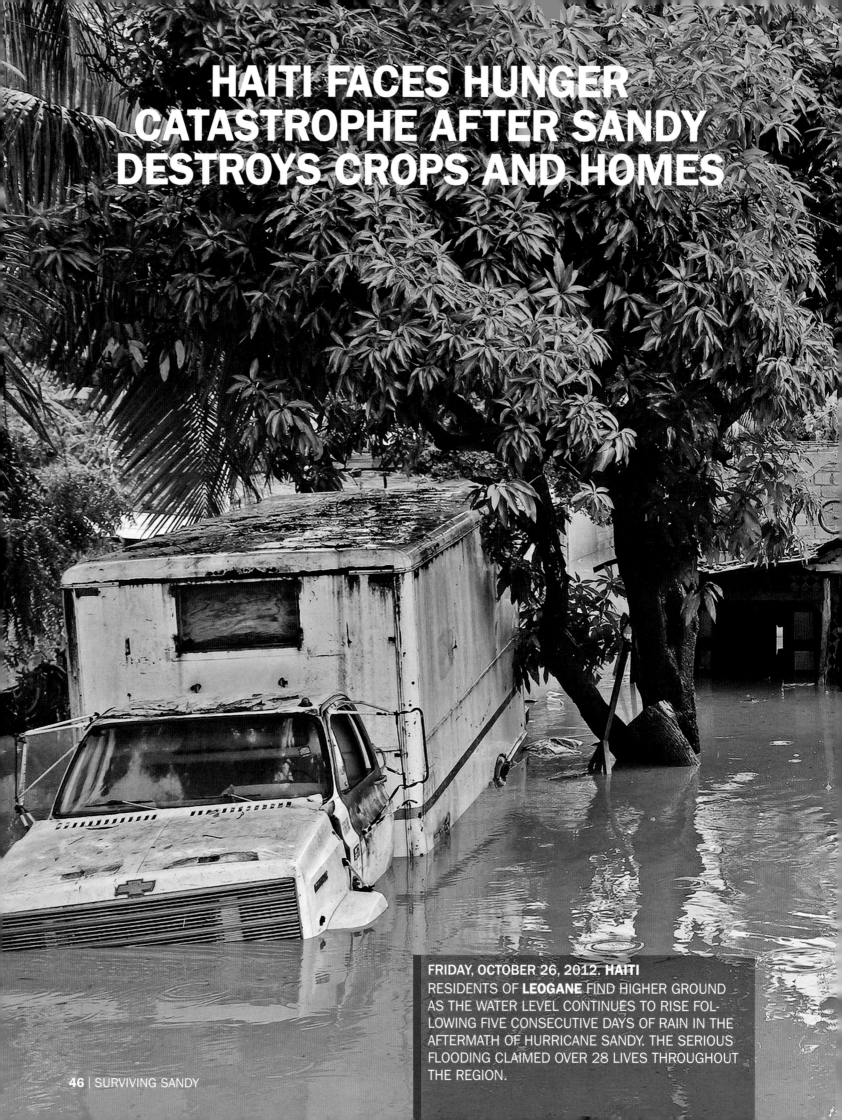

HAITI FACES HUNGER CATASTROPHE AFTER SANDY DESTROYS CROPS AND HOMES

FRIDAY, OCTOBER 26, 2012. **HAITI**
RESIDENTS OF **LEOGANE** FIND HIGHER GROUND
AS THE WATER LEVEL CONTINUES TO RISE FOL-
LOWING FIVE CONSECUTIVE DAYS OF RAIN IN THE
AFTERMATH OF HURRICANE SANDY. THE SERIOUS
FLOODING CLAIMED OVER 28 LIVES THROUGHOUT
THE REGION.

HURRICANE SANDY ROARS INTO CUBA AND DOMINICAN REPUBLIC

THURSDAY, OCTOBER 25, 2012. **DOMINICAN REPUBLIC** A WOMAN OBSERVES FROM HER FLOODED HOUSE IN THE NEIGHBORHOOD OF **LA BARQUITA, EASTERN SANTO DOMINGO.** HURRICANE SANDY BARRELED TOWARD THE BAHAMAS AFTER BATTERING JAMAICA, HAITI AND CUBA AND CLAIMING SEVERAL LIVES.

WEDNESDAY, OCTOBER 24, 2012. CUBA
STORM CLOUDS FILL THE SKY OVER **HAVANA**. HURRICANE SANDY BATTERED JAMAICA WITH FEROCIOUS WINDS, WAVES AND RAIN, KNOCKING DOWN TREES AND POWER LINES ACROSS THE CARIBBEAN COUNTRY BEFORE IT CUT A PATH ACROSS CUBA AND TOWARDS THE BAHAMAS.

TUESDAY, OCTOBER 30, 2012. CUBA
A FLOODED NEIGHBORHOOD AFTER THE UNDOSO RIVER BURST ITS BANKS DUE TO RAINFALL FROM HURRICANE SANDY IN THE VILLAGE OF **SAGUA LA GRANDE IN CENTRAL CUBA**, AROUND 240 KM (149 MILES) EAST OF HAVANA.

(CUBA PHOTOS) Reuters/Desmond Boylan

MAKING HER WAY UP THE ATLANTIC COAST

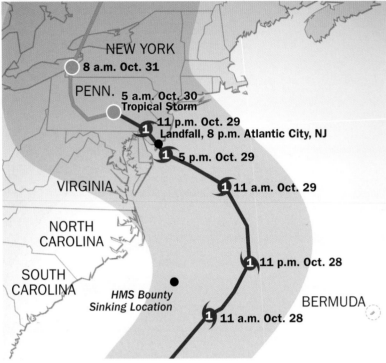

NEW YORK
8 a.m. Oct. 31

PENN.
5 a.m. Oct. 30
Tropical Storm

11 p.m. Oct. 29
Landfall, 8 p.m. Atlantic City, NJ

5 p.m. Oct. 29

VIRGINIA

11 a.m. Oct. 29

NORTH CAROLINA

11 p.m. Oct. 28

SOUTH CAROLINA

HMS Bounty
Sinking Location

BERMUDA

11 a.m. Oct. 28

GAINING STRENGTH AS IT TRAVELS THROUGH THE ATLANTIC, THE MEGA-STORM HEADS FOR NEW JERSEY

Hurricane Sandy forged an epic path of destruction in the Caribbean, leaving behind a death toll of 70 in Jamaica, the Dominican Republic, Haiti, Cuba and the Bahamas. She then moved on a northeasterly course up the Eastern Seaboard following the typical course of hurricanes that enter the North Atlantic. The typical behavior didn't last long as a growing number of factors developed that made this storm incredibly dangerous. The waters of the Atlantic were warmer than usual, which increased Sandy's strength to a Category 2 hurricane with sustained winds of almost 100 mph. Off to the west another storm loomed, a winter Nor'easter, which joined forces with Sandy to create the dreaded superstorm. Typically these storms would head out into the North Atlantic, losing strength as the waters grew colder, but Sandy was blocked--a high pressure system far to the north had weather experts across the globe predicting that Sandy would make a sharp westerly turn and smash headlong into the highly populated Eastern Seaboard.

October 27, 2012 (LEFT) Large waves generated by Hurricane Sandy crash into Jeanette's Pier in Nags Head, North Carolina.

October 30, 2012 (BELOW) The media names Hurricane Sandy "Frankenstorm" as she continues up the East Coast. A pounding surf tells the story at Mirlo Beach in Rodanthe. Even though there was significant damage on North Carolina's Outer Banks, emergency management officials say it could have been worse.

AP/The Virginian-Pilot/Steve Earley,
(ABOVE) AP/Gerry Broome

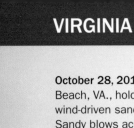

October 28, 2012 Matt Francis, of Virginia Beach, VA., holds on to his hat, as the wind-driven sand and rain from Hurricane Sandy blows across the beaches of Sandbridge in Virginia Beach, VA.

October 29, 2012 (BELOW) Waves crash on shore from high surf ahead of Hurricane Sandy at the pier at Virginia Beach.

Reuters/Rich-Joseph Facun
(ABOVE) AP/The Virginian-Pilot, L. Todd Spencer

October 29, 2012 (ABOVE) Glenn Heartley pulls on a rope attached to his car in preparation for getting it towed from a creek in Chincoteague, VA. Heartley and his wife were swept off the road into the shallow creek during Hurricane Sandy's arrival Monday.

October 29, 2012 (BELOW, LEFT) A worker retrieves a grappling hook on the dock next to Bubba's Restaurant on the water in Virginia Beach, VA. (BELOW, RIGHT) A car sits in water after a road was flooded by rain from Hurricane Sandy in Virginia Beach, VA.

November 5, 2013 Members of the West Virginia National Guard work to clear the road to a remote emergency radio repeater site in Tucker County in Parsons, West Virginia.

SNOW IN A HURRICANE?

This unprecedented storm continued to set records.

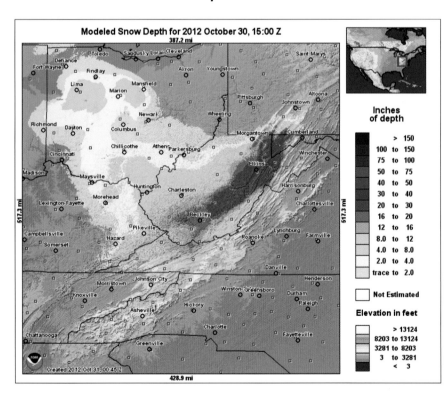

Modeled Snow Depth for 2012 October 30, 15:00 Z

Inches of depth

	> 150
	100 to 150
	75 to 100
	50 to 75
	40 to 50
	30 to 40
	20 to 30
	16 to 20
	12 to 16
	8.0 to 12
	4.0 to 8.0
	2.0 to 4.0
	trace to 2.0

☐ Not Estimated

Elevation in feet

	> 13124
	8203 to 13124
	3281 to 8203
	3 to 3281
	< 3

Combining forces with the Nor'easter that was looming across the Appalachian states, Sandy's moisture and high winds resulted in blizzard-like conditions and up to three feet of snow in parts of West Virginia. "Essentially, you took a hurricane's moisture, wrapped it into the Appalachians where the air mass was cold enough for snow," said Weather.com meteorologist Jon Erdman. Roofs collapsed under the weight of the wet heavy snow and trees snapped, causing widespread power outages across the state. Governor Earl Ray Tomblin issued a state of emergency on October 29th, which, remaining in effect for almost 2 months, provided the hard-hit communities with additional time and assistance to return to everyday life.

October 31, 2012 Rob Kohler, an electrical line worker from Kokomo, Indiana, clears snow-laden power lines in Terra Alta, West Virginia. Superstorm Sandy mixed with colder temperatures in higher elevations and dumped as much as 3 feet of snow in some places.

October 30, 2012 (BELOW, LEFT) A lone parked car is draped with snow-covered branches south of Morgantown, West Virginia. Drifts 4 feet deep were reported at Great Smoky Mountains National Park on the Tennessee-North Carolina border. (BELOW, RIGHT) An ambulance is stuck in over a foot of snow off of Highway 33 West, near Belington. Superstorm Sandy buried parts of West Virginia under more than a foot of snow cutting power to at least 264,000 customers and closing dozens of roads.

October 30, 2012 (ABOVE) Jenna Webb (L), 18, and Zoe Jurusik, 20, paddle-board down a flooded city street in the aftermath of Hurricane Sandy in Bethany Beach, Delaware.

October 29, 2012 (OPPOSITE, TOP) Streets of Bowers Beach flood as Hurricane Sandy hits Delaware. (OPPOSITE, BELOW) October 30, 2012 Homes in Bethany Beach, Delaware, are surrounded by floodwaters from Hurricane Sandy. Officials said Bethany and nearby Fenwick Island appeared to be among the hardest-hit parts of the state.

October 29, 2012 (ABOVE) A marina floods onto the road as Hurricane Sandy hits Ocean City, Maryland. About 50 million people from the Mid-Atlantic to Canada were in the path of the nearly 1,000-mile-wide (1,600-km-wide) storm, which forecasters said could be the largest to hit the mainland in U.S. history.

October 30, 2012 (LEFT) Lauren Sinnott walks her dog Becca in a flooded street in downtown Annapolis, MD, in the wake of Superstorm Sandy. (BELOW LEFT) Sveinn Storm, owner of Storm Bros. Ice Cream Factory, measures the flood waters outside his store in Annapolis, MD. (BELOW) A National Guard humvee travels through high water to check the area after the effects of Hurricane Sandy in Ocean City, MD.

October 28, 2012 (OPPOSITE, BOTTOM, LEFT TO RIGHT) DC Water employees fill bags with sand in downtown Washington, DC, ahead of Hurricane Sandy's landfall; A digital road sign warns drivers of severe weather conditions to come.

OCTOBER 28, 2012 Whitecaps break in the Tidal Basin as high winds from Hurricane Sandy head into the DC area. US emergency officials braced for the potentially massive impact of a so-called 'Frankenstorm' Monday as Hurricane Sandy lumbered north in the Atlantic Ocean, poised to hit the Eastern Seaboard with torrential rains and gale-force winds. The superstorm caused panic across both political aisles as she hit during the frenzied last days of the November 6 presidential campaign. Republican challenger Mitt Romney would later say, "Sandy made Obama look presidential and understanding." Some political analysts say the storm damaged Romney's chances.

SANDY CLAIMS THE HMS BOUNTY

A story of heroism, survival against all odds—and devastating loss.

HALIFAX, CANADA. July 23, 2012 (ABOVE) Sailing majestically in Halifax during Tall Ships 2012 Parade of Sail, the HMS Bounty is a replica of the Bounty that was built in 1784 at the Blaydes shipyard in Hull. The original Bounty was known as the collier "Bethia" until purchased by the Royal Navy on May 26, 1787, when it was refit and renamed Bounty. The new ship shown above was constructed for the 1962 film, Mutiny on the Bounty. It was built in Nova Scotia, a place whose history is shaped by the sea. The vessel was also later used for the film Pirates of the Caribbean. This tourist attraction sank in Hurricane Sandy's high seas off the coast of North Carolina on October 29, 2012. (OPPOSITE) **July 19, 2012** During the Tall Ships 2012 event in Halifax, the HMS Bounty is docked at dusk.

(ABOVE) The aircrews and operation experts who were directly involved in the HMS Bounty crew recovery, pictured with Commandant of the Coast Guard Adm. Bob Papp, Vice Adm. John Currier, Vice Commandant of the Coast Guard and Capt. Joseph Kelly, Commanding Officer of Air Station Elizabeth City, NC.

SURVIVAL STORY ATLANTIC OCEAN OFF NORTH CAROLINA

Daniel Todd, U.S. Coast Guard

The developments around the HMS Bounty wreck, including the amazing rescue by Daniel Todd, a rescue swimmer with the U.S. Coast Guard since January 2007.

Anxiety rose among the crew of the HMS Bounty, as howling wind and pelting rain continued unabated. After more than a day of fighting for their lives on the waterlogged ship, the seasick sailors became desperate, realizing they were losing the battle. The pumps and generators, essential in saving the ship, were clogged. Was there any hope left for the 16 crew members or for their beloved ship? On October 28, this was the scene aboard the 180-foot vessel, a replica of the legendary HMS Bounty, depicted in a novel and several movies.

The new Bounty, a three-masted ship, set sail from

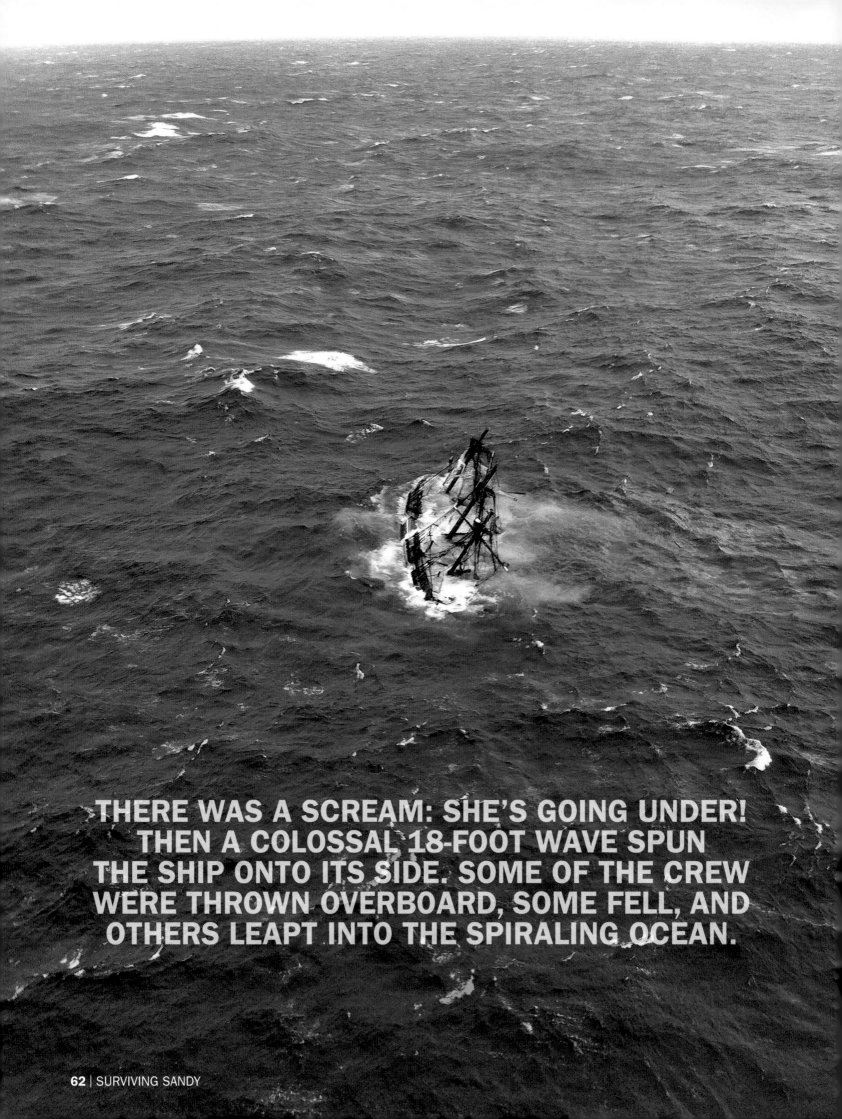

THERE WAS A SCREAM: SHE'S GOING UNDER! THEN A COLOSSAL 18-FOOT WAVE SPUN THE SHIP ONTO ITS SIDE. SOME OF THE CREW WERE THROWN OVERBOARD, SOME FELL, AND OTHERS LEAPT INTO THE SPIRALING OCEAN.

Photos by U.S. Coast Guard, Petty Officer 2nd Class Tim Kuklewski

October 29, 2012
As seen by the U.S. Coast Guard, the 180-foot HMS Bounty is submerged in the Atlantic Ocean about 90 miles southeast of Hatteras, NC. The masts point skyward as the Bounty's hull is dragged to the seafloor in powerful waves stirred up by Sandy. The sailboat's 63-year-old captain, Robin Walbridge, remained missing after the tall ship sank. Nonstop search efforts to find him continued for more than three days until the challenging decision was made by the U.S. Coast Guard to suspend the quest.

New London, Connecticut, on October 25, 2012. Its captain, Robin Walbridge, planned to avoid Hurricane Sandy by travelling swiftly as far east and south as possible on its southward course to St. Petersburg, FL. Fatefully, this plan changed, resulting in the vessel being caught up in the center of a destructive storm that eventually spanned 900 miles.

Traveling quickly, the ship sailed smoothly for the first few days - without sign of any looming danger. But anticipating rougher seas in the offing, the deckhands worked at securing gear. On Saturday morning, October 27, Walbridge ordered a change of direction. He made a right turn to head the boat in a westerly direction, hoping to utilize the storm's winds in speeding the ship. This fateful new course brought the Bounty and its crew straight into the hurricane's deadly path where it didn't stand a chance.

By Sunday, they were less than 200 miles from the eye of the storm. Seventy-mile-per-hour winds beat the ship, launching it through the 25-foot seas as if it were a toy. Huge sails were torn in half and furniture became unbolted. Violent waves churned the ship, pitching everything and everyone around, resulting in some serious injuries. The day dragged on as the crew fought frantically to pump out the rising water in the engine room. Floating debris destroyed the pumps, despite the attempts to keep this crucial equipment operational. By late afternoon, the engine room was submerged in at least four feet of water, causing electrical equipment to crack and explode. A few hours later, one of the two generators failed. Despite their best efforts, the crew was losing the battle. Orders were given for everyone to put on their emergency Gumby suits, and they began collecting

survival gear in preparation for the increased possibility of abandoning ship. It was then that the power went out completely.

At 9 p.m., the third effort to contact the Coast Guard was finally successful. Captain Walbridge learned that the Coast Guard wasn't planning to launch rescue helicopters until about 6 a.m. on Monday morning, so he instructed his crew to wait until daylight to abandon ship. But Hurricane Sandy had other plans. At the last minute the Captain finally ordered the crew to board the life rafts. There was a scream: "She's going under!" A colossal 18-foot wave spun the ship onto its side. Some crew members were thrown overboard, some fell, and others leapt into the churning ocean. Panic-stricken shouts pierced the air as they all desperately tried to swim away from the whirlpool into which the ship was sinking, and which would suck them down as well. Adding to the peril, the ship was rocking up and down, its broken wood and rigging thumping down on the sailors, relentlessly shoving them underwater. Despite their injuries and exhaustion, they continued to struggle for themselves and each other. It took an hour before they managed to get the life rafts inflated and climbed aboard.

Meanwhile, the Coast Guard personnel were anxiously preparing for the arduous rescue. Within 30 minutes, the first plane took off, and 30 minutes following that the second plane departed. Flying low to stay beneath the seething clouds, it took the USCG Search planes an hour to get out to the shipwreck, 90 miles off Cape Hatteras, NC. The survivors in the rafts heard the welcome sound of a search plane overhead. The HC-130J Hercules rescue planes stayed on the scene through the night deploying flares, additional life rafts, and a self-locating

A screenshot from a U.S. Coast Guard (USCG) video in which USCG members use a hoist cable to rescue the Bounty's crew from the 25-foot life rafts and hoist them to the USCG helicopters. Fourteen of the crew members were rescued after their ship was swallowed by 18-foot waves.

the helicopter steady. Instructions, given by the rescue swimmer, were carefully followed as the survivors were safely situated in the rescue basket. One, and then two, were carried up, but then Todd realized his raft had been flipped by a 30-foot wave. Swimming hurriedly, he came back to find the remaining four hanging on to the side of the raft. Soon he had six people safely in the helicopter, and deflated the raft so that no passing boat would see it and call in another emergency.

By now, rescue swimmer Randy Haba had successfully moved five people up into the first helicopter but it was running low on fuel and couldn't stay long enough to get the last three survivors. As worn-out as he felt, Todd agreed to finish the rescues. The second helicopter flew over and lowered Todd into the raging seas a second time to pick up the final three people. He had spent at least 45 minutes in the rough waters and rescued nine of the fourteen survivors. Todd was utterly exhausted. With 13 total people in the cabin of the second helicopter, bulky Gumby suits and all, there was just enough room to breathe, but that didn't hinder the sailors from promptly falling asleep. Fighting a headwind, the journey took an hour and a half back to the base. On touchdown, the Coast Guard crew unloaded the survivors, slitting the feet of the Gumby suits to let the water drain out before hypothermia could conquer them. As the adrenaline wore off, reality set in: at least they were alive.

Fourteen of the Bounty's crewmembers were safely on land once again. That was the good news. But the bad news was that two lives were lost. Deckhand Claudene Christian, 42, had been thrown overboard, and she was last seen swimming near the ship's rear mast. Her body was found by a third Coast Guard helicopter later on Monday afternoon. The Captain remained missing; A search continued for four days as there was hope that the experienced seaman would be able to stay alive in the survival Gumby suit until they could find him. Unfortunately, this man, who had been the Bounty's captain for 17 years, was never found.

The HMS Bounty's October journey ended on the ocean floor, claimed by one of the largest storms on record. It is sorely missed by the crew who used to call the majestic ship 'home.' They continue to keep in contact with each other, and are deeply saddened when they think of the two members who passed on. It was because of the teamwork and determination of the ship's crew and then of the Coast Guard that 14 of them were brought home safely again. ●

marker buoy. While this sentry operation was in progress, the USCG rescue helicopters were being prepared. Twenty-eight-year-old Daniel Todd, one of the USCG rescue swimmers, was wakened by the urgent call at 4 a.m. and thought it was "a really bad joke because they said it looked like a pirate ship." He learned that the distress call was from the HMS Bounty, and it actually wasn't going to last until daylight. The first helicopter arrived on the scene while it was still dark. Todd, the rescue swimmer on the second helicopter, recounted that upon their arrival, "the sun had started to crack the horizon and we were able to see what was going on." The rescue swimmer of the first helicopter, Petty Officer 2nd Class Randy Haba, had already begun evacuating one of the rafts, so Todd's crew flew straight to the other raft, which was floating about a mile away.

Todd admitted he "was definitely nervous" when he saw the waves he would be lowered into. Donning his helmet, fins, mask, snorkel and gloves, he was lowered down via the hoist cable above the raging water. It took him a moment to make some headway as he was initially tossed about by the waves which pulled and pushed and sucked him back and forth.Then, completely free swimming, he pushed through the waves and caught hold of the raft's line, using it to pull himself alongside. The rafts have sea anchors, a small parachute that gets attached to a 50-foot line. Greeting the exhausted survivors, Todd lightened the mood as he jumped in with a smile and said, "Hey, I'm Dan and I heard you guys need a ride!"

Each person was rescued individually, swimming with their rescuer away from the raft as the aircrew moved in with the basket, focusing solely on keeping

Survivors of the HMS Bounty shipwreck are assisted out of the U.S. Coast Guard helicopter by USCG crewmembers. (BELOW) Coast Guard members from the Elizabeth City, N.C. Air Station aid one of the HMS Bounty's rescued sailors.

October 30, 2012 A parking lot full of yellow cabs is flooded as a result of Superstorm Sandy in Hoboken, NJ.

AP/Charles Sykes

NEW JERSEY

STRETCHING FROM CAPE MAY TO SANDY HOOK, NEW JERSEY BOASTS 127 MILES OF PICTURESQUE SHORELINE. AFTER SUPERSTORM SANDY CAME ASHORE, MUCH OF THE LANDSCAPE WAS NEARLY UNRECOGNIZABLE, COUNTLESS BEACHFRONT HOMES WERE DESTROYED, AND NUMEROUS BUSINESSES WERE CLOSED INDEFINITELY.

NEW JERSEY

2.7 MILLION
POWER OUTAGES

2.5 MILLION
YARDS OF SAND AND SILT DEPOSITED ON ROAD AND WATERWAYS

8.5 MILLION
CUBIC YARDS OF DEBRIS REMOVED

89,025
RESIDENTS VISITED FEMA DISASTER RECOVERY CENTERS

1.1 BILLION
FEDERAL ALLOCATIONS FOR RESPONSE AND RECOVERY

Reuters/Eric Thayer

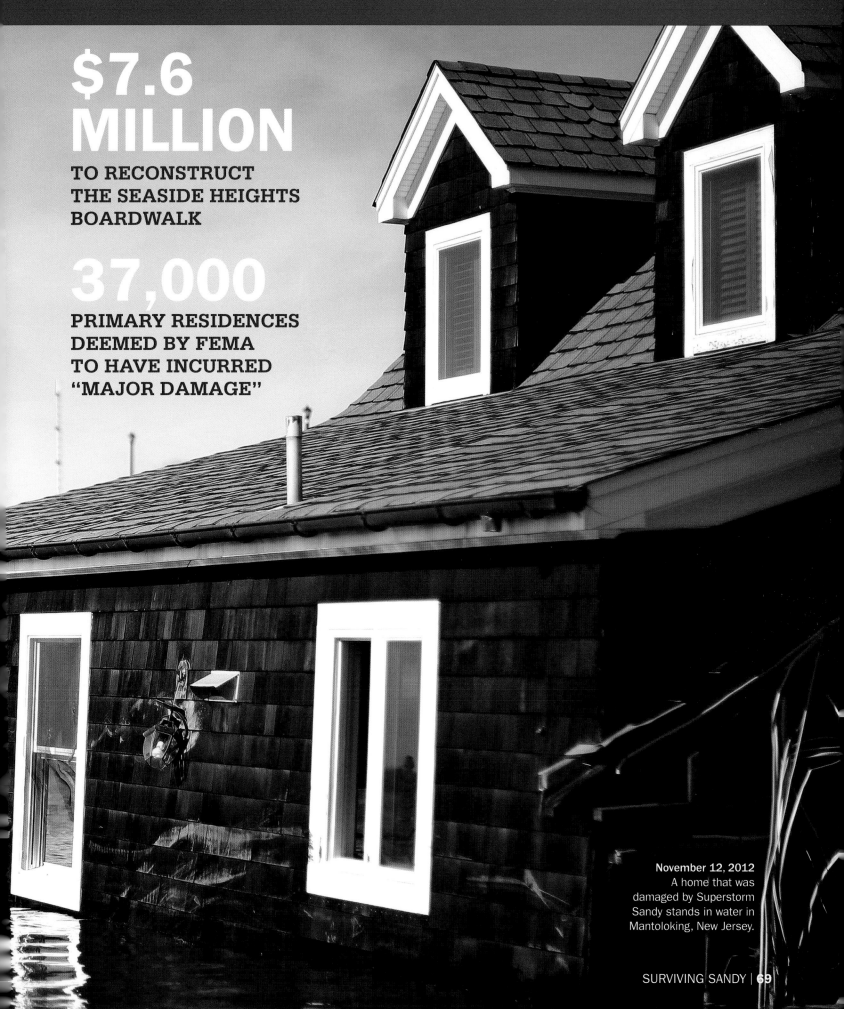

BY THE NUMBERS

$7.6 MILLION

TO RECONSTRUCT
THE SEASIDE HEIGHTS
BOARDWALK

37,000

PRIMARY RESIDENCES
DEEMED BY FEMA
TO HAVE INCURRED
"MAJOR DAMAGE"

November 12, 2012
A home that was
damaged by Superstorm
Sandy stands in water in
Mantoloking, New Jersey.

October 30, 2012
Brian Hajeski, of Brick, N.J., reacts as he looks at debris of a home that washed up onto the Mantoloking Bridge the morning after Superstorm Sandy rolled through in Mantoloking, N.J.

AP/Julio Cortez, Map by Steve Walkowiak/SWmaps.com

Miles of white sand beaches, tranquil beach towns, pristine summer homes, world-famous boardwalks, five-star waterfront dining, and endless opportunities for entertainment are some of the things that come to mind when we think of New Jersey. They are also what attract thousands to live, work, and vacation there year after year. As the summer of 2012 came to a close, tourists went home, and residents left their summer homes. No one could have begun to imagine what was soon to become of the Jersey Shore. Just two months after the season concluded, Superstorm Sandy had blazed a trail across the shore, unleashing its extreme strength and leaving behind untold destruction, loss, and devastation.

BERGEN

Little Ferry

Hoboken

HUDSON

NYC

LONG ISLAND

Breezy Point, NY

Lower New York Bay

Union Beach

South Amboy

Atlantic Highlands

Sandy Hook

MIDDLESEX

Sea Bright

Monmouth Beach

Long Branch

MONMOUTH

Asbury Park

Belmar

Spring Lake

Trenton

Manasquan

Point Pleasant

Bay Head

Brick

Mantoloking

Normandy Beach

Lavallette

PENNSYLVANIA

Ortley Beach

Toms River

Seaside Heights

NEW JERSEY

OCEAN

Philadelphia

Barnegat Lighthouse

Long Beach Island

Surf City

Ship Bottom

Beach Haven

Holgate

ATLANTIC

Brigantine

Atlantic City

Margate City

Ocean City

CAPE MAY

Sea Isle City

Delaware Bay

Avalon

Stone Harbor

DELAWARE

N

Atlantic Ocean

mi. 5 10

km 10 20

Wildwood

Cape May

Mark Wilson/Getty Images

CAPE MAY

October 29, 2012
The beach has disappeared, and water begins to gush out onto Beach Avenue as the Atlantic Ocean pushes inland.

ATLANTIC COUNTY

Atlantic County, famous for its vast array of recreational opportunities and lively atmosphere, was derelict and silent after Superstorm Sandy made landfall just south of Atlantic City causing extreme devastation.

October 29, 2012 (ABOVE) U.S. Route 30, the White Horse Pike, one of three major approaches to Atlantic City, was submerged by water overflowing from the Absecon Bay, during the approach of Superstorm Sandy. **October 30, 2012** (LEFT) An aerial view of Brigantine, NJ, reveals only a tiny portion of the ruin that Superstorm Sandy left behind on the Jersey shoreline.

October 28, 2012 (OPPOSITE, TOP) A seagull flies over breaking waves ahead of Superstorm Sandy in Atlantic City, New Jersey. **October 30, 2012** (OPPOSITE, BOTTOM) Nicholas Rodriguez stands on a fragile section of the world-famous Atlantic City boardwalk which was obliterated by the tremendous force of Superstorm Sandy.

ATLANTIC CITY

A depressing and eerie landscape is seen in this image of Atlantic City following the Superstorm. Foundations and pilings are all that remain of brick buildings and a boardwalk which was once bustling with tourists and cheerful activity.

AP / Seth Wenig

October 31, 2012 (ABOVE) U.S. President Barack Obama speaks in a neighborhood after he tours damage done by Superstorm Sandy in Brigantine, New Jersey. New Jersey Governor Chris Christie stands behind Obama. Putting aside partisan differences, Obama and Christie toured storm-stricken parts of New Jersey together on Wednesday, taking in scenes of flooded roads and burning homes in the aftermath of Superstorm Sandy.

DEVASTATION BRIGANTINE

Donna Vanzant

Donna Vanzant is owner of North Point Marina in Brigantine, NJ, which President Obama visited after it was destroyed by Superstorm Sandy.

Superstorm Sandy was a momentous event on our small five-mile long island in Brigantine, New Jersey. Many of the homes and businesses in our town were destroyed, but we are fortunate for the countless friends and neighbors who have pitched in to help us recover. Just a couple of days following the storm, President Obama visited here, including my own North Point Marina.

We did not evacuate for the storm; it was as if I thought that if I stayed, things would be fine. Floodwater had never entered the store or apartment before this, so we raised our belongings as high as possible, assuming we would be okay. We were not.

As the storm struck, we sat in our dark house and watched helplessly as water entered our home. I called a friend, Billy, who had also stayed back, and lives near the marina. I asked him how things were looking and he reassured me that "Donna, it is getting dark, but I think you will be okay." Even as I was on the phone, boats from my marina were floating past his house, and the last piece of my dock broke away. He did not have the heart to tell me how bad it really was.

Heading the four miles to the marina the next morning seemed to take an eternity. Our once serene community on the Atlantic had been transformed into a war zone. On the way, I saw our Director of Public Works who shook his head sadly. At the marina street, reality struck; 40 boats from my marina were strewn all over -- in between houses, in the streets, anywhere and everywhere. When we met my son, all we could do was hug and cry. My son lived on the first floor of a duplex with his pregnant wife; this was destroyed, as was the store, garage, and two sheds. The bulkhead was caving in and the docks were gone.

The Secret Service had arrived on the property and told us, "The President of the United States is coming here today." They asked that no one clean anything up, as President Obama and Governor Christie wanted to see the devastation. It was a very emotional day. Most would be familiar with the story from television reports, and my picture has gone viral; I am even on the cover of a Swiss newspaper!

The road to rebuild is going to be a long one. As others can attest, there were so many clauses in insurance policies that what we will receive is nowhere near the cost to rebuild. I truly believe in the human spirit and would like to share some things that have occurred during this journey. We have never been alone. Family, friends, customers, and strangers have reached out to us. From the very beginning cleanup stages, they brought us food. A local restaurant owner (who had just been released from the hospital), came not once, but twice, with a huge pot of hot soup and sandwiches for all the volunteers!

Assistance continued for weeks while volunteers wrote down all the part numbers on our inventory that was ruined. A friend spent three days cleaning tools that were battered by the salt water; during the storm,

(TOP LEFT) Reuters/Larry Downing

October 31, 2012 U.S. President Barack Obama hugs North Point Marina owner Donna Vanzant as he tours damage done by Superstorm Sandy in Brigantine, New Jersey. (TOP, RIGHT) The remains of North Point Marina's wharf after strong waves caused by Superstorm Sandy ripped the docks away.

U.S. President Barack Obama and New Jersey Governor Chris Christie (L) talk with survivors in a community center.

the water was chest high in the garage and seeped into toolboxes. Brother Bob, along with others, put the sheds back together by replacing walls and doors. My niece from Pennsylvania, who is in the seventh grade, took it upon herself to ask the Principal to have a fundraiser. I received boxes and boxes of toiletries, baby diapers (for my grandbaby, who was born on the 21st of November), baby wipes (all of them were destroyed in the apartment), and other baby necessities.

My son, Stephen, a Navy diver, came home on leave to help with the cleanup. He raised money for us through a Facebook page he created, "Rebuild North Point Marina"; every penny will help. With all our efforts focused on the marina, I had little time to concentrate on my own home. When I finally started assessing the losses, I found all my photo albums were ruined, including all my parents' memories and my children's pictures from childhood on. My sister-in-law made an album of photos she knew I would love; I will cherish them forever. I would have to write forever to list all of the people who helped.

Now, sitting in the remains of our store with everything off the pegboard in boxes, I still cannot believe that this all happened. I continue to wish it was all a dream. Last Wednesday, another miracle happened. A man whom I'd never seen before calmly came into the store and said "I would like to help you." He looked at the walls and at leftover sheetrock we had brought over and said, "I can do that." With only one day available to him, he got straight to work. On that particular day, it seemed that many people were stopping by to see how we were. He was amazed, commenting that we have our own little community here at North Point Marina! He asked if he could stay two more days to finish the job! It is no longer overwhelming for me to see that fabulous job he did. He was a stranger from Maryland and a volunteer for Operation Blessing! A blessing it was.

On May 6th, 14 local carpenters and friends brought their tools and re-decked the docks. They told me just to let them know when the wood was here and they would come. My brother and his girl Carmella came from Massachusetts and renovated the public bathroom. Customers, Brother Bob and my other son Thomas rebuilt the picnic area and walkways. Thomas did all the dock plumbing and Bob did all the electric on the docks.

It will not stop here, for in the near future there will be more family and friends who continue these unselfish acts. I hope and pray that this never happens again. We are safe. No one got hurt and that matters most! ●

OCEAN COUNTY

On October 29, 2012, the more than 30 mile coastline of Ocean County endured an unprecedented battering from Superstorm Sandy. Hundreds of coastal homes were reduced to ruins and the frequented beaches were destroyed.

Julie Dermansky/Corbis/APImages

November 15, 2012
A Bay Head beach house on the Jersey shore split in half by Superstorm Sandy. Sandy's surge flooded thousands of homes in the tri-state area and knocked out power to millions.

(RIGHT, TOP) Vinyl siding melted like cheese on one of the few homes still standing in the Camp Osborn section of Brick Twp. Sixty houses either burned to the ground in the raging fires or were washed away in the storm.

(RIGHT, MIDDLE) The remains of what had been a beautiful seaside home makes Brian Hajeski of Brick, NJ, turn away distraught.

(RIGHT, BOTTOM) A ruined beach chair ominously sits on a Seaside Heights beach not far from the Casino Pier, which was relocated with the fury of the storm surge.

(TOP TO BOTTOM) Jim Druckenmiller, AP/Julio Cortez, Jo Hendley

The front of the Bowker's Deli shortly after Superstorm Sandy had left the area heading inland.

SURVIVAL STORY HOLGATE

Eileen Bowker

Long Beach Island resident shares her experience during Superstorm Sandy and her faith in God that helped her through it.

On Thursday, October 25, my husband Brian and oldest daughter Kayle headed to Bloomington, Indiana, to watch Emily and the Hoosier field hockey team play against Ohio State. Since we knew a hurricane was predicted, my boys and I stayed on Long Beach Island to run the deli we own. Although the season was winding down, we were still opening on Saturday and Sunday mornings for the locals and the neighbors that were coming down to Holgate to close up their summer homes.

By late Friday I found myself checking with many of our friends to see who was planning to stay. Many of them were planning to stay—just like we have many times before. When the order was given for an evacuation I communicated with Brian in Indiana and let him know all our friends were staying and that we would be staying as well.

On Sunday morning, the winds were really starting to blow. I went to check out the surf and ran into a neighbor who was planning on leaving, but let me know his home was available should we need access to a third floor. Later on Sunday, my boys and I had talked about having a plan and working as a team, but I never thought we would really need to put anything into action. By late Sunday afternoon we learned that the road

to Beach Haven was under water at the marsh and they closed the bridge to incoming and outgoing traffic. We were officially in Holgate to stay.

Sunday night brought lots of rain and wind. We packed a change of clothes, our tent, sleeping bags, water purifier and other supplies in dry bags and had them by the door.

As I continued to receive calls from concerned family and friends, I tended to think this whole event was being hyped too much. Looking out the window it just seemed like other storms we've had—only with a little more wind and rain. My husband kept telling us to take pictures, but I have to admit the storm was paralyzing. On occasion I posted on Facebook and had quite a few friends sending messages and prayers. I did a lot of talking to God myself.

As the high tide came up we could see some water coming into the parking lot, onto Washington Avenue, north of us, and McKinley to our south. I went to bed about 12:00 and prayed for an uneventful night.

Monday morning brought much more rain and intense winds. Off and on throughout the morning the boys would go out on walks to check out the erosion and the condition of an oceanfront house across the street. The beaches were becoming more compromised as the hours passed. We heard that many of our friends that had stayed in Beach Haven had been evacuated to the Engleside for safety, as the flooding from the bay was bad. We had three to four feet of water on West Avenue, but only puddles in front of the store.

At some point on Monday as the severity of the storm was intensifying, I said to the boys, "We're in real danger, but don't panic - look to Jesus and He will help us." Like any teenage kids—they thought I was crazy but I just

Looking from the upper deck of the Bowker family's two-story home out towards the raging ocean in the hours before Sandy hit. The dunes, trees and grey bathhouse would be washed inland later that day as the full force of Sandy bore down on the community of Holgate.

didn't want them to be afraid. I know my words brought me comfort because at that point I was doing a lot of talking with God.

Around 4:30 I was standing at our kitchen window and the waves were enormous, probably between 15-20 feet, and were breaking down McKinley and Washington. Waves were also breaking on the parking lot to the south. My boys and I talked about the importance of moving as a team. We felt safe and ready for whatever was going to come. Brian said we would get some type of a sign as to what to do next. After a monster wave broke over the bathhouse and washed it right down the street, my son Seon exclaimed, "That's a pretty good sign." The next set of waves broke across all three driveways across the street and we all agreed we would move one house closer to the bay and further from the ocean. The boys got into their wetsuits and I got on my gortex. I turned off the main breaker, took the cake I was baking out of the oven and leashed up our dog. With the water level at about four feet deep, Brian unclipped the kayak we had and we used it to float one of the dry bags. I went first, we put Seon in the middle and we slowly and cautiously began making our way to our safe house. Now the water was surging and was chest high. It took us 40 minutes to move one house away.

Adventure at its best.

When we arrived at the "safe" house, we quickly got out of our wet clothes and into dry ones. The electricity was still working, so I put the clothes in the dryer and filled up as many containers of water as I could fill. I sent a text to Brian telling him we had moved. The power finally went out at 7:30 and around 10:00 the windows

and walls downstairs broke out and the house began to fill with water. Each wave would surge water in and then out of the garage. The wind was whipping and it was pouring rain. That's when I really began to pray for God to keep us all safe and to stay with us.

I woke up the next morning at 7:20. It was so quiet. We were able to go right outside as the water had receded, but nothing could have prepared us for the destruction. My husband had sent a text saying the road to Beach Haven was breached. We spent the early part of the morning moving back to our home and then began to assess the damages. Around 11:30 we discovered that many gas mains were broken and natural gas was leaking into the air. We were told the National Guard would be making their way down to get everyone out of Holgate. Until they arrived we got what water we could out of the store downstairs and picked up some of what was left of the yard.

There was a point in the morning when I went to the beach alone and thanked God for sparing our lives. I cried—partially in thanks and partially in knowing that the losses we had experienced were only material things. I also had the thought that the next months and years would provide work for many people who had not been working.

We caught a ride out with the National Guard and made our way to the mainland where my husband picked us up. We spent a few days with friends and then a few weeks with family. In hindsight nothing could prepare us for the work it would take to get home and get our little store open again, but thanks to the prayers, volunteers, family and friends, it has happened. ●

CASINO PIER DEVASTATION

Seaside Heights: Entertainment mecca to disaster area in less than 24 hours.

AS TOLD BY LOU CIRIGLIANO, DIRECTOR OF OPERATIONS
AT CASINO PIER AND BREAKWATER BEACH

The sun rises on the remains of the Jetstar Roller Coaster in Seaside Heights after Sandy devastated this once bustling pier.

Photograph By Jo Hendley

U.S. Vice President Joe Biden reviews the damage at Casino Pier on November 18, 2012. Seaside Heights Police Chief Tommy Boyd is standing to the left.

Reuters/Eric Thayer

I admit—I'm a weather geek. I have more than 14 weather apps on my cell phone that I check regularly. I live near the ocean and, as such, was always prepared in the event of an emergency. When the storm first showed up on the radar, I noticed that one of its projected patterns had it passing right through the heart of New Jersey. But this was around eight days before it hit, and no one was really serious about Sandy at that point.

On Sunday, October 28, 2012, the storm was indeed serious business and the major subject of conversation. At work, we finished preparations and since the weather was still fair, we continued operations as usual that included a birthday party in the Pier Grill. My manager, Jack Burke, and I surveyed the property. We went under the log flume and to the back of the Stillwalk Manor (amusement ride) and the storm surge could already be noticed. Water was considerably higher under the pier even though the storm was more than 30 hours away. We left Seaside Heights around 4 pm. That was the last time I saw the pier intact.

The scenario couldn't be worse. High tide—with full moon—was expected around 8 pm on Monday, October 29. Two storms were on a collision course, one coming in from the west and Sandy coming up along the coast. They joined together to form a Superstorm of immense proportions—820 miles in diameter.

The pier and the coastal towns never stood a chance against the 40-foot waves and 95—mph winds. I am grateful I had the foresight to stock up on extra food, batteries, gas and water. But there were so many others in need. In the wake of the storm throughout Seaside Heights, there were cold nights and long lines at gas stations, but it was nothing compared to the hardships of many other New Jersey communities.

Often, the worst of times brings out the very best in people. The spirit of goodwill was alive and well and thriving in our community and my family and I were grateful recipients—like when a Good Samaritan gave Halloween candy to my daughters, another brought me hot chocolate when I was cold, and another gave me a five-gallon gas container so I could get more gas. I considered these people "angels" who gave us strength and hope.

On November 12, businesses were allowed back into

Seaside Heights. We were able to survey our damage. In addition to the rides we lost, all the basements were flooded by the storm surge. The north basements took on about five feet of water. All items there were lost, as well as the electric service for the entire property except for Breakwater Beach Waterpark. Despite all this, we eventually got to work cleaning out the south arcade basement, storing damaged items into clear bags for the insurance companies to assess. The basement smelled foul and we were working at a feverish pace. It took only a short time for my clothes to become soaked with sea-water and my arms to ache from all the lifting. But this was only the tip of the iceberg. There were many more basements to tend to.

In the dark days of winter, there was light since electricity had been restored to the area by mid-December. By January 2013, officials lifted the curfew. State troopers who patrolled our property each day were replaced by sightseers who wanted to see the JetStar roller coaster in the ocean.

All during the remaining winter and spring, it was surreal going to work each day, but our team continued

(ABOVE) The aerial view shows damage over the Atlantic Coast in Seaside Heights, N.J., **Wednesday, October 31, 2012**, taken from a helicopter traveling behind the helicopter carrying President Obama and New Jersey Gov. Chris Christie, as they viewed storm damage from Superstorm Sandy.

the "Jersey Strong" mentality. They showed up early, did backbreaking work in unfriendly weather conditions, and showed up again the next day. These were the pizza makers, arcade workers, waterpark staff and others who all pitched in to do whatever it took to get the properties of Casino Pier open once again. They did it not just for themselves, but also for the millions who spend time at the Jersey Shore every summer. They are the heroes of the property.

The JetStar was removed from the water on May 14 and boardwalk properties opened to the public on May 24. Remarkably, the 103-year-old carousel, which remained intact, began humming again. Our work will continue for months and years to come, but we'll soldier on until the job is done. It turns out that we were "Stronger than the Storm." ●

RESCUE STORY SEASIDE HEIGHTS

Tommy Boyd

Definition of Hero: A person of distinguished courage or noble qualities.

On October 29, Seaside Heights Police Chief Tommy Boyd and Fire Chief James Samarelli became heroes 36 times. That's the number of lives they saved when Sandy came barreling straight for Seaside Heights.

The iconic shore community is known for many things but the famous photo of its famed rollercoaster submerged in waters is now the one that is logged in people's memories.

"We will rebuild," says Chief Boyd. "We have no choice. This is our home."

Police Chief Tommy Boyd takes a breather to address the media after a grueling week of rescue and recovery work.

AP/Julio Cortez, (ABOVE) Julian Simmonds

Chief Boyd has lived at the shore his entire life. His family ran the beach patrol for decades and he has been on the police force for nearly three decades. He's been on a lot of rescues but he never saw anything like this.

No vehicles could get into or out of Seaside Heights.....something that never had happened before. The Route 37 bridge was closed and Route 35 was flooded.

"We were debating evacuating the police and fire departments and I gave my officers the option of leaving. But they said "If you stay, we stay," says Boyd. "Every officer is a hero."

On the night of the hurricane, thirty-six people were trapped in their homes as the waters rose. The firehouse had become an emergency shelter to seventy people at one point. And all through the night, the rescues continued. Both Boyd and Samarelli risked their lives to search for victims in a 5-ton army truck.

"The water was pushing this huge truck back and parts of homes and the boardwalk were hitting us on the side. I thought we were going to flip and die but by the grace of God, the wheels stayed on the ground," Boyd adds.

Boyd has been honored for his efforts at the 12-12-12 concert and was even brought onstage by Sir Paul McCartney. But the next day, it was back to business and back to the seaside town that will likely be rebuilding for years.

"The boardwalk and the rides are our lifeline. Now I look at the rollercoaster in the water and it breaks my heart. But we're from Jersey.....we'll fight back." ●

October 30, 2012
Downed power lines and a battered road is what Superstorm Sandy left behind as people walk off the flooded Seaside Heights island.

After the Storm: Matt Kelly looks in disbelief at the damage in Seaside Heights, NJ.

October 30, 2012 The Lavallette boardwalk sits in ruins when the sun finally shines for the first time after Sandy's fury.

SURVIVAL STORY LAVALLETTE

Matt Kelly

Matt Kelly didn't take the weather warnings seriously, or prepare for a storm; but Superstorm Sandy was no joke.

I grew up in Lavallette, New Jersey where I learned to surf with my brother Paul. We often watched the weather reports hoping for good waves. We heard the warnings about Sandy but we didn't view them seriously or do anything to prepare for it. Every year we would prepare and nothing had happened in more than 100 years.

On October 29th, we realized this storm was different. We could see the waves rising and grew anxious. We drove around eager to see what would happen. As I look back, I realize how foolish this was.

My sister and her husband lived in Ortley, which is just one mile south of us. Three feet of water came rushing into their house and my dad drove through it to go and rescue them.

Around 8:00 p.m, the water started to come into our house. We tried to bail it out of our garage, but did not make much headway. Fortunately, most of our house is above ground level. Between the wind and rising waters, the night was the longest I had ever known.

When morning finally came, I saw that the water around our house was about five feet deep. There was also a red pigment in the water. I discovered it was some heating oil that was leaking from a tank from a laundromat behind our house. My dad and I swam over pieces of wood and fences to reach what turned out to be a 500-gallon tank. We managed to flip it over so that it would stop leaking.

After the water receded, Paul and I toured the towns of Lavallette, Ortley, and Seaside. At first we used a kayak, and later we rode bikes or just walked. The towns smelled like natural gas and oil. There were houses, boats, and pieces of the boardwalk everywhere.

It was heartbreaking to see the damage but people begged us to take photos. To make matters worse, the municipal department shut the natural gas lines off because of fears of explosions. We weren't able to take showers for more than one week.

We worked countless hours for weeks and months trying to regain some sense of normalcy. While I'm not certain when the Jersey Shore will return to normal, I am certain that I will always respect the storm warnings. I never want to go through this experience again. ●

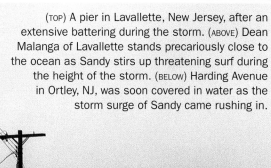

October 30, 2012 Philadelphia Avenue in Lavallette, NJ, is littered with debris, a broken boardwalk and piles of sand. Two church steeples in the background give reason for hope after the damage done by Sandy had taken it all away.

(TOP) A pier in Lavallette, New Jersey, after an extensive battering during the storm. (ABOVE) Dean Malanga of Lavallette stands precariously close to the ocean as Sandy stirs up threatening surf during the height of the storm. (BELOW) Harding Avenue in Ortley, NJ, was soon covered in water as the storm surge of Sandy came rushing in.

SURVIVAL STORY TOMS RIVER

Frank & Jacqueline D'Antonio

It was not a matter of how I was going to die, it was a matter of when...

(ABOVE) A boat awaits passengers looking to escape flood waters on Buchanan St. in Toms River.
(LEFT) Frank and Jacqueline D'Antonio

It's something we'll never forget. Superstorm Sandy and the havoc it wreaked on me and my wife, Jacqueline, is indelibly etched into our memories.

I owned a house in Toms River, New Jersey for 30 years and we were no strangers to East Coast storms, strong winds and heavy downfall. We were lucky that all during those times, we never experienced any property damage. But then came Sandy.

On Sunday, October 28, 2012, we were warned that a hurricane was making its way up the East Coast—and that it was heading our way. On Monday, the City Fire Department officials recommended a voluntary evacuation. It seemed odd, because the weather that afternoon was clear and sunny. My wife and I were both experienced swimmers, closely affiliated with the Coast Guard. All things considered, we decided to stay.

Evening rolled around, bringing with it rain and in-creasingly strong winds—80 or 90 mph. Behind our house, we could see the tide rising and coming closer. I walked around the outside, checking everything including our cars parked out in front, but all seemed okay. Around 8:30 pm, the weather news report on TV indicat-ed that the storm had passed Toms River and would reach New York City in about an hour. This meant the worst was over for us. The winds and rain were slowing down, and I told my wife we were going to be all right. How wrong I was!

About 11:00 pm we suddenly lost our electricity and by 2 am, water started coming into the lagoon behind our house in two- to three-foot swells. Although it was dark, I could still see the tide rolling in. I phoned 911, but even though I tried three times, there was no answer!

By 2:30 am, the water was rising fast and coming inside the house, so I knew we had to get out of there. Then our next-door neighbor phoned and invited us to

November 1, 2012 Only 3 days after the storm and this picture reveals entire first floors wiped out in these beachfront homes. (MIDDLE) Boat damage was extensive amongst Toms River's many inlets along Barnegat Bay. (BELOW) Sandy didn't even knock when she came charging into these beachfront homes, taking away entire walls of houses and dragging the contents hundreds of yards away.

his house, as he had a two-story dwelling.

Leaving our house proved to be a challenge. In only 20 minutes—from 2:15 to 2:35 am—we acquired four feet of water inside and it was quickly rising. As we got to the door, it was already above my knees. I could hardly get the door open because of the force of the water currents, but I finally managed it.

My wife and I tried to walk up to the front of our house. When we got there, the water was up to my armpits! The current was so strong that I knew if either of us fell down, it would sweep us away and we would drown. This was the first time in my life that I was really scared—VERY scared! It occurred to me that it was not a matter of how I was going to die, it was a matter of when.

It took us 35 minutes to walk the 60 feet to our neighbor's house. We arrived there at 3:10 am, and we were safe. I thank God we were able to do it.

After the storm, the damages to our home were great. We lost everything inside in addition to our three vehicles—a Honda Accord, a BMW 3 series, and my restored 1988 Chevy Corvette. But those were only material things and replaceable. My irreplaceable loved ones and friends survived the ordeal and for this, I am grateful.

A verse from the Bible reminded me how God helped us through that storm. In Isaiah 43, verse 2, it says: "When thou passest through the water, I [will be] with thee; and through the rivers, they shall not overflow thee." ●

(TOP AND BOTTOM RIGHT) Debbi Winogracki

October 31, 2012 This aerial photo was taken from a helicopter behind the helicopter carrying President Obama and New Jersey Gov. Chris Christie, as they viewed storm damage from Superstorm Sandy along the Atlantic Coast in Mantoloking, New Jersey.

MANTOLOKING

THE JERSEY SHORE'S "GROUND ZERO"

The small barrier island community is cut in half during the storm, but comes back stronger than ever.

Chris Niebling works for the Office of Emergency Management in Mantoloking, New Jersey – a quaint, Jersey Shore community where it is a short walk to the beach and bay. The area is home to Chris, who has prepared nearly his entire life for disasters but nothing prepared him for Sandy, which destroyed nearly the entire town. Mansions were cut in half. Others vanished from the face of the earth. "It was incomprehensible," according to Chris.

"When the sun finally came up, the only way emergency teams could get into the town was by boat. Gas was spewing out of the homes left standing and I just stared in disbelief wondering how we would ever rebuild."

On October 29, Mantoloking had 520 homes. On October 30, 56 of those homes disappeared without a trace. More than 300 homes were destroyed and the remaining were severely damaged. Mantoloking became the "Ground Zero" of the Jersey Shore. "Every home suffered damage," said Chris. "No one escaped Sandy's wrath."

Around 10:30pm on October 29, Sandy was at its peak, with water swells as high as 17 feet. Two major breaches occurred on Herbert Street and Lyman Street—cutting the island town into thirds. Experts say the water was traveling at a velocity of 20.3 knots, or the equivalent of 23 miles per hour. Sandy also brought the worst of all natural combinations—high tides, a full moon, and powerful winds. In addition to the homes destroyed, Mantoloking also lost its infrastructure of electric, phones, sewers, water and gas lines.

"There were four feet of sand, live wires, and water everywhere so emergency vehicles couldn't move.

AP/Doug Mills

New Jersey Governor Chris Christie (center L) and New Jersey Lieutenant Governor Kim Guadagno (center R) speak to the media while surveying Superstorm Sandy damage at the Mantoloking Bridge/Herbert St./Rt 528 along Rt 35 in Mantoloking, New Jersey,

We finally had to rent ATVs," explained Chris.

A retired firefighter of 36 years, Chris says the department rescued 15 families that stayed during the storm. He calls it a miracle that no one was living in the homes that were washed away—and that there were no deaths or injuries.

In the days that followed Sandy, emergency teams had a new battle: pressure from property owners and politicians to let people back into their homes. They had to keep people out because nothing was structurally sound. In the end, they set up tours for the politicians so they could survey the damage.

"When the tours were over, the blank stares told the story," said Chris. The level of destruction was so severe that the politicians went back and explained to homeowners how bad it was. After that, the pressure stopped and we went to work."

It took several weeks to pave the roads of Mantoloking, and eventually residents were allowed "controlled access" to the area. Emergency officials taking homeowners to their damaged properties remained the most heartbreaking of tasks. "There were photo albums on the streets, toys covered in mold. I don't think there was one person who didn't shed a tear," said Chris.

Eight months later the extent of the damage was still astounding. Hundreds of damaged homes lined Highway 35, still cut in half. Mantoloking became a kind of tourist attraction and people were curious," he said. "Still, there's an eeriness to it. The homes are half missing but when you look inside, you see beds still made and clothes in the closet. It's mind-blowing."

The recovery process was slow but steady. By mid-December, utilities were back on. By mid-March, the first resident officially moved back home. And on June 15, the beaches opened for business. While there was concern about debris in the water, crews combed the sand

and searched the waters for months. The items found have been incredible, says Chris. Crews have "fished" out microwaves, beds, cars, and much more. And there are also tales of how far some items have traveled. One of Mantoloking's heavy road signs was found 20 miles away. Part of a railroad also washed ashore, though no one is quite certain where it came from!

Because of the incredible devastation Mantoloking suffered, it has also gained international attention. Emergency teams from all over the world—from Singapore to British Columbia—have come here to study how to handle a disaster when everything is wiped out.

"The range of emotions these past couple of months has been intense, ranging from fear and sadness to the exhilaration of rebuilding and reuniting with people," said Chris reflectively. "While the shoreline will never look the same and some people who are uninsured or underinsured will likely walk away, we will rebuild. It will take a few years, but Mantoloking is stronger than the storm." ●

A home that was damaged by Superstorm Sandy is seen in Mantoloking, New Jersey.

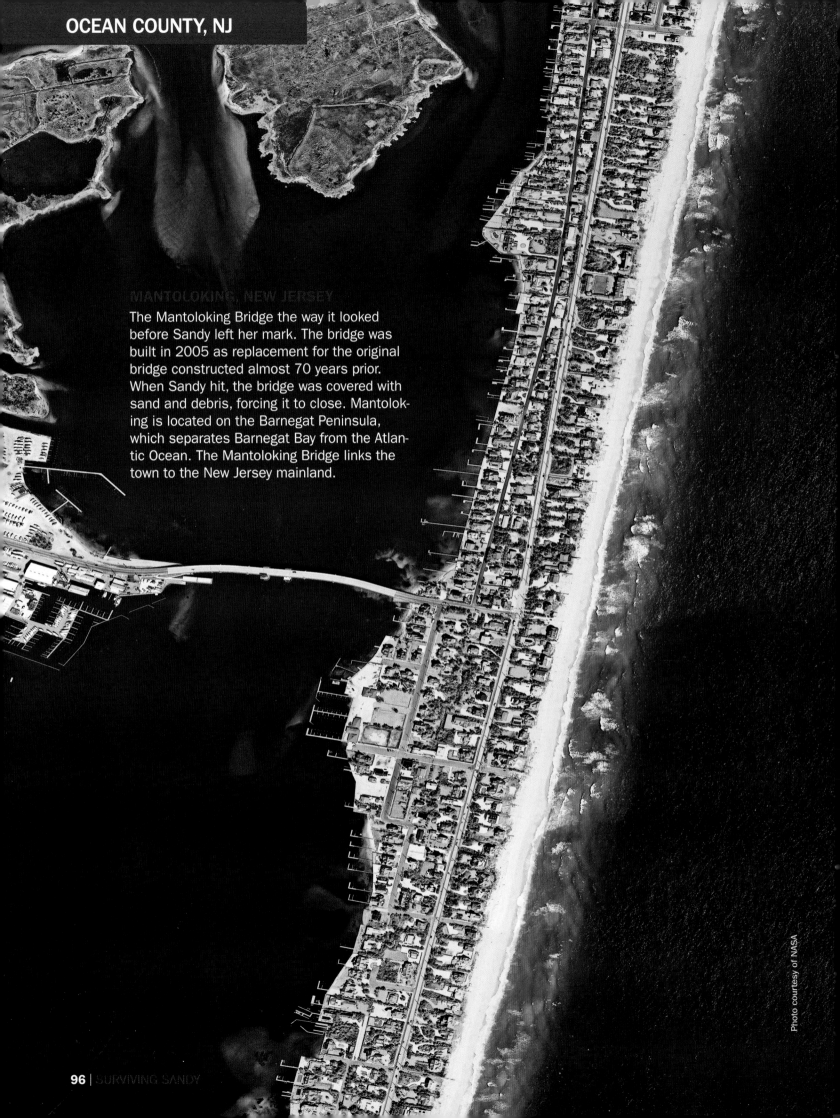

MANTOLOKING, NEW JERSEY

The Mantoloking Bridge the way it looked before Sandy left her mark. The bridge was built in 2005 as replacement for the original bridge constructed almost 70 years prior. When Sandy hit, the bridge was covered with sand and debris, forcing it to close. Mantoloking is located on the Barnegat Peninsula, which separates Barnegat Bay from the Atlantic Ocean. The Mantoloking Bridge links the town to the New Jersey mainland.

Photo courtesy of NASA

(ABOVE) A closer aerial perspective of Ocean Boulevard before Superstorm Sandy, where the distinction between water, homes and roads could easily be distinguished. Contrast that to the storm's aftermath (BELOW) where damaged homes, soil erosion and charred remains are evident. A new inlet was cut across the island, connecting the Atlantic Ocean and Jones Tide Pond.

(THIS PAGE) Aerial photography courtesy of the NOAA Remote Sensing Division.

SURVIVAL STORY MANTOLOKING

Larry Nelson

With water levels on the rise, Larry recalls the frightening events that unfolded in quick succession.

Homeowner Larry Nelson and his dog Sadie who weathered the storm together.

It was like a tsunami—nothing like I had ever seen before," said Larry Nelson, resident of Mantoloking, New Jersey. At 4 o'clock in the afternoon on October 29, 2012, he watched as bay water receded and then burst back with a vengeance. "All of the water was sucked out of Barnegat Bay—it was over 3 feet, and earlier my garage had filled with 6" of water from the ocean, "he said.

On Monday afternoon, Larry thought the worst was over. The water level was at an all-time low and, as Larry noted, "You could literally almost walk across to the other side of the bay. Everything was incredibly shallow." But in reality, it was just beginning. The storm hit with all its intensity that night and into Tuesday morning; and then the storm surge came rolling in.

Inside Larry's house the water was a foot deep, coming in and splashing up against the sliding doors, which really took a beating, as did the porch furniture. Like many families in the area, the Nelsons did what they could to protect their property but they lost a lot—furniture, electronics, and appliances.

Larry notes that about 50 houses were gone immediately after the storm and about 140 to 150 houses were demolished later on—they were beyond restoration.

Political activist and author Thomas Payne once coined the phrase "These are the times that try men's souls." America has certainly had its share of trying times, and now Superstorm Sandy could be added to that list. Despite the hardships, the power of the human spirit overcame all obstacles. Members of The Army Corp. of Engineers, the National Guard and the Department of Transportation worked diligently before, during, and after the storm to ensure the safety of the small Mantoloking community. Once the area was deemed safe enough, Larry and his family were afforded the opportunity to take a tour by Army truck as a result of his wife's position on the Town Council. "We were literally the first civilians allowed back in," says Larry, "and we're all grateful it's over."

Looking out the back door of Larry's house at the recedingbay waters the Tuesday morning after the storm.

LARRY'S DIARY
Highlights During Superstorm Sandy

MONDAY, OCTOBER 29

> About 2 o'clock, Larry walked 2 blocks to the beach and noticed the dune was half gone.

> By later afternoon, surge in garage breaks garage door. Six inches of water flood garage. Took small power tools out of harm's way. Car was in a safe place inland.

> Wind gusts over 50 mph.

> That night noticed whitecaps. Not big waves, on what had been dry land. Water was coming into the house. I took an old towel and stuffed it under door.

> I took Oriental rugs up in addition to any other items I could, and brought them to a higher level in the house.

> Wife evacuates the island, about noon, to Glen Ridge.

> Brought up as much as I could from the first level, including furniture from the living room, kitchen items, paintings, etc.

> I was living on adrenaline while Sadie, my dog, just slept.

> Waves were 1 - 2 feet on the bay.

> Barometric pressure drops 28.40" at 9:30 P.M.

> My wife was staying at a friend's house in Glen Ridge. She was on the front porch when she noticed the branches were starting to break because of the high winds. She decided to move her car from where she had parked it in their drive. Walking to the car, her cell phone rang, and my son was calling her. She stopped to answer and seconds later, a large branch crashed down onto her car. The call from my son really saved her life!

TUESDAY, OCTOBER 30

> At around 7 am, the water was gone from the first floor, but still about 3 feet in the garage. Winds from 30-40 mph from southwest, and some showers. The sun came out and there was a beautiful double rainbow.

> Around 11 am, the first sound of human life I heard was a Black Hawk helicopter, about 300 - 400 ft. off the ground. Most likely it was the National Guard doing surveys.

> I had gas, so could light the stove burners. I was able to cook and stay warm.

> The forecast was for wind and rain showers into the evening. The driveway was completely covered.

> Saw a small boat going south with four people in it. Second sign of life at 11:30 am.

> At 1 pm, I noticed the Black Hawk was back. Soon after, there was a police boat on the scene, along with Coast Guard helicopters and TV crews.

> By evening, I put on my waders, because the water dropped down significantly, and I walked around town and observed the utter devastation.

THURSDAY, NOVEMBER 1

> Bad move: I went to Emergency Management to charge my cell phone. They said "You're here? You have to leave!" So I got a free ride out of town in a police car and my wife picked me up. ●

A sign off Nejecho Beach warning looters. (BELOW) Water starts to seep into the first floor of Larry's house as raging flood waters roll by. (BOTTOM) The Durling House on Old Bridge Street in Mantoloking, which was smashed by Sandy, will be saved and put on a new foundation.

Daring Coast Guard Rescues at the Jersey Shore

Coast Guard Team Members:

Dan Wishnoff, Operations Petty Officer; Chris Henry, Petty Officer; Nick Gera, Petty Officer

A view of the USCG at Manasquan Beach out the door of a Coast Guard helicopter in the aftermath of Sandy.

The United States Coast Guard Station in Manasquan Beach, New Jersey, is staffed by approximately 30 men and women and they are responsible for the waters stretching from Spring Lake down to Seaside Heights, and up to 48 miles offshore. This station played a vital role during Hurricane Sandy and the timeline below details how these brave men risked their lives to save victims along the coast.

Reports of Superstorm Sandy began to come in and they were clearly preparing everyone for the most extreme conditions. Operations Petty Officer Dan Wishnoff began attending regular meetings with the Borough of Point Pleasant in view of creating a hurricane survival plan. All but seven members at the station were evacuated to safe territory. The plan was to ride out the storm, but as conditions began to worsen another four left, leaving just Dan Wishnoff, Chris Henry, and Nick Gera. Due to the lunar tides, coupled with the approaching storm, the water level began to rise earlier than usual. By Saturday night the tide had risen 4' above the normal high tide, and water was rushing through the boathouse and was flooding the streets. This was approximately 60 hours before the storm hit.

The three members who stayed behind decided to retreat to the shelter of the Point Pleasant Fire Station, which is on the west side of the railroad tracks. The local firefighters immediately saw the potential that the Coast Guard members had in assisting with rescues and requested them to return to the Coast Guard Station and gather their dry suits, helmets and rescue gear. As Dan neared the Coast Guard Station, he noticed the water level had increased significantly since they had left only a short while before. Even driving in his Ford F350 dual wheel truck, he felt himself beginning to get caught in the flood waters but managed to reach the station and obtain the equipment needed for the team. He then began his short but extremely treacherous journey back to the fire station.

The Coast Guard crew members and the local firefighters formed an immediate bond, despite having never met before. Their instincts took over and they felt like they had a strong team to handle the imminent calls. The Borough of Point Pleasant had a deuce and a half (Army Transport Vehicle) that was immediately dispatched for use in rescues. This became the Team's home for the next 2-1/2 days.

FIRE DEPT VEHICLE RESCUE

29th October 2012 09:30

The first call came in around 10:00 AM on Monday, 29th October 2012. The Fire Department's Dodge Durango was immobilized in the water while attempting to get to the fire station. Donning their dry suits and protective gear, the Coast Guard members waded towards the trapped vehicle with winches and towlines, with which they successfully hauled the stranded vehicle from the water. This was the beginning of the longest 2-1/2 days ever experienced!

TRAPPED IN SUV

29th October 2012 17:00

The second call came as a result of a downed power pole. Even though this did not involve a personnel rescue, the Fire Department was responsible to ensure that anyone or anything in proximity to the pole was safe. While performing this mission, the men came upon a Ford SUV with 2 occupants that were trying to escape the rising water, and had become stranded. They were successfully rescued and transported to safety.

Chris Henry (LEFT) bringing one of the USCG boats to Cape May to dodge the winter storm that came shortly on the heels of Sandy.

A view of the devastation at Hoffman's Marina from the window of a USCG boat.

OFF DUTY FIREFIGHTER RESCUE
29th October 2012 18:30
A call came from two persons who were stranded in their home on the east side of the railroad tracks. As the rescue team approached the intersection opposite the residence, they could faintly make out 2 persons wading through chest-deep water with a flashlight. Suddenly the flashlight went out and the Team was no longer able to locate them. With power lines and traffic lights swinging dangerously low overhead, trees bending under the forces of the severe winds and their rescue vehicle beginning to float, the team had to make split-second decisions. They reluctantly concluded that they would have to leave the area. In the back of their minds, they couldn't help but wonder what might have happened to these poor persons in the hazardous conditions. They were greatly relieved when they learned later on that these persons were rescued by another boat.

CHRISTINE COURT RESCUE MISSION
30th October 2012 01:45

The Team was dispatched to rescue eight persons from a flooded home. Upon arrival, the Team waded through chest deep waters, only to find out that a forced entry was required. One member quickly kicked down the door and rushed inside. All eight persons were successfully rescued, which included elders and children, and were transported to safety.

POINT BOROUGH RESCUE
30th October 2012 02:00
Immediately following the Christine Court rescue mission, the team was dispatched to rescue three persons in distress. As they approached the location where the persons were stranded, they were all crying in desperation to be rescued. After this mission was complete, the team had successfully rescued a total of 20 persons.

HIGH PRIORITY MEDICAL PATIENT RESCUE
30th October 2012 02:30-04:30
Located in nearby Lagoon, was a bedridden man and his family. With water levels rising rapidly

and the family's inability to move him, they had become trapped and were getting desperate! After several attempts to reach the residence by land, the team had to resort to a waterborne rescue in a Zodiac boat supplied to them by a neighboring town. After an hour of navigating through the ominous surf and physically hoisting the dinghy across non-flooded areas, the team finally reached the home. Upon arrival, they found the man still lying in his bed, which was now floating, with very little clothing and rapidly progressing towards hypothermia. The dangerously ill man and three family members were quickly loaded into the dinghy, and transported to safety.

30th October 2012 6:00
Becoming extremely fatigued from their strenuous duties, the team was forced to return to Fire Station 33 to regain their strength. They managed to get a couple hours of sleep before heading out again into the storm's mayhem.

With the Storm now reaching full intensity, the influx of calls for help became overwhelming.

The team was now faced with an entirely new challenge—the relatively small team of rescue members—compared to those needing assistance, forced them to "pick-and-choose" which calls they could respond to. This was determined by the level of urgency, location, and lives in immediate risk, without endangering their own lives.

RETIREMENT HOME RESCUE
30th October 11:00
An urgent call for help came in from a nearby retirement home where many elderly patients affected by Alzheimer's were located. Leaving the safety of the fire station, the Rescue Workers headed out again on what would end up being their final rescue mission. When they arrived, they maneuvered the Rescue Vehicle up to the front porch area which appeared to be the easiest point of access. Tearing down the railing was required to complete a quick and effective rescue of the many in need. The elderly persons were carried and placed in the back of the rescue vehicle. They were then transported to safety. ●

A NIGHT TO REMEMBER
AT JENKINSON'S AQUARIUM

As others were fleeing, a team of eight guardian angels were just arriving.

BY KATIE GILLIS, MARINE BIOLOGIST

There was an ominous feeling going through our minds as the eight of us hunkered down at Jenkinson's Aquarium as we watched everyone else leaving town in preparation for Superstorm Sandy. Foremost in our minds was the safety of the animals. We had more gas and batteries than we did for past hurricanes, but we didn't really know how to prepare for the forecast of what newscasters were calling "something worse than we have ever seen before."

On Friday, October 26, in preparation for the onslaught, we tested our three gas-run generators, which we would use to run half-life support to the large main tanks, and the battery-operated air pumps to be used on the small tanks. We purchased as many gallons of gasoline and batteries as we could, and all the pumps that ran our filters were hardwired into the electric system.

The ride-out team arrived by 2:00pm on Sunday. Point Pleasant Beach was shutting down. Monday was eerily quiet, but overcast, windy, and rainy. Around 4:00 pm the wind picked up. Telephone poles were swaying. Shingles and siding were flying off houses. Later, I saw that two of the poles had broken and were hanging by their wires. Surprisingly, the aquarium still had power but not for long.

At 6:15 the power went. In an instant, we were thrown into a darkness that lasted for two weeks. We expected

(OPPOSITE) Seaquin, the 22-year old seal at Jenkinson's Aquarium, came through the storm fine, thanks to the watchful eyes of Katie Gillis, who was among the staff that agreed to stay at the aquarium during the storm.

The storm surge comes in with a fury, ultimately surrounding the aquarium and leaving the dedicated staff with a sense of helplessness.

Seven of the guardian angels pose for a picture amidst the wind and rain as the storm approaches.

this, and we were ready. Air-breathing animals, the penguins and seals, would be fine in the blackout, but those that live in tanks must have water that is filtered of waste and freshly re-oxygenated in order to survive. This requires electricity. We raced against time to ensure the survival of thousands of fish. Operating in darkness, we fired up the generators to get air into the large tanks. Next, we worked on unwiring and rewiring one filter on the local and coral tanks. Other team members were lighting our way with flashlights and glow sticks, and putting battery-operated aerators into the smaller tanks on the exhibit floors.

Around 6:45pm, 12 inches of water had collected inside the employee entrance door, right by our basement, and we then saw ocean water streaming down the back wall. The aquarium had borrowed a trash pump and we had it up and running by 7:35pm. As we headed to the shark tank, we heard a loud bang. Fire alarms went off and the water that had been holding steady at 12 inches was now rising quickly. We went up to the top floor where our "command center" was set up, and then determined that we would leave the building. The ocean had broken through our basement and there was concern about the stability of the building itself. We relocated the penguins, moving them upstairs to our quarantine room. We grabbed our essentials and headed towards the bathhouse, connected to the aquarium through the gift shop, and about five steps above the parking lot.

Standing in the pitch black, as we awaited the own-

ers, sea foam showered down on us. The ocean was pounding, the back bays had flooded and Ocean Avenue was under water. To our right what appeared to be a river was running out of our basement and we could just make out the outlines of holding tanks, scattered all over the parking lot. This was probably our scariest moment, as we seemed to be surrounded by water. We were not able to see the damage that we knew was less than 50 feet from us. Soon we realized that the owners could not make it to us; they had been forced to abandon the vehicle and swim back to their houses.

The eight of us sat in the bathhouse, and the stark realization that no one could get to us suddenly overwhelmed us. The cell phone service was spotty, so not all of our texts got through. One of the owners called to explain that the walls in the basement were designed to break away to let the ocean through. If the ocean was flowing in the parking lot, we were completely safe; we could go back upstairs, restart the generators, and try to get some rest. Once back and settled in for the night, we heard the voices of two police officers that had followed our path of glow sticks, and asked if we wanted to be rescued. We declined, and they told us that in actuality, we would probably be better off in the aquarium than anywhere else in town.

The next morning, we surveyed the damage before the next high tide. The crisis was not over. Not only did the ocean break through the wall and fill the basement—destroying pumps, filters, tanks and a quarantine room—

A large diesel generator helps to get the aquarium back up and running, ensuring that the animals have what they need to survive.

(BELOW) Camp Jenkinson's: with the penquins and the seals not too far away, the staff hunkered down to ride out the storm.

All photos by Katie Gillis

it had also pushed 90 percent of our holding tanks out into the parking lot and surrounding neighborhood, and deposited four feet of sand throughout the entire basement. With food and supplies running low, we managed to keep all of the animals on their regular feeding and lighting schedules. We even spent some time playing with the penguins.

Around 4:00pm the construction company arrived to help with the cleanup. We checked generators, air pumps, and the animals' behavior throughout Tuesday. For animals dependent on generators to breathe, the situation remained serious. Other staff entered town on Wednesday to assist us. Many people came forward to help, and at midnight on Thursday, a green diesel generator finally arrived. By the time we lay down to get some sleep, we had lights and all tanks running on full life support for the first time since Monday.

The damage took its toll on Jenkinson's Aquarium, which was not able to reopen to the public until February, 2013. But the experience was one of collaboration and perseverance. Many people brought us supplies and were there when we needed them. Thanks to the team effort there were no lives lost—neither of the animals or the dedicated staff that faithfully cared for them. ●

MONMOUTH COUNTY

*The rescue efforts undertaken were truly heroic
and were successful due to the coordination, cooperation and collaborations
of all agencies that came together in treacherous conditions.*

(THIS PAGE, ABOVE) Miles of empty framework for board-walks are seen along the Shore, thanks to Sandy.
(LEFT) Businesses are closed and covered with plywood along the main street in Sea Bright, N.J.

(OPPOSITE PAGE, CLOCKWISE FROM TOP LEFT) Debris from Sandy is seen on a beach in Long Branch; The destroyed Riverside Cafe on the Manasquan beachfront; **December 5, 2012,** FIrefighters begin to pour water on two houses as they burn on First Avenue in Manasquan just south of Pompano Avenue in an early morning blaze that heavily damaged or destroyed five houses on the Manasquan beachfront; A row of beach homes rest off their founda-tions after Superstorm Sandy came ashore in Sea Bright; Waters flood Ocean Avenue in Sea Bright; The remains of the Avon boardwalk and inlet gazebo looking north from the Shark River Bridge.

THE MONMOUTH COUNTY SHERIFF'S OFFICE OF EMERGENCY MANAGEMENT (OEM)

Sandy brings out the best in emergency response and recovery teams.

BY MICHAEL OPPEGAARD

We knew it was coming several days before the storm even hit the Atlantic Seaboard. The Monmouth County Sheriff's Office of Emergency Management (OEM) team watched the storm's progression and the forecasting models and hoped that the track of the storm would miss us.

As the last weekend of October approached, it became increasingly clear that the likelihood of the storm hitting New Jersey was not only likely, but probable. Following the lead of Governor Christie, the Monmouth County Board of Chosen Freeholders along with Sheriff Shaun Golden, who oversees the Office of Emergency Management, issued an Emergency Declaration for the entire County on Saturday, October 27, 2012, which paved the way for the OEM to direct resources and assistance as deemed necessary.

The Emergency Operation Center, located in Freehold, became operational and was fully staffed by 9:00am on Sunday, October 28. The Emergency Operations Center was staffed by more than 60 people from various County departments and agencies. With the center remaining in operation on a 24/7 basis for the next several weeks, County emergency management staffing was beefed up by a 20-person Incident Management Team from Missis-

sippi that helped us maintain assistance and guidance on recovery missions.

On Monday, October 29, the devastating impact of Superstorm Sandy was being felt all along the Jersey Shore. The morning high tide brought water from the ocean and back bays into communities that would normally flood during full moon and astronomical tide cycles. But Monday night's high tides would bring record-breaking storm surges in excess of 13 feet and sustained hurricane-force winds to the shore communities of Monmouth.

The water levels were unprecedented and quickly flooded communities, leaving those who chose not to evacuate the area stranded in their homes, requiring emergency personnel to assist in rescue efforts.

At the height of the storm, the Monmouth County Sheriff's Office 9-1-1 Communications Center was buzzing—receiving 300 rescue calls—with several more requests for assistance coming into the EOC from many towns along the coast. Most of the calls for assistance were coming from the Bayshore community, while the town of Belmar also had many residents stranded.

Without hesitation, Monmouth County OEM dispatched five high-wheel vehicles to both areas. Over the next several hours, and into Tuesday morning, emergency

(OPPOSITE) **October 26, 2012** A fisherman surveys the oceanfront at York Avenue in the south end of Spring Lake, New Jersey, as Superstorm Sandy makes its way up the coast. (BELOW) Not much remains intact in the devastated neighborhood along Raritan Bay in Monmouth County.

At the height of the storm, the Monmouth County Sheriff's Office 9-1-1 Communications Center had over 300 rescue calls stacked within the Computer Aided Dispatch system and several more requests for assistance were coming into the EOC from many towns along the coast. The majority of the calls for assistance were coming from the northern section of the County known as Bayshore while the town of Belmar also had many residents stranded.

December 11, 2012
Night photo of Front Street,
Union Beach, NJ.

personnel performed over 200 rescues using boats, scuba divers, flat-bottomed boats and the high-wheeled vehicles. The rescue efforts were truly heroic and made successful because of the combined efforts of the agencies.

The Monmouth County Sheriff's OEM, with assistance from the County Health Department and Department of Human Services, operated two evacuation shelters during the storm. The primary shelter at Monmouth University was able to shelter 1,200 evacuees spread out over two adjoining gymnasiums on the West Long Branch Campus. This shelter would see visits from state and Federal officials including Secretary Napolitano from Homeland Security.

The second shelter, located at a defunct troubled-adolescence center in Wall Township, housed 300 evacuees and an assortment of pets, 75 in total, including a snake, two iguanas and a rabbit. This shelter remained in operation until November 19, at which point all evacuees were finally able to find temporary housing or other assistance through FEMA programs.

By late on Tuesday, the 30th, the remnants of Superstorm Sandy were clearly evident, with massive destruction along the coastal communities. Ninety-two percent of the 650,000 residents were without power. There

were downed trees and utility poles strewn all over the County. The first formal damage assessments from the shore towns indicated that 10,000 homes and businesses had been impacted in varying degrees—from broken windows and missing roof shingles to homes being leveled and some washed away altogether by flood waters. Boardwalks that once lined the 27 miles of coastline were completely gone and several feet of water—up to six feet in certain areas—covered Ocean Avenue. Eight separate sewerage authorities reported catastrophic damages to much of their infrastructure. That, coupled with the power outages, made it very difficult to safely monitor, treat and dispose of the waste. As local officials and emergency management personnel toured the area, it was quite evident that Monmouth County's shoreline would never be the same as many landmark locations that held generations of stories and family memories had been washed away.

In the weeks and months that passed since Sandy, many residents remained in over 250 hotels scattered across the state, while others sought new places to live within the County. This proved to be a challenge as the home rental market had a limited supply of available units due to the economic climate of the past few years. As

Large pumps help to lower the water levels in Lake Como, which is between Belmar and Spring Lake.

Silver Lake in Belmar overflowed as a result of the storm surge leaving many residents surrounded by water for days after the storm.

FEMA set up Disaster Recovery Centers at four locations within the area, residents and business owners stood on lines and called 800 numbers to register for assistance. The total number of residents seeking Federal aid reached over 32,000, with well over $100 million being provided to survivors of the storm.

Additional housing help for displaced residents came on December 28, when the first families were moved into renovated housing on an old Army Installation known as Fort Monmouth. Initially there were 42 units renovated into one- and three-bedroom units and as the next few weeks ensued, over 80 more units were made available. By renovating these units on the base, which had just officially closed in September, 2011, FEMA and the U.S. Army Corps of Engineers were able to provide a longer term housing solution to many residents throughout the area. They also provided 11 Temporary Housing Units (THUs) or mobile homes, which were set up in three mobile home parks within the County.

As Monmouth and its 53 municipalities strive to rebuild, many not-for-profit groups have been formed or have changed their focus in an effort to assist those impacted by the storm. Long Term Recovery Group is one such organization, whose primary mission is to provide assistance to those who have unmet needs after receiving assistance from FEMA, insurance companies and other methods of assistance.

One thing for sure is that Monmouth County, like other shore communities, will be working on recovery efforts for many years to come. It will be interesting to see how these shorelines will be rebuilt in a stronger and more resilient manner, so new memories of family vacations can be generated for years to come. ●

(BELOW, LEFT TO FAR RIGHT) A destroyed boat sits atop a ruined pier in front of the Shore Casino in Atlantic Highlands, New Jersey. Boats lay ruined in another example of Sandy's extensive battering on boat owners. A painted fence in Union Beach expresses gratitude to emergency personnel for their heroic efforts during the storm.

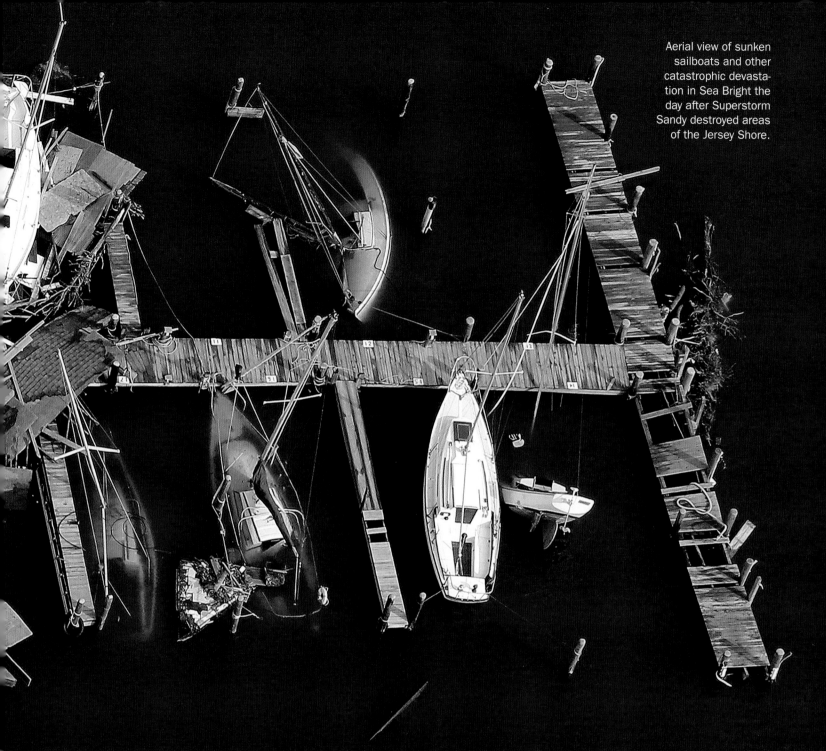

Aerial view of sunken sailboats and other catastrophic devastation in Sea Bright the day after Superstorm Sandy destroyed areas of the Jersey Shore.

GOD BLESS union BEACH Great Job UB Pride
#Sandyprobz
Thank you all Emergency Services
family

SEA BRIGHT

October 31, 2012
Boats are strewn among houses amid wreckage from Superstorm Sandy in Sea Bright, New Jersey.

An aerial view of the swollen waters of Silver Lake, looking east towards the ocean. The Magovern's house can be seen on the southern shore, with the flooded 7th Avenue behind. (LEFT) Brian Magovern's home in Belmar taken a day after Sandy Hit.

SURVIVAL STORY BELMAR

Interview with Brian Magovern

Nothing could have prepared Brian and his wife Jane for the experience that awaited them.

Brian Magovern is no stranger to the hazards of big weather. He grew up in Belmar in his family home at 207 South Lake Drive, across the street from Silver Lake, which runs perpendicular to the coast and is separated from the ocean by only a small strip of land.

In his 60 years at this address, he had been through hurricanes, blizzards, a tornado, and many serious storms. Never once did he have to evacuate: not in 2005, when the banks overflowed after two weeks of solid rain; nor in 2011 when Hurricane Irene left devastating floods in her wake, leaving Brian with water lapping against the home's outside steps.

But then came Sandy.

Brian knew this particular hurricane would be like none other. In preparation, the Borough of Belmar, of which Brian is a Council member, drained the lake to minimize the flooding. Brian worried that maybe they had drained it too low, but as it turned out, he could not have been more wrong. During high tide on October 29, Brian and his wife Jane noticed something very peculiar—white foaming water from the ocean coming up over Ocean Ave. and filling up the lake.

What had taken the Borough almost three days to empty was now filling up in a matter of minutes. They watched the lake break its banks, come across their street and right up to their front steps. From his back door, Brian stared in disbelief at rising floodwaters that had quickly blocked in his pickup truck and car in his driveway, which backed out onto 7th Avenue.

"Never in all my 60 years of living in Belmar have I seen anything like this," said Brian. Quick inspections of his basement and his worst fears were realized—small but steady trickles of water were coming in through the masonry foundation. In front, the water was now up to the third step of his porch. A strong smell of gasoline fumes permeated the air, a result of leaking cars.

It was flooding and it was dark, as power was cut off hours earlier. From out of the darkness, Brian heard something unexpected: "I heard shouting coming from the back of the house, and I wondered if someone was in trouble," he said. "I called out to ask if anyone needed help. But then figures appeared out of the darkness and it turned out to be Belmar rescue personnel coming to help anyone who wanted to be evacuated."

Jane jumped at the opportunity, having had enough of the rising floodwaters and strong fumes. Brian, however, was determined to stay with the house. The rescuers told Jane, "Prepare to get wet - it is about waist-deep on 7th Avenue."

Brian watched his wife and the two rescue personnel walk down beside his house in knee-deep water and disappear into the black darkness. When they reached the back of their property, the floodwaters had risen and the water was now neck-deep.

(ABOVE) A damaged pier at the northern end of Belmar's beach. (LEFT) Brian and Jane Magovern standing in front of their home in Belmar. (BELOW) An aerial view of the flooded waters on 7th Avenue behind the Magovern's house. Jane Magovern was taken out by the rescuers and down this street toward the ocean, which was where the boat was supposed to be waiting for them.

Portrait by Joyce Garlic

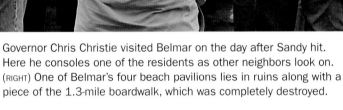

Governor Chris Christie visited Belmar on the day after Sandy hit. Here he consoles one of the residents as other neighbors look on. (RIGHT) One of Belmar's four beach pavilions lies in ruins along with a piece of the 1.3-mile boardwalk, which was completely destroyed.

The rescuers told Jane that there was a boat to pick them up about 100 yards away at 7th Avenue and A Street. They helped her up onto a lifeguard torp and pulled her towards the boat. They got to the corner where they expected to see the boat but it was not there. It had moved on.

While the rescuers were dressed suitably in wetsuits and life jackets, Jane was hampered by her boots and a heavy down jacket that was soaked through. The swirling waters were cold, and large sections of the Belmar boardwalk and other debris were swiftly passing them as they struggled through the strong current.

The rescuers assured Jane that everything would be alright and guided her down through the dark waters to the next rendezvous, which they hoped would be one block to the south. No such luck. The boat once again moved on. The rescue personnel had no radios and couldn't contact the boat so they moved to the next block, the corner of 9th Avenue and A Street. Once again, the boat was not there. By this time Jane was starting to lose strength from the cold water and

the strong current, so they decided to head west on 9th Avenue and seek higher ground. After about two blocks they reached shallower waters and were able to wade their way through. At Main Street, five blocks away, the rescuers were able to get Jane out of the water and into a waiting ambulance. She had been in the cold floodwaters for over 40 minutes.

It wasn't until the next morning that Brian heard of the harrowing experience his wife had endured at the hands of Sandy. In the storm's aftermath, he used his kayak to travel back and forth to his house. His basement had filled up with six feet of water, just shy of the floor joists of his first floor. It took four days for the water to recede around Brian and Jane's house, two weeks to restore power and 18 days to restore heating. Both vehicles were lost.

Despite it all, "there was no loss of life in the town," said Brian thankfully. "While Hurricane Sandy caused widespread destruction, it brought out the best in Belmar's community spirit—with neighbors helping neighbors get back on their feet again." ●

(ABOVE) Workers pumping water out of Silver Lake across Ocean Avenue and back into the ocean. It took about four days of around-the-clock pumping before the floodwaters started to recede and people could return to their homes. (BELOW) Belmar's iconic boardwalk shows nothing but the framework. The floorboards were made from composite wood lumber that proved to be a challenge to dispose of. Some pieces of the boardwalk were found a quarter-mile away from the beach.

(BELOW) An aerial view of Belmar's beach, showing a sand-filled Ocean Avenue, no boardwalk and a beach house moved up on the road. In the background is the swollen Silver Lake, with its floodwaters blocked in.

Lieutenant Katherine Ustler of the United States Coast Guard stands aboard the Sailfish, an 87-foot coastal patrol boat.

SURVIVAL STORY SANDY HOOK

Katherine Ustler
Lieutenant, Sandy Hook Coast Guard

Katherine Ustler leads her crew to navigate the stormy waters of Superstorm Sandy—learning valuable life skills along the way.

Katherine Ustler has the sea in her blood. Shortly after graduating from the Coast Guard Academy where she majored in marine and environmental science, she was stationed on a 270-foot median endurance cutter, the Thetis, in Key West, Florida. From there it was on to Bahrain, in the Arab Emirates, where she was the executive officer of a patrol boat relief crew, providing security for oil platforms in the Persian Gulf. "That was a pretty cool experience," she said.

Her next port of call took her home—to Staten Island, where she was stationed on the Sailfish—an 87-foot coastal patrol boat. "We work for Sector New York and all of District One," Katherine explained, "which goes from Long Branch, New Jersey, to Maine." The primary missions of Sailfish are port security, fishery enforcements and search and rescue efforts.

On the Sunday afternoon before the storm, the Sailfish crew of 11 was positioned in Sandy Hook, New Jersey, to maintain search and rescue coverage. They then went to a mooring ball in the Hudson River just south of the George Washington Bridge. "Our mission was to moor south of the bridge, and to be on standby for search and rescue," explained Katherine.

On Monday night about 9pm, she got a call from Sector New York saying there was a report of 20 people in the water, in Graves End Bay, just south of the Verrazano Bridge. "So we got the boat underway, untethering it from the mooring ball, which proved a little dicey. I felt really bad for the guys out on deck—60-knot winds hitting you in the face, it is raining, and it is dark," Katherine said.

> "Cars were piled up on top of each other, barracks and housing would have to be condemned, and the pier had floated off its pilings."

The journey down the river through New York harbor proved to be an obstacle course: "We had about six-foot seas in the harbor and the boat was rocking pretty hard. There were full trees in the water at this point. We had heard a report of shipping containers that had broken loose. The debris in the water was a lot more than I expected. We never actually saw any of the containers… you didn't know exactly what was there, or what wasn't there."

Adding to the eeriness was the darkness. Staten Island had lost power; most of lower Manhattan had lost power. The crew watched as neighborhoods in Brooklyn sequentially lost power as they passed by.

The sturdy Sailfish finally arrived at its destination, just south of the Verrazano Bridge, where there were ten-foot seas. Katherine then got in touch with the Command Center only to learn that the people who had been stranded in the water had made it back to shore. "From what I was told, it was a handful of people on a pier taking pictures and the pier collapsed." So back the Sailfish went, up the river to the mooring ball—which is where they stayed until just before dawn on Tuesday morning, when they set out for Coney Island.

"We had heard reports…Breezy Point and Coney Island were constantly calling for help. I can only think back to Katrina, where people were stranded on roofs and being washed out. We figured if we could get there by sunrise, we could assess the situation from the shoreline, and do whatever we could to help." It turned out, however, that there weren't as many people trapped

as originally estimated. When the tide went out, most of the floodwaters went with it and so there was little Katherine and her crew could do. So they set their sights on Sandy Hook.

The scene there came as a real shock. For starters, the pier was gone so they sent a small boat in with three crewmembers. They managed to tie the boat up to a small pier that was still standing. They came back with pictures that showed utter devastation: "Cars were piled up on top of each other, barracks and housing would have to be condemned, and the pier had floated off its pilings," said Katherine. "That is when we realized how big the storm actually was."

The crew stayed on for three more days to help with search-and-rescue operations. But thoughts about the fate of their own homes were on their minds. The few crewmembers that lived on the base knew that at least their homes were standing but had a lot of water damage. Little did they realize that their homes would shortly be condemned.

"I live on the boardwalk about 12 miles south of Sandy Hook and I had no idea if my building was even still going to be there. The people who lived further south didn't know if they had homes to go home to or what they were going to face. And we didn't have cars, so we were stranded," said Katherine.

Katherine and her crew stayed on "immediate recall" status for a week after the storm, where they performed looting patrols along the Shrewsbury River, in the towns of Monmouth Beach, Sea Bright, and others. This vigilance was necessary: "A couple of days after the storm,

(ABOVE) The CGS Sailfish docked in Bayonne, New Jersey, where it was transferred after the Sandy Hook facility was put out of commission as a result of damage from the storm.

(RIGHT) **October 29, 2012** The CGS Sailfish is secured to a mooring ball in the Hudson River just south of the George Washington Bridge during the storm.

some people were taking kayaks and running up to the homes and taking money, jewelry and prescriptions," said Katherine. "We were helping out the New Jersey State Police who were just overwhelmed. Luckily we didn't have to apprehend anybody."

As for Katherine personally, it took about a month to get power and water back in her home. She moved in with her parents on Staten Island and the Coast Guard officially changed her crew's homeport to Bayonne, New Jersey, as Sandy Hook's pier was still being repaired. "We were able to get the crew members funded to move so they could be closer to Bayonne versus Sandy Hook, too," said Katherine. "But when you look at all of the expenses involved—car mileage, gas, tolls, etc.—it has been a real hit on the personal lives of everybody here." They have every intention of returning to Sandy Hook once reparations are complete. ●

SURVIVAL STORY UNION BEACH

Joe Argentina

Joe Argentina, whose home was destroyed and relocated by Superstorm Sandy, begins to rebuild.

Joe Argentina is the owner of a two-story house formerly located at 710 Front Street in Union Beach, NJ. When Sandy came thundering in on October 29, 2012, it brought a devastating tidal surge and fierce winds, gathering everything in its path. Joe's house was destroyed washing up some 200 yards away from its foundation, and finally, settling in a nearby marsh area. Luckily Joe and his family had heeded the warnings from officials and escaped the storm, but he returned to find nothing resembling his home where it once was located.

Although the storm did not spare many of Joe's possessions, his rebuilding process began with a search for any he could save from the wreckage. Like much of the Union Beach community, the road to recovery will be a long one and will require much patience, diligence, and hard work. ●

(ABOVE) The main story of Joe Argentina's house, which is now located in a marsh 200 yards away from its original location at 710 Front Street. (BELOW, LEFT TO RIGHT) The foundation of Joe Argentina's house was all that remained in its original location; Joe Argentina and his wife Lori with children (left to right), Jessica, Veronica, and Katrina Ramos; Joe retrieves some personal belongings from the remains of his home.

Ferocious waves crash through walkway rails along the Shore.

RESCUE UNION BEACH

Chief Robert Laberta

Fire Chief Robert Laberta and his team are on duty—and on top of their game—during Sandy.

October 29, 2012. To say that it was not business as usual for Fire Chief Robert Laberta would be an understatement. On that fateful day, while Superstorm Sandy pounded the region, rescue workers at Union Beach's fire station performed 77 water rescues, fought countless fires, and were faced with many heartbreaking challenges and unthinkable devastation.

In the days before Superstorm Sandy made landfall, Chief Laberta and his team worked to gather resources, and to be prepared to fulfill their huge responsibility of keeping the residents of Union Beach safe. The Chief never wanted to play catch-up during emergency management, so reverse 911 systems were put into place to notify everyone of the serious danger that lay ahead, and authorities went door-to-door to demand evacuations. Resources were commandeered such as boats, front-end loaders to aid in the rescue efforts, dump trucks and loaders to assist in the rescues.

Flooding caused by high tide began the night before, on the 28th, as the storm reached New Jersey. As weather conditions steadily deteriorated, the number of 911 calls steadily increased. Residents called as they watched their neighbors in danger, and were unable to help themselves. Families were holding babies above their heads in the first floors of their dwellings. Firemen were up to their necks in water putting their own lives at risk to rescue others. On Brook Ave., every house was in danger of collapsing; many homeowners could be seen swimming out of their homes while others were floating down the street on rooftops.

While the rescue workers toiled to save those endangered by flooding, including an 80-year-old woman in an attic who decided she was going to die in her home, numerous structure fires were breaking out simultaneously posing further threats.

Flooding forced firemen from Union Hose's 2nd Station to abandon the firehouse, while their brush truck was stuck on a small island. The stranded firemen took shelter in Pluggies Deli, until a fire broke out just across the street in a two-story frame house/motorcycle shop. They managed to fight the fire back until the pump blew out. Good luck was with them at that time: If they hadn't been so close when the fire broke out, there would have been no way to reach it because the other trucks were broken down.

Later, in the early morning hours on 9th Street, a car ignited setting a nearby house on fire and once again, Chief Laberta and his firefighters were quickly dispatched. When it rekindled and the structure collapsed hours later, Holmdel and Aberdeen Fire Departments, realizing that the Union Beach men were on the verge of exhaustion, came in to assist.

These courageous firefighters are family men in their

On Brook Ave., every house was in danger of collapsing; many homeowners could be seen swimming out of their homes while others were floating down the street on rooftops.

Two weeks post-Sandy, homes shattered by the Superstorm are seen strewn throughout Union Beach.

(RIGHT) Devastated residents of Union Beach search through the remains of their storm-battered homes.

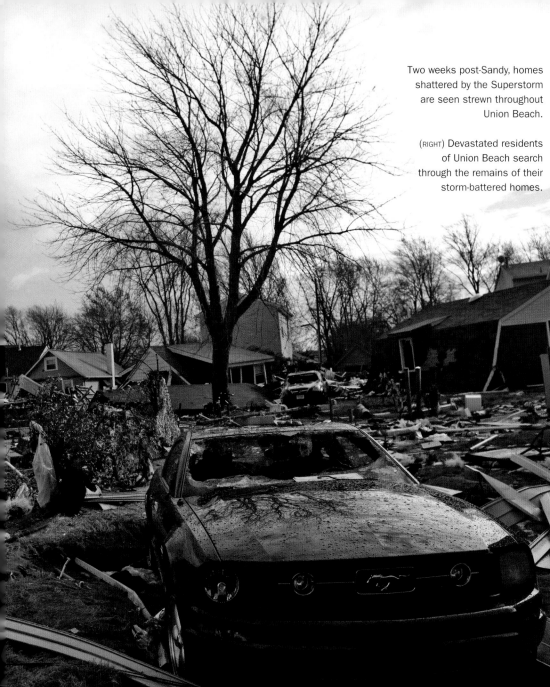

Photos by Reuters/Eric Thayer

own right and although they were on the job to save others, they also faced dangers and hardships on their own home fronts. Lieutenant Justin Visajio needed to rescue his own wife and children; Union Hose's captain got the news that his family was attempting to escape and their vehicle was floating away. Throughout the duration of the storm, five firemen were taken to the hospital suffering from hypothermia.

At the firehouse they raced against time to save equipment from the quickly approaching floodwaters. The water rose so fast that they barely made it out and had no choice but to abandon the ladder truck. All told, Harris Gardens had over seven feet of water in the firehouse. Residents who had been taken there, and to other public facilities, had to be moved as the floods approached. All of the residents who were sheltered at the Memorial School on Morningside Ave. were shuttled away in school buses

until those buses broke down.

Desperate for more equipment to aid in the rescues, the firemen tried to reach Monmouth County Radio Room requesting for help in treading water. Eventually, the Monmouth County Highway Dept. dispatched two trucks with drivers who accompanied the Union Beach firemen in rescue efforts. Many other towns also came to the aid of Union Beach including the fire departments of Holmdel, Aberdeen, Cliffwood Beach and North Centerville — in addition to four men from Missouri, one from Bristol, PA, and one from Philadelphia.

It was around 2am on Tuesday morning when Superstorm Sandy began to subside. A total of 60 men were on duty all through the night. They had performed a whopping 77 water rescues. Although Union Beach largely lay in ruins, no lives had been lost. And that, according to Chief Laberta, made the operation a resounding success.

Union Beach Rescue Timeline - Chief Robert Laberta

October 29, 2012

7:18 am	820 Prospect needs to be evacuated – Fire truck dispatched for manpower
7:35 am	820 Prospect evacuated, occupants en route to shelter
10:17 am	No motor vehicles on roadways – essential personnel
10:20 am	Union Avenue flooding between the bridge & Jakeabobs – person needs to be evacuated
10:46 am	208 Union Avenue is evacuated and unsecure
10:55 am	65-66 711 Front Street is evacuated
11:02 am	Wires down at 506 Union Avenue
12:38 pm	Emergency sirens activated
12:46 pm	Code Red message being updated
12:53 pm	Wires sparking behind McDonalds

2:16 pm
Tree fell on the house at 1708 Florence Avenue

2:17 pm	330 Prospect Avenue needs to be evacuated
2:31 pm	41 people in shelter
2:54 pm	Snapped pole at Shore Road and Poole Avenue
3:03 pm	Tree down by Scholer Drive
3:33 pm	Shelter is out of power
3:34 pm	Tree on a house with children inside at 523 Columbia Avenue
3:43 pm	Smell of gas at 805 4th Street
4:30 pm	Tree down, wires arching at 434, 431 & 428 Clark Ave residents will be evacuated
4:30 pm	Several transformers popping on Clark Avenue
4:37 pm	Occupants of 431 & 428 Clark Avenue are evacuating – trying to reach others on block
4:48 pm	Wire cut at 519 Park Avenue
4:57 pm	Wires arching at 813 3rd Avenue and 525 Washington Avenue
5:02 pm	Florence and 3rd Ave flooded out – can't get to 813 3rd Avenue
5:05 pm	Transformer fire behind 519 Cambridge Avenue
5:32 pm	FA Building being evacuated
5:34 pm	Three residents at 431 Clark Ave and five residents from 428 Clark Avenue evacuated
5:54 pm	Transformer blew at Dock and 3rd Street
6:02 pm	4 adults, 3 children need to be evacuated at 933 6th Avenue
6:09 pm	402 Campbell Street - transformer

	fire with wires in water & burning side of the house is inaccessible. 2 ½ ton truck dispatched to 402 Campbell Street, but cancelled – water is 2 feet deep
6:39 pm	Two front end loaders are needed for evacuation - put call to County for 833 3rd Street
6:54 pm	719 7th Street calls for evacuation and 5 people evacuated on Rte. 36 North - all are safe
7:20 pm	Call for evacuation at Poole and St. James Avenue
7:24 pm	7 rescued people being transported to shelter
7:28 pm	Mayor needs evacuation
7:45 pm	People at 322 Broadway calls for evacuation. Arrived at Police Dept Station for safety
7:58 pm	8 people need to be evacuated at 818 Prospect Avenue
8:02 pm	Vehicle with trapped occupants on Heckleman Street
8:05 pm	Pole down across Stone Road
8:10 pm	A car floating on Poole Avenue – unreachable. The people self-rescued and are safe
8:18 pm	Heckleman Street residents are rescued

8:21 pm
46 Scholer Drive house under water - infant being held in the air

8:42 pm	18 Marine One is in water heading to 8th & Florence Avenue
8:53 pm	Electrical fire at 229 Broadway
9:04 pm	Elderly resident at 611 Poole Avenue is in the attic needing rescue
9:38 pm	Marine Boat rescued resident trapped in attic at 7th & Florence Avenue
9:53 pm	Structure fire at 915 Florence Avenue

9:48 pm
Bayshore Hospital being notified of the amount of victims and asked if they're capable

9:56 pm	Resident at 719 7th Avenue is in boat and rescued
10:08 pm	Victims on roof at 800 Brook Avenue
10:23 pm	Victim in front of Pluggys Two having seizures
10:32 pm	Missing children at 818 3rd Street
10:35 pm	Smell of gas at 27 Scholer Drive, residents are light headed
10:45 pm	People in water at 800 Brook Avenue
10:49 pm	7 people in custody at Union and Bayview Avenue needing transport
10:55 pm	Florence & 9th Street - structure on fire collapsed
11:06 pm	340 Front Street calls for evacuation
11:14 pm	Structure collapses at 820 Brook Avenue with one victim on roof and other in water
11:16 pm	Heading back to EOC with 13 victims in a 2 ½ ton truck
11:20 pm	Multiple structure collapses on Brook Avenue, search for missing victims. None in sight
11:26 pm	House floating on Brook Avenue towards Union Avenue with victim on roof
11:33 pm	Ruptured gas line at 725 Brook Avenue

October 30, 2012

12:29 am	Car fire up against house at 9th & Florence Avenue
12:31 am	Firefighters/EMT coming from Carlton, PA
12:50 am	Condos collapsed at Pine & Front Street
12:58 am	932 Center Street calls for evacuation of two people in the attic
1:00 am	Car & structure fire is being fought at 9th Street and Florence Avenue
1:35 am	Jakeabobs main is leaking – everybody's gas main in that area is leaking

2:30 am
Two adults and pets rescued at 211 Gateway Way

The right side of the house at 705 Front Street remains standing after its left half crumbled in the wake of Sandy's storm surge.

New York City and the Verrazano Bridge can be seen on the horizon from the shores of Union Beach, littered with debris from this beachfront property.

(ABOVE) After Superstorm Sandy, the destroyed Jakeabob's restaurant is seen from Front Street. (BELOW) Jakeabob's staff poses for a group photo prior to the unexpected devastation of their livelihoods.

DEVASTATION UNION BEACH

Jakeabob's Restaurant

Popular local eatery, well-known for its casual water-front dining, was nearly washed out to sea in Superstorm Sandy's wrath.

Gigi, the owner of Jakeabob's, left her restaurant that day never to return to the same tranquil atmosphere again. Gigi recalls waiting out the storm in anticipation, expecting to see damaged carpets and substantial flooding damage whenever she could return. At midnight she tried to no avail to reach the restaurant. Finally at 3:00AM, Sergeant Chuck Ervin drove Gigi down to see what was left of it. Utter devastation met their eyes. The water had risen over the top of the building, and all of the contents had been washed out the front door. The restaurant was in splinters.

In the days following Sandy, Gigi organized and ran a pantry with the pastor at Boro Hall to provide food and relief for displaced residents. She also set up a nonprofit charity www.giveub.com. Red Cross came to the restaurant 15 days later but didn't offer much help. Gigi is now working to rebuild the old bar to be called "Jakeabob's Off the Bay." ●

(ABOVE) Before facing the forces of Sandy, Jakeabob's seaside restaurant rests against a tranquil sunset, providing an exquisite atmosphere for customers (BELOW) After Sandy ripped through the area, this seaside restaurant portrays an extreme contrast to that seen above. It is now a scene of disaster and despair.

MIDDLESEX COUNTY

An amazing story from the county at the mouth of the Raritan Bay, which absorbed a hard hit from Sandy's storm surge.

(LEFT) Ten members of the Lockwood Boat Works crew stop for a photo in between the many hours of post-Sandy cleanup. Behind the crew are the new 50-foot pilings that will be used to replace the ones damaged in the storm.

DEVASTATION SOUTH AMBOY

Lockwood Boat Works

When devastation and loss came thundering in, the Lockwoods sprang into action and were able to resume normal operations quickly.

When **Ellen Harrigan**, manager of Lockwood Boat Works in South Amboy, N.J., heard of Superstorm Sandy's approach, she knew that flooding was inevitable. Just one year earlier, during Hurricane Irene, the Lockwoods had experienced flooding at their boat yard and every report was promising that Superstorm Sandy would be worse.

Before the storm arrived, the staff worked quickly to fulfill the requests of anxious boat owners, and to get as many boats as possible out of the water. With boating season coming to an end, many existing customers requested that their boats be moved to winter storage.

The Lockwoods moved as many boats as they could but it proved impossible to get all the boats on dry land before the storm arrived.

As weather conditions worsened on Monday, the Lockwoods operated as normal for as long as they could. They kept the store open, laid sandbags, and dug a ditch to protect the store, shop, and boat yard. The paint shed floor was burrowed out to circulate air, so they placed a pump in the bottom and swept water into the hole as it came in. As the storm gained strength, the water rose faster. By 2:30, they were forced to shut the store. The pump was completely overrun and the shed had 4 feet of water inside of it by 6:30pm. The Lockwoods had never experienced anything like it before! As it got dark, the workers rushed around laying sandbags and moving equipment to higher ground in an attempt to save everything they could. It became obvious to Ellen that major destruction awaited.

The horror was only just beginning. As Ellen stood back to examine the situation, she saw a shower of sparks coming from the electrical transformers as the

A twisted mangle of sailboats seen by Ellen and her sister as they reached the bottom of the hill on their way to the dock.

water reached them. The police and fire department arrived and told the Lockwood crew to leave. They cut off the power and the transformer smoked, ready to blow up. With no lights there was little they could do so Ellen instructed her team to go home.

Later, Ellen's two brothers went back to the dock in a rowboat. They first noticed the diesel tank starting to shift. Before they could react, a 48-foot boat floated off its jacks and shot across the yard. Then another boat, and another. Feeling helpless, the brothers returned home.

At dawn, Ellen and her sister returned to the docks to begin the arduous process of cleaning up. The ruin was overwhelming. Not sure how to begin, Ellen's brother Mike offered his advice, "Start like any other day, turn on all the machines." The crew started cleaning up debris. A crane arrived on Wednesday and they began to move some of the smaller boats that had been strewn all over — some as far as a mile away from where they should have been. A 500-ton crane was brought in later to lift the heavier and longer boats and some that had landed in the marshland.

Although the phone lines were down, the Lockwoods' cell phones rang constantly with anxious customers inquiring about their boats. By a stroke of good fortune, the Lockwoods managed to save most of them. Some things couldn't be saved and the family faced a financial loss of approximately $1 million in the yard.

With seven feet of water in the shop, everything was soaked. The upper part of the shop that had never seen damage before was underwater. The team got right to work to save everyone's tools. They set up an assembly line, and every tool and drill was washed, rinsed, greased, and left to dry all week.

After a short time, the hard work paid off and Lockwood's Boat Works was back up and running. Using gas-powered generators for electricity, the store opened the next day. It was the only store open in town, and it hardly missed a beat. On Thursday, they were fortunate enough to receive a shipment of fuel tanks and jerry jugs, becoming the only ones in the area with any stock.

A boat lies beached on the slope, not far from the highway barrier, indicating the height of the record storm surge. (BELOW, LEFT TO RIGHT) Several Lockwood workers try to salvage a fishing boat that had become a victim of Superstorm Sandy. Two sailboats float on their sides after being blown over by Sandy's violent winds.

Friends and neighbors came from all over to make coffee and cook with the gas oven. The Lockwoods had become the community heroes.

The first customer to arrive at the dock was one who lost a 48-foot boat to Sandy. Seeing his family's boat at the bottom of the pile, he and Ellen started to cry. They were heartbroken but their spirits remained strong. The next day he brought pizzas and sandwiches to the family for all the work they were doing and other customers brought food to them as well over that difficult stretch of time. It was a great demonstration of the love and care in the community that the Lockwoods share.

Lockwood Boat Works is already prepared for the next storm. The plan includes taking the equipment up to the second story if flooding is predicted, hoisting the transformer on a pole away from the water, and resting the dock on 50-foot pilings—10 feet higher than before.

The Lockwoods lost much in terms of machinery. Through hard work, dedication and a passion for what they do, there is no doubt in anyone's mind that Lockwood Boat Works will be an anchor in their community for many years to come. ●

A 500-ton crane removes some of Lockwoods' displaced boats from the nearby marsh. (BOTTOM) After being torn from their 40-foot pilings, sections of the Lockwood's dock float in a jumbled heap.

HUDSON COUNTY

Nearly half of Hudson County became part of the Hudson River for a few frightening hours as Sandy brought water levels to a record-breaking height.

HOBOKEN

(ABOVE) **October 31, 2012** Two days after the storm, a man standing on a flooded street stops to speak with someone who is left inside the building.
(ABOVE, RIGHT) **Oct. 29, 2012** The Hudson River expanded its borders, flooding the Lackawanna train station during Sandy's approach.
(RIGHT) **October 31, 2012** The National Guard comes to the rescue on a flooded street, evacuating residents from their apartments.

October 30, 2012 Across the river from New York City, twisted ruins are all that is left of the Hudson River marina in Hoboken, New Jersey.

U.S. COAST GUARD   109

AP/Charles Sykes

(ABOVE) **October 30, 2012** One day after the storm, cyclists make their way through the floodwaters in Hoboken, New Jersey.
(BELOW, MIDDLE LEFT) **October 30, 2012** Mike Donofrio, a resident of Hoboken, is stranded after his car stalled in the floodwaters.
(BELOW, MIDDLE RIGHT) **October 30, 2012** With only a few belongings and their dog, Blaine Badick and Andrew Grapsas cross a flooded street after leaving their Hoboken home.

(BELOW LEFT) **October 31, 2012** After evacuating a flooded building with its owner, a dog named Shaggy is carried off of the National Guard truck. (BELOW RIGHT) Heartbroken residents of Weehawken, New Jersey embrace before beginning the daunting task of cleanup from Superstorm Sandy. Some homes in their low-lying community known as "The Shades" were deluged with as much as six feet of water. Residents who had chosen not to evacuate this neighborhood before the storm were later rescued by boat.

STALLION
AUTO SERVICE INC.
• Domestic & Foreign Cars
• Transmission and Engine
  Complete Service
201-229-0038

BERGEN COUNTY

*Although largely protected by steep cliffs that line the Hudson River,
even New Jersey's most northeastern county experienced severe flooding and ruin.*

AP/Craig Ruttle

LITTLE FERRY

(ABOVE) **October 30, 2012** As the aftermath of Sandy looms, rescue workers transport residents out of town by boat.

(RIGHT,TOP) **October 30, 2012** A fireman carries a resident's dog to safety from flood waters. (RIGHT,MIDDLE) After being rescued, this woman's emotions display the trauma and sadness that thousands of people were feeling after realizing the toll the storm had taken on their lives, and belongings. (RIGHT) Residents, including a young child, are rescued by emergency personnel from flood waters.

NEW YORK

AS THE SUN ROSE ON TUESDAY, OCT. 30TH, ONE OF THE WORLD'S LARGEST CITIES, HOME TO 8.2 MILLION PEOPLE, AND WELL-KNOWN AS THE CITY THAT NEVER SLEEPS, STOOD STILL AND SILENT IN THE AFTERMATH OF SUPERSTORM SANDY.

NEW YORK, NEW YORK

On the morning after Superstorm Sandy ravaged the City, the Brooklyn Bridge stood strong and bright against the backdrop of a dark and silent NY skyline. A record-breaking surge and violent winds shut down the city's electrical system leaving the Big Apple in complete darkness.

NEW YORK

5.3 MILLION

CUBIC YARDS OF DEBRIS WERE
REMOVED FROM NEW YORK

80

HOUSES BURNED
TO THE GROUND
IN THE BREEZY POINT
NEIGHBORHOOD
OF QUEENS

10,000

CALLS PER HALF-HOUR
WERE RECEIVED
BY 911 DISPATCHERS
ON THE NIGHT
OF OCT. 29

BY THE NUMBERS

670,000
CON EDISON CUSTOMERS WERE WITHOUT POWER IN NEW YORK CITY

15
DAYS OF GAS RATIONING TOOK PLACE IN NEW YORK CITY

124
YEARS SINCE THE STOCK EXCHANGE HAD LAST BEEN CLOSED DUE TO WEATHER

57,000
UTILITY WORKERS FROM 30 STATES AND CANADA CAME TO NY TO RESTORE POWER TO THE CITY

AP/Mark Lennihan

BREEZY POINT, QUEENS, NEW YORK

Tuesday, October 30, 2012
A devastated firefighter studies the smoking remains of one of 80 houses in Breezy Point, NY, that were ravaged by a fire which broke out the evening of the hurricane.

(ABOVE) Richard B. Levine/The Image Works
Map by Steve Walkowiak/SWmaps.com

LONG BEACH, LONG ISLAND, NEW YORK
This 2.2-mile boardwalk, built in 1917 and enjoyed by thousands of people year round, was battered to splinters by Superstorm Sandy. It will now be torn down and rebuilt at an estimated cost of $25 million.

AS SUPERSTORM SANDY TOOK AIM AT THE COAST, New Yorkers prepared for the worst, but devastation that far exceeded anything they imagined was in store. An overwhelming storm surge combined with high tide forced water levels 9-14 feet above normal, flooding the New York area. Battery Park on the tip of Manhattan lay beneath 13.88 feet of water! A 32.5-foot-high wave—the second largest recorded during Sandy—crashed just outside the NY Harbor! Could we have imagined that 35 blocks of Manhattan from Battery Park to 14th Street would be under water? In addition to flooding, wind gusts up to 95 mph tore through the area bringing down countless trees and power lines, leaving thousands indefinitely in darkness and danger.

"DON'T BE COMPLACENT, NEW YORK"

— MAYOR MICHAEL BLOOMBERG IN THE DAYS BEFORE SUPERSTORM SANDY STRIKES

Mayor Michael Bloomberg's office was on full alert days before Sandy ever made landfall. Addressing the nation's largest city, the Mayor delivered the first of many updates to New Yorkers on October 28 from the Office of Emergency Management in downtown Brooklyn.

"They now are talking about a surge from six to eleven feet. The gale-force winds are going to start late this afternoon. The worst of the storm will still be on Monday night; tides overnight will lead to flooding in low-lying coastal areas—those designated as Zone A," Bloomberg said.

Twenty-four hours before Sandy made its way to the City, Mayor Bloomberg placed an Executive Order mandating the evacuation of Zone A areas. He ordered schools to be closed and announced subways would shut down and buses would stop running. The closure of New York City's transit system, the largest in the world, set new records. It was only the second time in history and it meant that almost 12 million people would not be going to work. It seemed unthinkable that Sandy could wreak such havoc before making landfall.

During the next 12 hours, Sandy brought sights to the City that were never before seen. More than 375,000 New Yorkers became refugees—fleeing their homes. It was the largest number of people to evacuate since September 11, 2001, and only the second time in history. Police used bullhorns to send out warnings. Others went door-to-door to make sure everyone was out. The roads were jammed and lines were long at supermarkets and gas stations. Thousands went to emergency shelters set up by the City. Mayor Bloomberg provided safety tips that had rarely been heard, but there was no denying the weather maps: Sandy was heading straight for the Big Apple.

"We will pull through this," the Mayor said. "But now is the time to take the kind of sensible precautions that we said yesterday, even outside of

October 26, 2012 (ABOVE) New York Mayor Michael Bloomberg speaks to the media during a news conference about the City's preparations for Superstorm Sandy.

October 29, 2013 (ABOVE) Mayor Bloomberg updates New Yorkers on the City's response to Superstorm Sandy.

October 30, 2013 (BELOW) New York City Mayor Michael Bloomberg views damage in the Breezy Point area of Queens after fire destroyed about 80 homes as a result of Superstorm Sandy, which hit the area on October 29.

Zone A. Make sure you have drinking water. Clear storm drains and rain gutters of debris. Secure outdoor items that might blow away in high winds. And stay away from windows and close your drapes," he added.

New York City is known as the city that never sleeps—and there were few people who did sleep that terrifying night when Sandy finally did blow in. As strong and commanding as Mayor Bloomberg was in his pre-Sandy press conferences, there was a bit of sadness in the post-Sandy updates. The numbers were unimaginable.

Sandy brought 23 serious fires. Eighty homes were lost in Breezy Point. Four thousand trees were down. There was an estimated $19 billion in damage and economic loss. Forty-four lives were lost.

MTA CEO Joe Lhota described Sandy as the "worst disaster the agency has seen in the 108 years the subways have been running." The two biggest challenges now facing New York City were getting the mass transit system operating and restoring power.

Millions of people shivered in the dark, supplies were short, and patience was turning to anger and fear. Most of the people without heat or power were concentrated in lower Manhattan—from the Empire State Building to the New York Stock Exchange.

Remarkably, Wall Street opened after two days. The last time markets shut down for 48 hours was in 1888. After four days, the lights went on in Soho and Chelsea and screams of joy could be heard. After 13 days, New York utilities restored power to more than 95 percent of their customers.

But there were new challenges: Tens of thousands of homes were destroyed or damaged so it was imperative to get Sandy victims back on their feet. The Mayor signed two Executive Orders to help New Yorkers rebuild. The first Executive Order allowed home and property owners to meet new flood standards without violating zoning codes. The second waived fees for businesses that were rebuilding, but the greatest challenge remained–Mother Nature herself. As Mayor Bloomberg told New Yorkers, his team is now studying how to cope with extreme weather events and how to keep gas stations open, ensure hospitals maintain power, and guarantee a working transportation and power system if—and when—another storm hits.●

FDNY

THE NEW YORK CITY FIRE DEPARTMENT (FDNY)

FDNY Commissioner Salvatore Cassano

Cassano began as a probe in Manhattan in 1969 and has since advanced through every rank in the fire department.

Aside from 9/11, October 29, 2012, was certainly the busiest night of my 43-year career. During Hurricane Sandy, storm-related emergency calls relentlessly flooded the FDNY as rapidly as the storm surge flooded New York City. Our resources became taxed as major events developed simultaneously in every borough, something our department had never experienced. However, as chaotic as it may have seemed, the FDNY was well prepared for that wild night.

October 29th was a quiet morning at our Brooklyn Head-quarters. As the afternoon unfolded, the action began. At 2:30pm, Hurricane Sandy's winds toppled a crane on a luxury condo high-rise under construction in Uptown Manhattan. It dangled above the 90th story, threatening many surrounding buildings. The news spread rapidly throughout our office and immediately the decision was made to send a number of our units and more than 150 firefighters to help evacuate people from the neighboring buildings. We were handling that when the façade of a four-story apartment building came crumbling down on 8th and 29th street in midtown Manhattan—while some of our members were in it. They had gone to examine the building when suddenly the front of it ripped off.

All too soon, the fires and flooding conditions began. At 6:30pm, there was a fire on City Island. Then there was flooding at the Battery and in the Rockaways. Fires started burning unchecked in Breezy Point. There were people trapped in their homes. Traumatic events were occurring in Staten Island as well. There was the collapsed house in Tottenville, where we rescued a mother—the daughter and father were lost. Another terrible scenario was the woman who was escaping a home on Father Capodanno Boule-vard (it turned out she would have been fine where she was), when the surge came in and the water reached the roof of her car. She had her two kids by the hand and they were swept away from her. We found them three days later in marshland.

My greatest concern was at the peak of the storm, when

(ABOVE) Fire Comissioner Salvatore Cassano (RIGHT) Memorial Day 2011: Mayor Michael Bloomberg, Fire Comissioner Salvatore Cassano and Chief of Department Edward Kilduff watch as thousands of members march up Riverside Drive.

all the incidents were occurring simultaneously. When we got the call about the fire on City Island, they were still dealing with the crane collapse, others were still at the building collapse, and a large number of firefighters had been sent to deal with the fires and flooding conditions in the Rockaways. Manpower went down to 9% availability. We have 198 engines, 143 ladders, five rescues, seven squads, three boats, 49 battalion chiefs and nine deputies. An additional 500 members had also been deployed before the storm. Even with that kind of a staff, I was down to 9% availability. I was thinking, one more operation and we may not be able to respond to it, or at least would have a delayed response. As quickly as companies became available to serve, they were dispatched because the calls for help were coming from Breezy Point, Gerritsen Beach, Sheepshead Bay, Coney Island, all the way to Manhattan, South Beach, Tottenville.

Sometime around one o'clock in the morning, I went downstairs to get away from the bustle of the room and just walked outside with some firefighters. There was no rain, yet I knew all the tragedies that were going on in the city. I was saying, "What is going on here?" It was very bizarre – there was only a drizzle of rain at about 12:30 that night, yet a large proportion of the city was submerged in flood waters. The storm surge is what did it. As we looked to the east, we could see a number of transformers going off. All of a sudden there was a huge

flash and then everything went dark. I said, "Guess we put that fire out!" Whenever one of the transformers blew, the fire would go out. To see Manhattan in darkness was an eerie sight.

I was concerned about the safety of our firefighters in conditions that we hadn't before faced in our department: operating in waters up to their shoulders, knowing that they had people trapped. From the reports we were getting, there were cars floating down the streets and electrical wires arcing, so we knew these were the conditions our crews were operating in. Our EMTs and paramedics were jumping on tops of cars to get down the street to get people out. I told them to hang in as long as they could, and if someone was trapped they had to get them out of there, but once they started to get trapped themselves, they had to get out.

We had a fire in Breezy Point at the far end of the peninsula, where we lost 120 homes. Not one person was killed. It took us a long time to get through because the flooding was preventing our rigs from getting across the bridges onto the peninsula. Our members in each borough were pretty much on their own during the storm since travelling between them was nearly impossible that night.

The amazing part of the whole event was that we didn't have any serious injuries with any of our people that night. Even with all the rescues that were going on, we didn't have one severe injury. It is a testament to the

Even with that kind of a staff, I was down to 9% availability. I was thinking, one more operation and we may not be able to respond to it, or at least would have a delayed response.

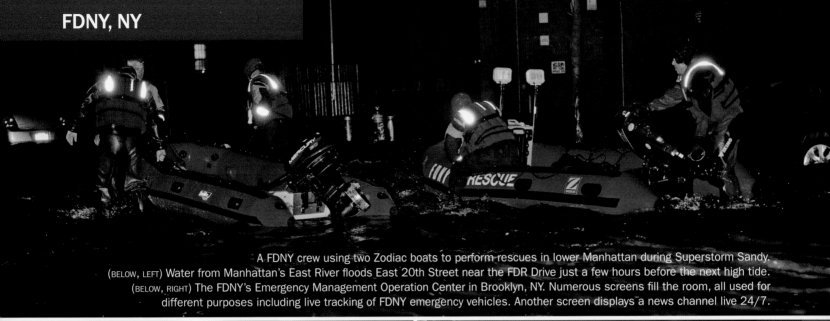

A FDNY crew using two Zodiac boats to perform rescues in lower Manhattan during Superstorm Sandy. (BELOW, LEFT) Water from Manhattan's East River floods East 20th Street near the FDR Drive just a few hours before the next high tide. (BELOW, RIGHT) The FDNY's Emergency Management Operation Center in Brooklyn, NY. Numerous screens fill the room, all used for different purposes including live tracking of FDNY emergency vehicles. Another screen displays a news channel live 24/7.

great safety command; we stress safety. A few days before the storm we put out a message of possible safety conditions that could be faced while operating during the storm, and pretty well, those were the conditions. They were cognizant of it, but they still did their work.

We had some people off-duty that were working, and others working even though their homes were affected. Folks were out helping others while their own homes were flooded. Out of 15,500 members of our department, over 1,000 of their homes were affected. Even though they knew that their home was being destroyed and their wife was on the second floor, they bravely focused on their job until we got through the worst part of the storm.

When the sun came up the next morning, we knew we had survived it. I got off lucky at my home, where I only lost of couple of shingles due to the extreme winds. My sister and nephew were both wiped out of their homes. It really was a very harrowing night for every part of the City.

We have a special operations command consisting of probably the most qualified firefighters in the country. I am extremely proud of what they did; in terms of how proud – I am beaming now! Our line troops performed outstanding work too – our firefighters in companies that

don't get that specialized training. They operated under extraordinary and dangerous conditions. I don't know how many lives they saved; it would have been hundreds, thousands. They got people out of their homes, working with makeshift boats. We didn't have enough boats, only around 30 small craft. The Police Department had about that many as well; they were pulling people out left and right.

We had put together a planning team on the Thursday before the storm, and brought them in on Saturday. It was a 35-member management team that worked 24 hours around the clock and helped create an instant action plan for any event that we do. They plan the next 24 hours and sort out what our mission is, the logistics and safety message, as well as giving the road conditions and weather. It is a full plan that we learned from September 11th when people came in and helped us. We met Thursday and Friday, and then they were in place on Saturday planning for the storm on Monday. They had to plan for evacuation of the homebound, make a strategy for the people to be evacuated in the A zone (which had expanded by that point), and then work through the storm. We kept them on for two months afterwards, helping other agencies plan their response

October 29, 2012 FDNY firefighters respond to the collapse of a facade of a four-story building on 14th Street and 8th Avenue.

to future storms. This team was a tremendous asset to us during Sandy; it gave us the ability to deal with that gigantic storm.

Sandy was the worst storm this city ever experienced, and as a result, we have learned that we need to increase our logistical supplies. We thought we had a lot of boats, but we need more smaller craft, 33-footers, 28-foot boats, etc. Right now we are compiling a stockpile, and we are not going to give them to anybody, but will hold them in POD (point of distribution). Then when a storm is going to hit, we will disperse them to the areas we think are going to be hit. We are also going to get some more water equipment that our Special Operations people have. For example, they have different types of boots which are needed for operating in high water conditions. I don't feel enough of my units have them, so we are going to prepare.

Humvees worked – the National Guard brought in large 2 ½-ton trucks. I ordered 6-10 of them; I am getting them from army surplus. I knew we needed them right away, might need them if we have a blizzard. I am getting them as quickly as possible; two in each borough, and a spare or two.

From 9/11 until now, we have seen how hope comes out of the darkness. 43 people passed away during Hurricane Sandy, with 23 of them being on Staten Island. We're sad about the 43 that were lost, but I think of the thousands that we saved. However, I think that with the conditions we were faced with, and the overwhelming odds facing our first responders, it is a proud day for the city, and a proud day for the FDNY. We knew what could have happened. To not have lost any of our first responders, EMTs, or our firefighters is an amazing feat. We stress safety to our members. If you aren't safe yourself, you can't help anybody through all those life-threatening circumstances. The fact that none of our members got seriously hurt is a testament to the character, dedication, and qualifications of the people who work in this department.

I would never compare this event to September 11. Firstly, because of the substantial casualties that the City suffered, but also because of the casualties this department suffered. On 9/11, we lost 50 more people in one hour than we had lost in fifty years. I believe that it is the training that we have implemented since that violent attack that gave the FDNY the capacity to carry out the wide-ranging rescues during Sandy, and as a result, save so many lives. ●

MONDAY October 29, 2012

1432 HOURS
Crane collapses and hangs from 90th story of 157 West 157 Street in Manhattan. 4th Alarm response (40 units/170 firefighters) to evacuate 1000 people from surrounding buildings.

1837 HOURS
Partial building collapse at 92 8th Ave in Manhattan. Facade from 4-story apartment building collapses to street. 25 units/100+ firefighters respond.

1900 HOURS
Swift water rescue boat teams in operation in Queens, Brooklyn and Staten Island. FDNY members will rescue 500 people from flooded streets and homes using these boats.

1930 HOURS
Multiple homes and businesses on fire at Beach 114 Street and Rockaway Beach Blvd.

1958 HOURS
Fire in a restaurant at 1 City Island Avenue, Bronx. 3rd Alarm response (33 units/140 ftire-fighters)

2000 HOURS
Multiple homes and businesses on fire at Beach 130 Street and Rockaway Beach Blvd

2053 HOURS
Fire in a 2-story home at 2800 East 29th Street, Brooklyn. 2nd Alarm response (25 units/100 Firefighters).

TOTAL
STORM INCIDENTS
4125 FIRE   5681 EMS

2149 HOURS
Fire in first floor
and basement of
2-story home at
88-21 186 Street,
Queens. 2nd
Alarm response
(25 units/100
firefighters).

2237 HOURS
Fire in basement
and 1st floor of
1424 East 87
Street, Brooklyn.
2nd Alarm response
(25 units/100
firefighters).

2239 HOURS
Fire throughout
a commercial
warehouse at
141 6th Street,
Brooklyn. 2nd
Alarm response
(25 units/100
firefighters).

2334 HOURS
First FDNY units arrive
at Breezy Point Fire,
which grows to a 6th
alarm response
(50 units/200+
firefighters).
111 buildings
destroyed by fire.

1158 HOURS
Fire on 3rd floor of
231 Butler Street,
Brooklyn. 2nd
Alarm response
(25 units/100
firefighters).

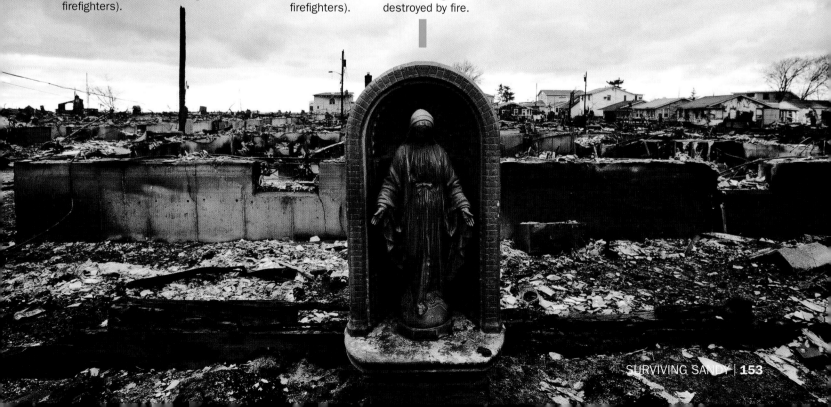

"THIS AREA IS FLOODED; DO WE NEED TO SEND MORE ASSISTANCE? WHERE ARE OUR AMBULANCES NOW? SHOULD WE PUT MORE HERE? WHERE ARE OUR RESOURCES?"

FDNY EMERGENCY MANAGEMENT

Director of the FDOC

Tim Herlocker is director of the FDNY Emergency Operations Center in Brooklyn, NY.

These were some of the many imperative questions circling through our crowded office during Hurricane Sandy. Through planning ahead and bringing in additional staff before she struck, we were able to oversee all of our fire and EMS units in the entire city that night. Nevertheless, as much as we prepared, I do think the force and impact of Hurricane Sandy actually took everybody by surprise.

Management of resources is our responsibility in the FDNY Emergency Operations Center. To fulfill our task, we try to understand how the various units are operating, and keep an eye on what is happening around the city. In simple terms, it is a big common operating picture of what is going on in the City. We are constantly looking at our resources to be sure they are in the right place at the right time.

Our EMS team eats, sleeps, and breathes response time - performing about 3,500 runs per day. Big red arrows on their screens tell them how they're doing: whether they're up or down on response time. Every one of our ambulances is tracked live, so they can actually give orders from here to relocate ambulances on street corners in order to reduce that time getting from A to B. If you've ever been walking around the City and see an ambulance idling on the corner, you've probably wondered why it's there. They are placed in strategic locations based on call volume. The Fire Department, whose members perform about 1400 runs per day, largely operates the same way as EMS, except they respond from stations, not from street corners.

In preparation for Hurricane Sandy, I tripled staff. Once they arrived, they were here for the duration - we worked the same crew for two and a half days straight! Although some could get home, most of the staff couldn't have gotten home even if they wanted to. One of the guys here that night lives in Breezy Point—we were trying to follow the fire, but we couldn't figure out if his house was involved or not. Fortunately his family wasn't there.

One thing we implemented during Sandy that really worked well was to set up each borough to oper-

(ABOVE) The Emergency Operations Center in Brooklyn, NY, was in full swing during Sandy, with various monitors displaying real-time situations.

(LEFT) October 30, 2012 1am: A massive fire in Breezy Point, NY, burns as the FDNY grapples with flood waters coupled with low water pressure for their hoses.

ate almost independently. Generally, if there is a fire in Washington Heights, units are sent in from the Bronx; if there is an incident on the Manhattan side of the Koch Bridge, units come in from Queens to assist. However, during Sandy, they put additional resources in place in each borough and told them, "You are operating independently. You are not going to have someone coming over the Verrazano Bridge. [We're] not pulling resources from different boroughs." They put on additional chiefs as borough commanders. Some of the chiefs would be stationed here normally, but they were put to work out in the field. Hospital evacuations became a big thing that night. We had to sort out whether the hospitals had their own resources, or if they needed us to send ours.

In our office, we have an overview of the entire City on our screens. Every corner of every building in the City is photographed. When a fire reaches a certain level, the guys start data mining it and employ a lot of baseline data to send it in to the Commander. The information gained includes what it looks like from a map point, any dangers we are aware of in the building, pictures of the building - the roof, the front façade, etc.; that's just Google, it's amazing. The main video room was ex-

tremely crucial during the storm because we could pull up images and plot maps of where houses were. We also have a news station live 24/7. If something blows up, we know about it right away.

The evening Sandy hit, I was upstairs. Our cable went out, but our main control room is always going, so I went down there. I'd seen where my in-laws lived on the East side of Manhattan. On the screens, I saw the water over the cabs. It was the first time I have seen the flooding that high. They could see it on the monitors and could get it out right away to the field. There were chiefs in the room making decisions and filtering them down to the field.

It's rare for the fire department to have these mass military types of movements, where all their resources are in fighting, but then they have to pull everybody out and stage them, waiting to go back in. It's not an ordinary thing for us to do; it was kind of cool to see.

After any fire, we analyze it to see if we could have done better. We look at the things that worked well; can we perfect them? Companies working today are the same as those tomorrow, same location, and same operation. Tactics that worked on a top-floor fire, how we can perfect them? What could we do better? What can we learn?

My operations teams all wrote down ideas and suggestions following Sandy, and I got up to two pages of bullet points. Some we have been able to address already and others will need some money thrown at them. We try to concentrate the decision-making based on what they do have, and what they do need. We had a good primer the year before with Irene, which turned out to be a benefit. There were lessons for us in those experiences, and therefore, we were better prepared for this massive event. ●

RESCUE STORY ROCKAWAYS

Swift Water 6 Unit

FDNY Lt. La Rocco and his team Swift Water 6 battled fires and floods in the Rockaways during Sandy.

Out of his **32 years** of experience with the FDNY, Lt. Robert La Rocco said this was one of his "most defining adventures." He led the members of Swift Water 6 (a unit put into service during emergencies like hurricanes) – including firefighters Jonathan Hoffman, Edward Morrison, Christopher Rooney, Thomas Fee and Michael Wood – to rescue dozens of people trapped by flood waters and fire on the night Superstorm Sandy hit.

Lt. La Rocco said for about 12 hours before the storm even hit, they responded to several calls on the bayside of the Rockaways, and removed approximately 12 stranded people using their Zodiac boat.

"We knew by the weather reports that the storm was going to hit later in the day," Lt. La Rocco said. "We had it in the back of our minds that high tide was at 7:30 p.m., so we knew it would get worse."

He was right.

At around 8 p.m., Swift Water 6 was headed down Rockaway Beach Boulevard, about to drop off two people they moved from a retirement center nearby. At that time, they remembered the water was moving over the tops of cars, so they headed toward higher ground, at around Beach 116th Street.

As they moved in that direction, they saw a fire in several buildings at Beach 114th Street.

So they quickly dropped off the two victims and then sped in the direction of the fire. When they arrived, they found four buildings fully engulfed with fire and 13 people trapped on the roofs of several two-story structures nearby. The high winds were pushing the fire like a blow torch over their heads.

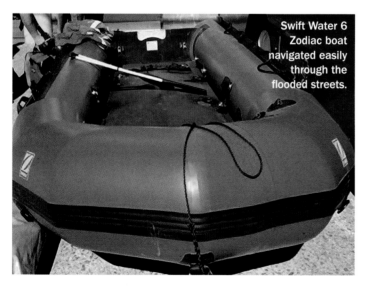

Swift Water 6 Zodiac boat navigated easily through the flooded streets.

"They were beyond panicked," Lt. La Rocco said. "We had our hands full."

As their boat approached, two victims immediately jumped into the water and were pulled into the boat by firefighters.

The firefighters then jumped into the five-foot deep water that they described as moving like rapids. Then they either scaled the awning to get to the roof or forced open the door and took out windows to reach the victims.

There was a two-foot gap between the buildings, so they jumped to the next building to reach the victims. They then took doors off their hinges to lay them atop the gap, to safely move the victims back.

They then lowered the scared victims into the water and Firefighter Woods then moved the individuals to the boat using a tether. The others also formed a human chain, moving the women and children to the boat first. As firefighters continued to move people to safety,

(LEFT) FDNY

October 30, 2012
FDNY fights a battle on a
street of utter devastation.

Lt. La Rocco was on the boat, shielding the victims from the flames with his body. He said the flames were so close, it singed the back of his neck.

They did not have a lot of room on the boat, but they knew the fire was moving so quickly that there was no time to leave some and come back for them later. So they moved the victims onto the boat, all of whom said they could not swim and knew limited English, and the firefighters walked alongside it.

"I couldn't believe the fire was roaring like it was," said Firefighter Rooney, who also noted that he was a lifeguard for 11 years and never saw water move like it was that night. "It was luck that we were there – we were in the right place at the right time. Anyone else in the same situation would have done what we did."

They then took them to Rockaway Beach Boulevard and Beach 116th Street, where firefighters and NYPD officers helped them evacuate the victims.

The firefighters then grabbed a portable ladder and took it back to the area to remove a few victims who were trapped in buildings down the block.

In all, about 35 victims were rescued on that night, including adults, children, an infant and a small dog. Nine structures burned.

Lt. La Rocco said the firefighters aboard Swift Water 6 did an outstanding job that night, working together to save multiple lives.

"When you do a rescue, and you know you're the only person to come between this person and their Maker, you know you did your job and you did it well."

But, he added, he has seen the damage caused in areas from the Rockaways to Staten Island and feels terrible for the people who have lost everything.

"There are so many displaced people in New York City, it's amazing," he said. "We'll just do everything we can now to make sure people can get back on their feet."●

STORY © THE FDNY

(TOP) Alan Chin

PREPARATION NYC

When the Big Apple Met Hurricane Sandy

By Joseph F. Bruno, Commissioner of the NYC Office of Emergency Management

In October 2012, Hurricane Sandy, a 1000-mile-wide extra-tropical storm, unleashed its fury and centered much of its anger on New York City. It was unlike any other storm in the city's history, and tragically 43 New Yorkers lost their lives.

A confluence of weather elements resulted in a worst-case scenario for the City. Sandy's arrival coincided with a full moon giving rise to astronomical tides, and its path was altered when it collided with a second weather front causing it to turn towards New Jersey, putting the City on the northeastern side of its winds. These factors led to massive surges that hit many beachfront neighborhoods. Water levels at Manhattan's southernmost tip, the Battery, reached an unprecedented 13.88 feet – a scenario that the U.S. Federal Emergency Management Agency (FEMA) estimated had a less-than-one-percent chance of happening.

To be sure, New York City has faced many major emergencies and even life-changing events, but the City has never experienced an event that damaged so many areas and impacted so many residents. Each phase of response and current recovery has taken a massive and coordinated effort. Sandy taught us that response and recovery from a superstorm required the City's response to get big enough fast enough to handle myriads of issues – almost all of which arrived at the same time as Sandy. This necessitated the City having in place the task forces, agencies, space, and structures long before Sandy's arrival to deal with the critical issues in the aftermath of the storm, including dewatering, power restoration, debris removal, and residential support.

As Commissioner of the New York City Office of Emergency Management I am paid to be a pessimist. I look to the worst-case scenarios and plan for them, and we did!

Preparations did not start the week before Sandy arrived; they started in the wake of Hurricane Katrina which devastated the City of New Orleans in 2005. NYC OEM studied the reports and analyses of Katrina and built the largest and most operational coastal storm plan

nationally. In 2007 OEM issued the NYC Coastal Storm Plan. This detailed plan is really a series of plans that guides the City's storm tracking and decision-making, response and recovery from the hazards that large-scale coastal storms like hurricanes bring. The plan addresses not just what we must do, but how to get it done.

The decision to activate the Coastal Storm Plan was made by the Mayor of the City. As Sandy approached, each of the plan's components were activated – from evacuation considerations for the general population, to health care facilities, to sheltering to recovery efforts including such task forces centered on downed trees, debris, power restoration, and the care and feeding of our residents. This plan guided New York City through a very difficult period: evacuations were ordered for more than 370,000 residents across many coastal communities, and 65 evacuation centers and 75 shelters were operational.

Certainly, life-safety was the first and foremost priority before and after the storm. Post-Sandy, the Police and Fire Departments initiated aggressive search, rescue, and security operations. Further supporting our efforts,

October 29, 2012 Waves pick up on the East River ahead of Superstorm Sandy on east side of Manhattan.

Michael Heiman/Getty Images

Urban Search and Rescue Teams conducted door-to-door searches of 30,000 homes in impacted areas before switching to an unprecedented humanitarian mission. Our federal partners, our communities and many others joined with us to execute the operation.

Over 2.5 million meals were distributed to those in need; disaster relief centers were established to offer cash assistance, food, and medical and prescription support.

Private facilities and public infrastructure were inundated with salt-water, requiring extensive dewatering and repairs. Approximately 600 million gallons of water infiltrated our nation's busiest and oldest underground mass transit system, tunnels and critical roads, the World Trade Center site, telecommunication infrastructure, Con Edison utility vaults, and many other parts of the City's infrastructure.

The storm surge and high winds led to an enormous loss of power across the five boroughs of New York City. Over seven hundred thousand customers lost power. The storm's impact on our power system was so pervasive that it destroyed existing power capability in a significant number of hospitals, nursing homes, adult care facilities, public housing residences and beyond, to the level that restoration would require much more than simply getting the utilities back up and running. It would require tedious, time-consuming and difficult rebuilding of the electrical systems within almost all of the flooded structures.

Debris immediately became a big issue. It was strewn across streets, on private property, in parks and public places, on beaches and in our waterways. More than 2 million cubic yards of debris were generated by Sandy's impact. To put that in perspective, it took only 62,000 cubic yards of concrete to build NYC's iconic Empire State Building.

An unprecedented life safety rescue mission began in mid-November. The National Guard and volunteers visited every residential unit under six stories. Teams handed out information, food, water, heaters, and blankets. As it got colder those impacted were offered warmer places to stay like hotel rooms. Residents were checked on multiple times until their homes had heat. In all, the teams made some 140,000 visits.

I am convinced from our work in New York City during Sandy we will learn that governments, along with all of their partners, can meet the massive and multifaceted challenges of high-impact events with an organized response and recovery effort. The effort will be coordinated by the fiercely resilient and innovative emergency managers who have the training and skills to think and act big when needed. We can and will get big and fast enough to protect those in our charge. ●

Joseph F. Bruno is the Commissioner of the New York City Office of Emergency Management. He was appointed by Mayor Michael R. Bloomberg in March 2004.

PREPARATIONS FOR THIS STORM DID NOT START THE WEEK BEFORE SANDY ARRIVED; THEY STARTED IN THE WAKE OF HURRICANE KATRINA WHICH DEVASTATED THE CITY OF NEW ORLEANS IN 2005.

NYPD

THE NEW YORK CITY POLICE DEPARTMENT (NYPD)

NY'S BRAVEST PROVED THEIR TITLE

The NYPD's essential role in Sandy saved lives and facilitated recovery efforts.

The New York Police Department played an integral role in the saving of lives during and after Superstorm Sandy. Recognizing the importance of their role in public safety during such a storm, the Department sprang into action. The NYPD participated in rescuing thousands of people from the threat of rising storm waters, and helped transport them to safe areas. The City's 911 emergency call-taking system recorded its highest call volume ever during the storm at 20,000 calls per hour, and not one call was lost or dropped. After Sandy passed, millions of New Yorkers were without power leaving street and intersection lights dark. The NYPD successfully executed the important task of traffic management and intersection control in areas with no functioning traffic signals. In the first weeks after the storm, the NYPD further facilitated recovery efforts by providing its 59 fuel sites to all City agencies and official vehicles. ●

November 1, 2012 An NYPD officer stands on top of the Rockaway beach boardwalk, devastated due to the effects of Superstorm Sandy, in the Queens borough of New York November 1, 2012. New York power company Consolidated Edison Inc. said Thursday it still had about 659,400 homes and businesses without power three days after monster storm Sandy slammed into the U.S. East Coast.

Reuters/Shannon Stapleton.
(OPPOSITE TOP AND BOTTOM) Stan Honda/AFP/Getty Images

October 30, 2012 (ABOVE) New York Police Department divers walk through a flooded area in the Breezy Point area of Queens, New York, that was hit hard by Superstorm Sandy. (BELOW) People affected by flooding and fire from Superstorm Sandy get a ride in a New York City Police Department truck in the Breezy Point area of Queens.

MANHATTAN

Very few things can stop the hustle and bustle of what is arguably the most vibrant city in the world. But... then came Superstorm Sandy.

Wednesday, October 31, 2012
Aerial view captured at night by architecture photographer Iwan Baan shows Manhattan in the aftermath of Superstorm Sandy, including the blackout from the power being cut south of 39th Street on October 31-November 1, 2012, in New York City.

Photo by Iwan Baan/Reportage by Getty Images

By all accounts, it was the perfect storm. Superstorm Sandy hit Manhattan with all its might, causing widespread flooding of the New York City subway system, roads, and tunnels, and widespread destruction of homes and neighborhoods. Its severity even forced the closure of the New York Stock Exchange for two consecutive days. No natural event in recent history has impacted the City quite like this particular storm—a storm that weather experts now say was a one-in-700-year event.

Iwan Baan

"With half of the city without power, I knew that from the air you would see this in a very dramatic way. Renting a helicopter was the only way to capture the massive impact that the storm left on the city,"
— Iwan Baan

This image, provided by AP, shows the front cover of *New York* Magazine released November 3, 2012.

"Iwan Baan's powerful and now iconic image brought to life one of the many devastating effects our city experienced in the aftermath of Superstorm Sandy."
— *Mayor Michael Bloomberg*

New York is loved for its greatness, and in many ways it is the American Dream all summed up in one city. To capture it in its most vulnerable state was something I will always remember," said renowned Dutch photographer Iwan Baan, who is known primarily for his stunning images of architecture. His studies took him to the Royal Academy of Art in The Hague and his work in documentary photography can be seen in New York and in Europe.

Superstorm Sandy came as a true photographic challenge for Baan, but it just may have been his finest hour. He succeeded in capturing the eeriness and silence that fell upon the New York area as it was under siege. While everyone was fleeing for cover, Baan was taking flight in a helicopter: "With half of the city without power, I knew that from the air you would see this in a very dramatic way. Renting a helicopter was the only way to capture the massive impact that the storm left on the city," he said.

Baan had photographed New York from above many times, so he knew which perspectives to capture. "I always turn to aerial shots to reach deeper into the context of a building or space. In this case, shooting from the sky was the only way to capture the magnitude and impact of the storm, and to clearly show the divided city—half of it lit, half in darkness." In addition to the aerial shots, Baan also spent time just wandering the dark, cold and virtually empty streets, capturing random moments as he discovered them. "It was such a surreal moment, where the city was totally quiet and still," he reflected.

Baan's Superstorm Sandy images have received widespread praise. Still, he maintains, the effect of the storm will last generations. His hope is that these images will carry a greater message to the global community "so that in the future, efforts can be made to prevent such a catastrophe."

Baan's photo on the cover of New York magazine shows a city divided by darkness and light. But as evidenced by countless survivor stories, one thing became clear: its people remained united. ●

(MAGAZINE COVER) AP/New York Magazine/Iwan Baan

MANHATTAN IN THE DARK | PHOTOGRAPHS BY IWAN BAAN

October 29, 2012. Rising water, caused by Superstorm Sandy, rushes into a subterranian parking garage in the Financial District of New York. Superstorm Sandy, which threatens 50 million people in the eastern third of the U.S., is expected to bring days of rain, high winds and possibly heavy snow. New York Governor Andrew Cuomo announced the closure of all New York City bus, subway and commuter rail service as of Sunday evening.

October 29, 2012 (ABOVE) A vehicle is submerged on 14th Street near the Consolidated Edison power plant. Sandy knocked out power to at least 3.1 million people, and New York's main utility company said large sections of Manhattan had been plunged into darkness by the storm, with 250,000 customers without power as water pressed into the island from three sides, flooding rail yards, subway tracks, tunnels and roads. (BELOW) Blackout conditions in Manhattan, after Superstorm Sandy hit.

October 31, 2012 (ABOVE) Joseph Leader, Metropolitan Transportation Authority Vice President and Chief Maintenance officer, shines a flashlight on standing water inside the South Ferry 1 train station in New York in the wake of Superstorm Sandy. A map of the original topography of Manhattan is seen on the wall behind Leader. **October 30, 2012** (BELOW) Cars floating in a flooded parking garage entrance in the Financial District.

Con Ed Gets More Than It Planned For: The Challenge to Power New York for Future Storms

Four of Con Ed's power plants were wiped out during Sandy, cutting power to millions.

With all the planning, and all the predictions, planning "big" was not big enough. Superstorm Sandy went bigger than New York's largest utility expected, bringing a surge of water 14 feet high.

According to the National Weather Service, the highest surge on record for the New York metro area was 11 feet during a hurricane in 1821. Consolidated Edison—which supplies electric, gas, and steam to millions of New Yorkers—thought the equipment would be safe. After all, the substation was designed to withstand a surge of 12.5 feet.

But between a high tide, full moon, worst storm surge in nearly 200 years, and the placement of underground electrical equipment in flood-prone areas, Con Ed experienced the most extensive storm-related power outages in New York City's history. At one point, nearly 1.4 million Con Ed customers were in the dark — a record number for the company. Even their own headquarters lost power.

The lights started going out when a surge of water poured over the banks of the East River near the substation on 13th Street. There was an explosion that lit up the most famous skyline in the world. These types of flashes usually last less than a second, but this one lasted for 30 seconds—a major predicament. The powerful spark created one of the most serious challenges the utility company would ever face.

Looking out his window, Con Ed's CEO Kevin Burke realized something was wrong on Monday night, October

October 29, 2012
Consolidated Edision partially submerged on 14th Street near the ConEd power plant in New York. After a gigantic wall of water defied elaborate planning and swamped underground electrical equipment at a Consolidated Edison substation in Manhattan's East Village, about 250,000 lower Manhattan customers were left without power.

29, 2012. A darkened City lay below him. He ran upstairs to the 19th floor auditorium, which served as a command center for Superstorm Sandy. The emergency back-up power had kicked in and the room was lit. But as the number of people losing power continued to rise, Burke would be faced with a heart-wrenching decision as to whether he should shut down power to tens of thousands of New Yorkers in order to save two substations. There were sick and elderly living in those homes…..young children, too, but if power wasn't cut off and the substations did flood, the result could wipe out part of Manhattan's power grid. It was a decision so big that Mayor Bloomberg received updates. In the end, Burke ordered the shutdown of two power stations south of 36th Street which cut off power to tens of thousands of people.

By mid-evening, conditions worsened. More than 150,000 customers in New York City and Westchester County were off grid. And the utility began turning off more power, as a precaution, to a section of lower Manhattan, including Wall Street, in an attempt to stem damage.

THE CHALLENGE TO RE-POWER NEW YORK
As the day broke Tuesday, Con Ed began assessing the damage, but downed trees made it hard for repair crews to reach some areas. The damage was massive and in the billions of dollars. At the substation, four feet of water had overwhelmed the control room and water began rushing over the 12-foot flood wall. Two Con Ed workers, an electrical engineer, emergency responder, and two

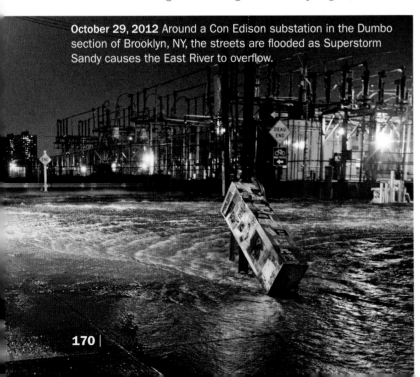

October 29, 2012 Around a Con Edison substation in the Dumbo section of Brooklyn, NY, the streets are flooded as Superstorm Sandy causes the East River to overflow.

October 30, 2012 Much of lower Manhattan is in the dark after the Consolidated Edison substation in East Village flooded. Transformers were exploding after the area lost power, as seen below.

firefighters used an inflatable raft to maneuver through floating cars, strong waves, and total darkness to rescue the 11 employees trapped there. Everyone was saved.

It was cold and dark in the City and the big question for Burke soon became: When can we get power back? Burke told reporters that Con Ed would have full power restored to Manhattan by Saturday night which forced workers to focus on priorities. It was determined that three of the eight high voltage lines would need to be working in order to get the substation running again. But, there was another challenge: Gasoline.

There were nearly 5,000 contractors called in to assist Con Ed's workforce of 13,000 and everyone needed to travel by car. Fortunately, the company was able to get an oil tanker to fill up Con Ed vehicles. Despite the enormous challenges, the utility was able to get more than 140,000 customers back on the grid within hours.

It was a cold and dark time in New York, but by Saturday morning, more than half of Con Ed customers in Manhattan were restored to full power once again.

The storm still isn't over - Sandy cost Con Ed more than 550 million dollars and now the question is: how to prevent power loss in the event of another major storm. Possible solutions include burying overhead power lines underground. Another idea is using reliable, tall brick walls to surround power facilities located near water. There have also been discussions about upgrading the region's power grids and technology, but all these options would cost billions of dollars and the question becomes: how to pay for prevention. ●

October 29, 2012 (ABOVE) A Consolidated Edison Inc. circuit breaker that caused a light arc at the 14th Street substation.

October 30, 2012 (BELOW) FDNY fire and rescue personnel lead a boat of ConEd power workers through flood waters after their power station was overrun by flood waters in New York.

October 29, 2012 Dozens of ambulances lined up outside NYU Tisch Hospital, as doctors and nurses began the slow process of moving patients out. (LEFT) October 28, 2012 In preparations for evacuations, ambulances gathered outside NYU Langone Medical Center.

NEW YORK UNIVERSITY HOSPITAL EVACUATION

DR. ACHIAU LUDOMIRSKY

Director of Pediatric Cardiology,
Department of Pediatrics, NYU Langone

I received a text saying there were reports of fire on the 6th floor! That was a very tense moment...

At the time of Superstorm Sandy, I lived on the 22nd floor of Skirball Tower, which was part of the NYU Medical Center campus in Manhattan. When our hospital team heard the warnings about the storm, we were afraid that the hurricane winds might blow out some windows; so early on October 29, we evacuated one PICU (Pediatric Intensive Care Unit) to another building.

Around 8:30 that evening, I was back in my apartment and the power went off. The building was on the same backup generator as the hospital, so I knew the hospital had lost power as well. The elevator in my building did not work, so I walked down the dark stairwell to the ground level where the Nursing Vice President asked me to check on the Pediatrics unit on the ninth floor. There was more light on that floor, and the Cardiac Intensive Care Unit on the 15th floor still had power.

Amazingly, no one panicked—neither the staff nor the patients nor the parents. Some of our team reviewed the situation with the Communication Center on the first floor. The NICU (Neonatal Intensive Care Unit) had 22 patients, of which four were on ventilators. The PCICU had 11 patients, of which three were on ventilators. The PCICU on the 15th floor had one patient on a ventilator. It was a question of what our next step should be.

We had so many patients with some who were critically ill. We needed to prioritize, and determine where and how best to transfer the patients.

Working with the Communication Center, we finally made a decision to evacuate all 34 of the Pediatric

patients. Eight of them were on ventilators and these were the most critical, as the ventilators were running on backup batteries which lasted only four hours. It was going to be a difficult transfer, one that required a lot of trust and coordination.

We quickly assigned teams for each patient. Since we had no computers, we instructed the residents to hand-write a half page of medical records for each patient, slip it in a plastic bag, and attach it to the patient's bed.

Moving an adult was actually easier than moving a baby down the staircase, as we could not put babies on the hard transport boards. We assigned a team to move each patient, and these included physicians, nurses, respiratory therapists, and residents. Since many of the Pediatric patients were hooked up to multiple monitors, oxygen or ventilator tanks, it all presented a very unique and delicate situation.

When we finally got down to the first floor, the patients were assigned to various ambulances. A physician, nurse, and family member accompanied patients to their respective new hospitals but our choices were limited, as none of the bridges and tunnels in the City were open.

Back inside the dark hospital, it was only a matter of time before the 15th floor lost power and it went around 10:30pm that evening. Another evacuation was in order and we quickly assigned teams to each patient, with the most critical of them (the patient on a ventilator) being evacuated first. We managed to force open the door to a stairway and started making our descent. We worked

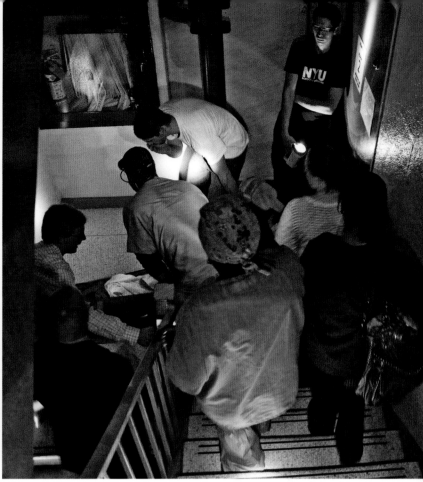

quickly, and in just 20 short minutes all PCICU patients had been taken downstairs.

By 4:30am, the hospital lobby resembled an Emergency Room—with all the lights, monitors, oxygen tanks, etc. There was amazing coordination and order on the part of the doctors, nurses and staff throughout the ordeal.

We were very fortunate in many ways. For instance, we were able to reopen the hospital only two months after the storm, and we were even able to perform surgery again.

I remember a father who was trying to get into the hospital during the storm. He wasn't allowed to, but we got him in anyway, as his son had open-heart surgery only three days earlier. To see father and son reunited in those circumstances was truly moving. The father was right there when his son was evacuated to Mt. Sinai.

Sometimes people ask me how many times I had to run up and down stairs when the hospital elevators weren't working. I don't remember exactly—I probably ran up and down nine to 15 floors at least seven or eight times. It was a great workout for me, and I never saw others complaining about it, either.

People ask me if we anticipated this storm, and the answer is no—it was a complete surprise. We had evacuated when Hurricane Irene arrived the year before, but we were able to do it in a much more controlled environment—complete with working elevators! Superstorm Sandy made Irene and past hurricanes pale in comparison.

In closing, I cannot commend enough the quality of leadership and the staff at NYU Langone. ●

October 29, 2012 (ABOVE) A patient was evacuated from the NYU Langone Medical Center during Superstorm Sandy. After backup generators failed due to flooding after a power outage, more than 200 patients were evacuated from the hospital.

Medical workers (BELOW) helped a patient into an ambulance during the evacuation of NYU Langone Medical Center on Monday evening. Two of New York City's most important medical centers lost power, and their backup generators proved inadequate. Nearly 1000 patients were evacuated.

Helicopters sit on the tarmac of the 34th Street Metroport on the edge of the East River. (OPPOSTIE TOP) The north Heliport terminal building after Sandy was finished with it. It was almost completely moved from its foundation and sits amidst debris washed up by the surge.

DESTRUCTION EAST 34TH STREET HELIPORT

Atlantic Metroport at East 34th Steet

Everyone expected that the Heliport would lose power…but the ensuing gigantic water surge was a complete surprise. By Pat Wagner

The East 34th Street Heliport is located on the east side of Manhattan, between the East River and the FDR Drive viaduct. It is a public Heliport that is owned by New York City, but run by the Economic Development Corporation. It opened in 1972, to provide charter, commuter, and sightseeing flights.

On Monday, 29 October 2012, the Heliport staff members prepared for what everyone thought would be a Nor'easter type of storm. As a precaution, they stowed all the ramp equipment, fire extinguishers, emergency equipment, and ladders. It was raining when they left the terminal on Monday evening.

It did not rain as much as anticipated that night, and the wind became more of a concern. Everyone expected that the Heliport would lose power—but that was not the worst. The ensuing gigantic water surge was a complete surprise.

Pat Wagner, one of the employees who lives in Valley Stream in Nassau County, did not lose power although some of his neighboring communities did. So on Tuesday morning he phoned one of her co-workers, Joe Cortez, to ask him to meet him at the Heliport and assess the damage. Joe phoned back and told her, "Do not come in, the place is totally trashed!"

The water had dragged the north Heliport terminal off its metal foundation base, and it was completely ruined. The exterior stairs and landscape items on the site had been thrown around like toys, and mixed in with the piles of debris, there were lumber bales from Brooklyn and railroad ties from Queens!

On Wednesday, Pat and Joe phoned the Heliport landlord to relay what had happened, and the reconstruction process began. This was a formidable job, because the southern part of Manhattan had been severely damaged. There was no electricity in the area, and it was difficult to see anything before 7:00 a.m.

In spite of this, carpenters and other construction workers came, bringing generators, dumpsters, and building materials. The workers had to bring flashlights, lunch coolers, cleaning materials, and whatever else they needed along with them. Pat and Joe and two other staff members came to the Heliport each morning at 5:30, to help with the cleanup.

The staff members' first mission was to salvage im-

portant documents and other items needed to resume business, and store them off site. Then they endeavored to get the telephone, electricity, and other vital utilities restored, so that they could reopen the Heliport service. They did as much as they could during daylight hours, and went home exhausted; this went on for days.

When the ramp was finally cleared and the building had been renovated, they made plans to reopen. They decided to offer temporary hours with limited service, use cell phones to communicate, and use hand-held radios to dispatch. There was no more fuel available, due to the water intrusion.

Amazingly, they did reopen the Heliport on November 5 the Monday after the storm—and were able to fly helicopters in and out of Manhattan. By the end of November, they had resumed fueling, and were able to reconnect to Con Edison. Their computers started working again, but they had to use back-up telephones for some time.

When asked to tell about his experiences, Pat Wagner commented: "I am thankful for the staff I work with and the resilience of the people of NYC, to be able to continue the business I have worked for over 31 years to procure. Many thousands of New Yorkers are still without homes and businesses, and have no means to recoup what they lost, but they will survive with the help of others. That it what is it all about." ●

Devastation reigns inside the office of the Metroport. The storm surge moved the entire building right off of its metal foundation base. (BELOW) A heavy bundle of lumber from a lumber yard in Queens was carried across the river and deposited by the Metroport.

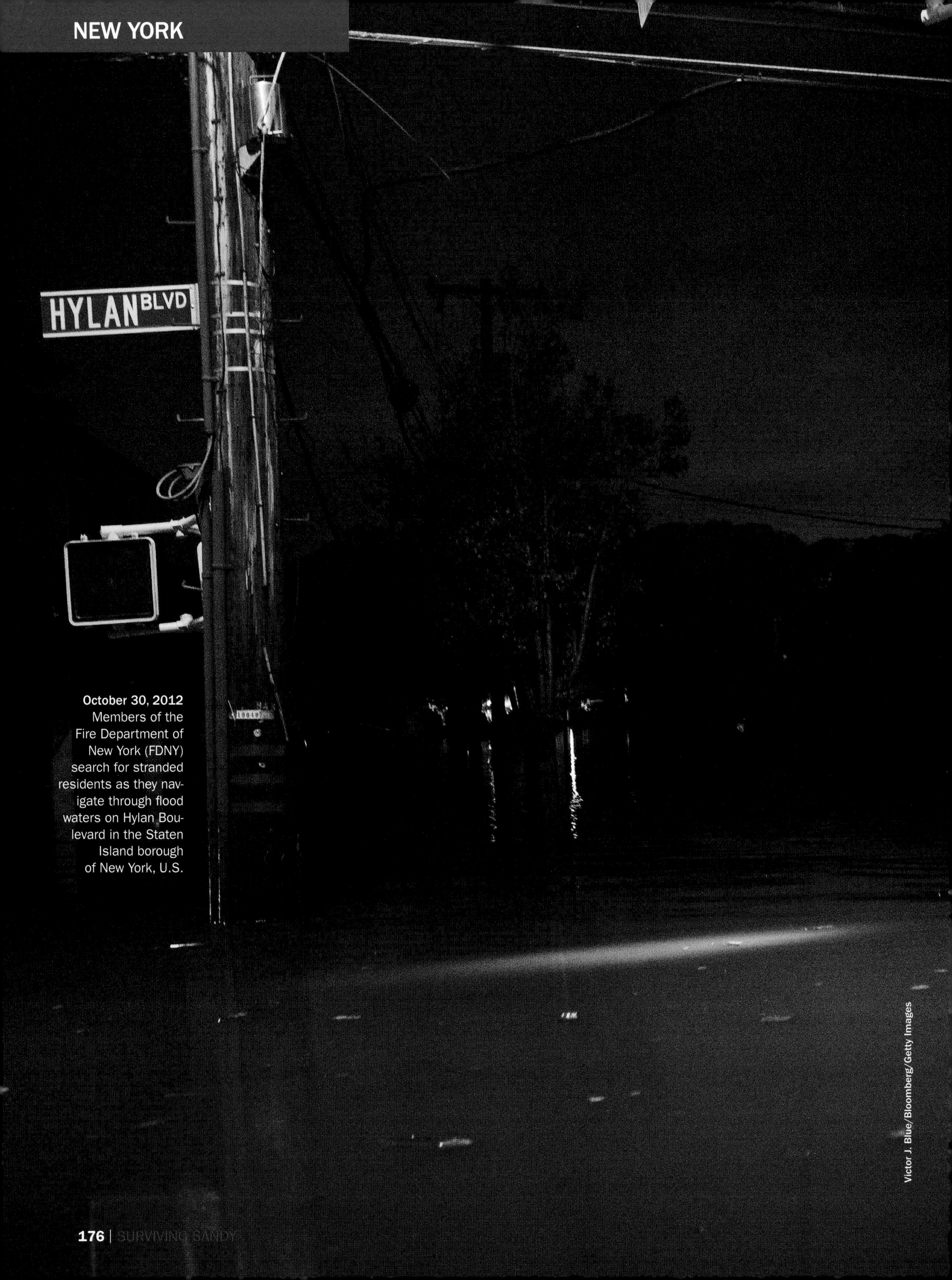

HYLAN BLVD

October 30, 2012
Members of the
Fire Department of
New York (FDNY)
search for stranded
residents as they nav-
igate through flood
waters on Hylan Bou-
levard in the Staten
Island borough
of New York, U.S.

STATEN ISLAND

Like other communities across the New York metropolitan area, Staten Island saw its share of devastation during Superstorm Sandy.

hey say that when the going gets tough, the tough get going. Perhaps at no other time in recent history has that adage been more true. Staten Island, the smallest of New York City's five boroughs, was particularly hard hit during Hurricane Sandy. Surrounded by water on all sides, its residents witnessed rapidly rising floodwaters, out-of-control fires and heartbreaking loss. But in the end, they discovered something else: the depth of their own courage and resiliency.

SURVIVAL STORY MIDLAND BEACH

Bill Connors

Staten Island resident reflects on the kindness of neighbors and the loss of his cats.

(ABOVE) Rescuers came by boat to take a pet out to safety.
(RIGHT) Bill in front of his renovated house.

On that fateful day I was working late and finished up around 6:30pm. When I got home, I thought it best to park my car up and away from the rising tide and out of harm's way. Once inside the house, power was failing and lights were flickering as my wife was trying to get one of our cats into the cat carrier. Meanwhile, we also had two cats that were up for adoption in a walk-in cage on the porch.

Then the lights went out. I could hear my neighbor yelling and as I looked out; I saw her in the street with water rising up fast. Help came for her but it was clear that the water was posing a real threat.

I went to the porch where the two cats were, to bring them into the house. Then I ran upstairs to find my cat Josie and get her into the cat carrier. That was a feat in itself, as she was so frightened. As I ran downstairs to get the other cats, water was coming in the window. One cat finally came inside but the other was afraid and wouldn't come in. The water was above the open window by then and I waded through it to open the top part of the window. As I returned to the stairs I saw the cat hanging on to the wall of the porch, and again I waded in to retrieve him. By then, the water was up to my armpits and everything was floating. I grabbed the cat and pulled him inside, but in his fright he would not go upstairs! I made my way back to the stairs; the water was getting too high for me and I was hoping that the cats would follow my lead as well.

I had a flashlight to contact my neighbors next door and we communicated that way all night. Then I heard people yelling for help! I couldn't do anything; it was too dark, and it looked to me as if we were in the middle of the ocean. From time to time I looked out to see my neighbors' houses; a few of them were still home.

As if things weren't bad enough, I saw a fire just a few blocks away and realized that I might have to leave the house with my cat Josie. I was trying to come up with a plan just in case and decided I would tie the carrier to me so I wouldn't drop it.

In the neighbor's one story house across the street the water was above the first floor windows. I wanted to make a call but my phone was wet. The water finally stopped just below the top stair!

As the sun came up I could see I was still surrounded by several feet of water. I could see my neighbors' son wading down the cross street calling out for his parents. From another neighbor's window, his father called out

that he had last seen his wife in their truck and it had washed away. As the son threw up his arms and cried out in grief, a woman called out that his mother was safe in their house, and the scene quickly changed from grief to joy.

The police came in rescue boats. I was happy that my neighbors had survived, even when the water had risen above their windows. They had managed to break into the crawl space above the first floor and waited there until the water receded. Another 66-year-old man was not so fortunate. His body was found along with the body of his cat several days later.

That afternoon, volunteers took my cat in the boat and I walked behind to leave. As we reached the street, I realized I had nowhere to go! I had no phone. I was wet! My neighbors kindly asked me to go with them because relatives were picking them up.

I returned to my house with my son Dave once the water receded, only to find the two cats, Bunny & Sylvester, dead. I had made it but the poor cats didn't.

The volunteers were great. They helped to clean up and they brought provisions. People came in the days after the storm offering food and coffee. One young couple unloaded a grill from their vehicle and started grilling food for anyone who might want some.

For the last three months I've been staying at my friend's house and I'm still waiting for money to fix my house. The churches and the volunteers have been terrific. I have flood insurance and I thought that I would be back by now, but unfortunately not. I have been forced to start rebuilding myself and continue to hope that the insurance funds come in. ●

FLOOD MAP OF STATEN ISLAND
The blue shaded land area on the map shows the
FEMA designated flood zone, which closely represents the
extent of the flooding caused by Sandy's storm surge.

**Blue shaded areas
represent FEMA
designated Sandy
flood zone**

Staten
Island

NEW
JERSEY

Elizabeth

Bayonne

Upper
New York
Bay

Linden

Brooklyn

Lower
New York
Bay

Rahway

Midland
Beach

Crescent
Beach

Atlantic Ocean

(BELOW) This house on Quincy Avenue is almost turned perpendicular to its foundation
as a result of the tremendous force of the storm surge.

(ABOVE) Looking out past a portion of Kim Joyce's rented home towards the bay that had days earlier decimated her house.

November 14, 2012 This bungalow-style house at 355 Tennyson Drive on Crescent Beach was Kim Joyce's home for 15 years before Superstorm Sandy demolished it. Joyce, (LEFT) who had to swim for her life when the storm struck, stands in front of her ruined home.

SURVIVAL STORY CRESCENT BEACH

Kim Joyce

A longtime resident of Crescent Beach, Kim Joyce lived with nine cats in her photo-filled home. She recounts her experience during Hurricane Sandy.

I lived in my rented house on Crescent Beach for 15 years with my nine cats. All during that time, there was never a flood. There were high tides, full moons, storms, and Hurricane Irene – but never a drop of water in the house. So why, I thought, should Sandy be any different?

I did take the warnings seriously enough, though. I boarded up the back and sides of the house, and I had packed a little overnight bag because I knew I'd be back in the morning. My boyfriend came over to pick me up but we stayed for a while, watching the storm and the TV broadcasts. About 3:30pm, the power went out and we lost touch with what was happening. We drove around to check out the scene in other areas and how high the water level was. We did know that around 8pm was when the real surge was supposed to hit.

We arrived back at home to see the water starting to come in from the north. In a panic, we ran into the house to quickly put the cats in their carriers and grab the basics. While we were inside, a huge wave hit the house and water poured in, slamming the front door.

"Swim for your life!" He had resigned himself to die in the house and called out to me, "Tell my boys I love them!"

This sealed off our one means of escape. My boyfriend went to the front of the house where there were two very small rollout windows, no more than 15" x 24". He opened one and managed to push me through, but then he couldn't fit. He told me to try to get around the side of the house to pull a piece of plywood off the kitchen window so he could escape. I was able to get to the window, but every time I tried to get the plywood off, a wave would knock me over. I got back around the front where my boyfriend handed me two of the cats and said, "Swim for your life!" He had resigned himself to die in the house and called out to me, "Tell my boys I love them!"

With that I started swimming as best I could in wild water over my head and two cats in hand. It was pitch black and the current was unbelievable, with the water pushing and pulling me. I had to let go of one of the cats just to try and survive. Fortunately, I'm a very good swimmer, because I wouldn't have made it otherwise. There were very large pieces of debris, including logs, appliances, and furniture, not to mention large pleasure boats swirling around in the frothing water. Miraculously, I escaped being hit.

I have no recollection of the temperature of the water, nor do I have any idea why I ended up where I did. I found temporary shelter approximately 1,000 feet away to the north. I actually swam through the house and then the owners let me come upstairs. My face was

The remains of Kim Joyce's rented house, which was one of the last few existing houses of its style on the south shore of Staten Island.

bleeding because my lip was cut through, and my remaining cat was dying in my arms.

Back at my house, my boyfriend had ripped the frame of the tiny rollout window out of the opening and this gave him just enough room to escape. He swam due west up the side street until he got to higher ground, calling out my name the whole way. When he reached the fire and rescue personnel, he asked if they knew where I was or if they had heard anything about me. No one had any information and they said nobody else had swum up the street. He then figured that I had been swept out to sea.

After four hours, the fire department came and rescued us. A kind-hearted policeman took me, along with my cat, to my mother's house. Sadly, the cat died on the way, meaning I had lost all nine cats. This was my greatest loss of all.

Six hours later, my boyfriend showed up at my mother's house. It was a joyous reunion, but dampened by the realization that none of the cats had made it.

The next morning, we returned to what was left of my house and absolute devastation awaited us. All that was left were the front and left walls and half of the roof.

The whole beach and yard were littered with everything from household items to vinyl siding that had been stripped from houses and left on the beach when the water receded.

I come back every so often to dig through the sand and try to find mementos such as the gold hoop earrings that my father bought for me before he died. I'm a big photo person and had many albums as well as pictures on the walls. I lost everything including all the photos of my grandmother and my father.

While I was digging there recently, I uncovered something that looked very familiar: my wallet! It still had $230 cash as well as gift cards and my Metro subway cards. I tried to locate any remains of the cats to bring some closure to the experience. We were only able to bury two of the nine; the one that died in my arms, and "Silly," who we found up the block.

After the storm, an amazing Buddhist organization called Tzu-Chi showed up on the island, making rounds of the neighborhoods and handing out $500 and $600 gift cards and a piggy bank to put coins in, requesting that it be set aside for the next victims in need. ●

October 30, 2012 Members of the New York Fire Department, concerned with the safety of the people, make their way through floodwaters on Hylan Boulevard, bringing Staten Island residents to dry ground.

SURVIVAL STORY CRESCENT BEACH

Leon Rose

A courageous Sandy survivor recounts the moments of fear, pain and destruction he endured during Superstorm Sandy.

Our house faces the bay on the east side of Staten Island and is approximately 500 feet from the waterfront. My wife and I spent the night of the storm at home on the second level of our house. The worst of it lasted about four hours with water levels rising so quickly—about 8 feet above street level.

When I first looked out the window, there was only a trickle of water, so I figured we could drive out. When I looked out a few minutes later, my car and garage were gone and the first wave of water crashed against the house, throwing the door open and hurling the furniture about. A piece of runaway furniture hit my leg with such force, it broke it—but I was still able to move to the upper level with my wife who suffers from a heart condition. I also have a son who was disabled in the army.

We listened as six feet of water went rushing through the house and the furniture bashing around. All the doors and windows on the lower level were blown out and we could feel the house swaying. A large pleasure boat that washed in from a marina a mile away was forced up against the side of the house, ending up in my yard when the water receded.

In the calm after the storm, I saw my Range Rover washed up behind my house along with the lower level deck. I also noticed a large piece of plywood wedged between the first floor joists and one of the concrete columns my house rests on, showing that the force of the water actually lifted the house enough to force the plywood in!

In the end, there was big damage to the house both inside and out — about $150,000 worth between the furniture, car and foundation. We were without water, electric and heat for over two months, but the important thing is that we survived. For that, I am grateful. ●

(ABOVE) When the water receded, Leon's Range Rover, and splintered remains of the lower level deck, laid in a pile of rubble behind the house. (LEFT AND BELOW) Leon's home is open to the outdoors after all of the windows were blown in and doors ripped off of their hinges during Sandy.

Mark Zolatares

While Sandy raged, Mark Zolatares and his wife remained in their home surrounded by blazing fires and raging floodwaters.

The house across the street from Mark Zolatares' where a couple spent the night of the storm. Water reached the roofline at the peak of the surge!

My home is a split level that faces north a block and half from the waterfront in the Midland Beach neighborhood of Staten Island. My wife and I spent the night of the storm in our living room, which was above the water level of the surge. Eventually, the water reached about nine feet above street level and came within a foot of the upper level.

It was a scary night to say the least. The first surge of water crashed against the house, followed by constant waves until the tide receded. At the height of the storm, the house next door and the two houses immediately behind caught fire and burned completely. We were now surrounded by fire—and making matters worse—the heat of the fire next door melted the vinyl siding on our house. We came so very close to losing our house and our lives.

As I was looking out my living room window, I saw my neighbors crawling out onto the roof of their one-story house as the water reached to the roofline. I felt so helpless as I watched them huddle together through the remainder of the night with 60 to 80 mile per hour winds

howling and fires burning just 100 feet away.

On the deck I saw a different but equally disturbing view: another neighbor standing in chest deep water at the front door of his one-story cottage with a flashlight. The water eventually came close to the top of his first floor, but he miraculously survived and was rescued the next morning when a team of volunteers made it onto his roof and pulled him to safety.

Like so many others in the area, we suffered loss of property and damage to the house, but the people of Staten Island are strong and we overcame this nightmare together. ●

With the Manhattan skyline shining in the background, the John B. Caddell tanker is seen on Staten Island after it was torn free of its mooring and tossed aground by Superstorm Sandy's record 13 ft. storm surge.

JOHN B. CADDELL

Andrew Burton/Getty Images

SURVIVAL STORY BUEL AVENUE

Ronald Forster

Ronald Forster and his family managed to survive Superstorm Sandy by retreating to a neighbor's two-story house. He recounts his tale:

WATER LINE DURING THE STORM

There was a lot of pre-storm activity on TV in the community as the threat of Superstorm Sandy loomed. I, along with my wife and two of our eight children, remained behind to watch the developments and listen to the evacuation warnings. Every few hours we would walk to the beach only 800 feet away from our house and survey the landscape. At around 7:35pm, I saw that water was trickling across the road that separates the beach from our community. It was time. We went back to our house and told our two children to pack a bag because we were going to evacuate.

In the ten minutes it took to get our bags packed, my wife noticed that there was a two-foot river running down the alley between the houses. I walked out to the street to see how strong the current was and noticed our car was submerged in water—and the level that was quickly rising. In five more minutes, the water level was at about four feet. As we were scrambling to leave the house, my wife and daughter reminded me that they did not know how to swim. Needless to say, panic set in.

My house is a raised ranch with the ground floor about five feet off the ground. But the water steadily rose, infiltrating the main floor and coming up from the basement. Walking out of the house was nearly impossible.

In a desperate attempt to find safer ground, we decided to break into my neighbor's house that had a second floor and finished attic. I went out on our side stoop and into the water, stepping down two steps that put me at a level even with their window. I broke the window with a flashlight and had my son cross the alley first. He went into the house and made a path to the upstairs. After clearing a path I handed my daughter over, then my wife.

And then came a shock: I quickly saw that the water in my neighbor's house was already four feet high on the first floor! We made our way to the second floor by about 8:00pm, only 25 minutes since we first noticed water on the street.

My son and I kept watch on the water level in the house, which rose a bit more, but did not cause us much alarm. There we stayed for 12 hours in a cold, wet house waiting for rescue. The wind was incredibly strong and we could feel the house swaying with each mighty gust. I realized it may have been the water causing the swaying as well, but I didn't dare mention that as the family was frightened enough!

By daybreak the wind had abated somewhat and we looked out on a scene of total devastation. Almost four feet of water blanketed the neighborhood. Debris was floating everywhere and a 12' x 12' room was gone off the back of our house. Only the roof remained hanging precariously off the back of the house until three days later, when a Nor'easter dumped a few inches of rain taking the roof off completely.

Across the street, a one-story house had shifted two feet off its foundation. I found out later that the 89-year-old woman who owned the house had perished when she fell off a couch that she and her daughter were standing on to escape the water. Her daughter survived and was rescued by boat the next day.

I returned to our house after the water receded, and the scene was overwhelming. Our minivan had been

The alley between Ronald Forster's house and the neighbor's house in which they rode out the storm. The four Fosters swam from this side stoop and broke into the neighbor's window directly across. (ABOVE, RIGHT) Ronald and Samantha Forster, with sons Steven -15, David - 11, and daughter Kylie -10. (RIGHT) The current that came with the tidal surge was extremely powerful cracking the foundation of the house the Forster's took refuge in.

washed to the end of the block and then halfway back, finally ending up in a neighbor's yard tangled up in weeds. The inside was a disaster of clothing, toys, furniture and food all jumbled on top of each other. It was nearly a week before any offers of help came in. We lived a couple of weeks with my family in my in-law's two-bedroom apartment, before renting a separate apartment for ourselves.

After weeks of hard work, we finally moved back the week before Christmas. It was a wonderful time for our family to reunite. The neighbor's house that gave us shelter from the storm remains vacant but repairable, as are many of the houses in the neighborhood. But amidst all of this hardship, the collective spirit of a community in crisis remained unbreakable. ●

(ABOVE) The house on Buel where the Foster family's elderly neighbor lost her life after being swept off the couch that she and her daughter were standing on to escape the water. (BELOW) An overturned workvan and car piled on the remains of a structure at the corner of Graham Bvld. and Father Capodanno Blvd.

AP/Bebeto Matthews

BROOKLYN

Brooklyn is underwater. Its legendary attractions are devastated. This chapter's life-or-death accounts tell us of people who survived Sandy's wrath.

Home to the **NY Aquarium,** Coney Island Beach, and Luna Park with its world-famous Cyclone Roller Coaster, Brooklyn is separated into 18 community districts and covers 71.5 square miles. Also known as Kings, it is New York City's most highly populated borough, with more than 2.5 million residents. As the Superstorm blasted through on October 29, it claimed seven lives: five were drowned and two others were killed by a falling tree. Sandy's relentless force created wind gusts nearing 40 knots, and her strength caused a 14.31 foot tidal crest – approximately 12.5 feet above average for Brooklyn.

October 29, 2012
Streets are flooded under
the Manhattan Bridge
in the Dumbo section of
Brooklyn, New York.

A deluge of water hits the seawall along the already flooded walkway in the Fort Hamilton section of Brooklyn. The Verazzano Bridge, which spans between Staten Island and Brooklyn, can be seen in the background.

Photograph by Carlos Ayala

Superstorm Sandy ripped through NYC with Red Hook, Brooklyn being one of the hardest hit.

Photograph by Daniel Krieger

FLOOD MAP OF BROOKLYN

The blue shaded land area on the map shows the FEMA designated flood zone, which closely represents the extent of the flooding caused by Sandy's storm surge.

October 29, 2012
1:50pm (BELOW)
Heavy winds and pounding rain gain intensity as Sandy pushes northward and closer to land. Lower Manhattan, seen in the background here, is becoming less and less visible from Brooklyn Heights, in the foreground. Rain streaming down obscures the skyscrapers of the Manhattan Financial District in the distance.

NEW JERSEY

Hoboken

Jersey City

Hudson River

Manhattan

East River

Greenpoint

Williamsburg

DUMBO

Navy Yard

Queens

Upper New York Bay

Red Hook

Gowanus

Sunset Park

Brooklyn

Canarsie

Bay Ridge

Blue shaded areas represent FEMA designated Sandy flood zone

Bergen Beach

Fort Hamilton

Mill Basin

Jamaica Bay

Staten Island

Bath Beach

Gravesend

Sheepshead Bay

Gerritsen Beach

Barren Island

Sea Gate

Coney Island

Brighton Beach

Manhattan Beach

Lower New York Bay

N

Queens
Rockaway Peninsula

Breezy Point

Atlantic Ocean

ml.
km   2   4

SURVIVAL STORY SEA GATE

The Paraisons

Dominique and Robbin thank a fire pole, a sanitation truck, and an open window for saving their lives.

When Hurricane Irene came one year ago, our family evacuated. When nothing happened the family was upset, so when Hurricane Sandy was coming we wanted to stay. Dominique and I were more concerned this year because the news channel was predicting a collage of weather forces, and National Guard trucks were in our neighborhood. When we saw them open the gates of the community and people leave, we decided to go while we still had the opportunity. This decision saved our lives.

The Atlantic Ocean is just east of us, the East River is on the west side, and the lagoon on the north side. All three of those collided on that day.

We left at 5:30 in the evening knowing that high tide was at 8 p.m. As we drove down the street, we suddenly saw water, and we noticed the bay had already started to rise. When we got to 22nd Street, a wave came from the opposite direction and pushed my Lincoln truck. The water was rising so quickly that Dominique opened the sunroof and climbed out. He didn't think we'd be able to open the doors, but when he pulled the passenger door and I pushed it, it opened. Ashleigh, my daughter, and I got out of the car and we walked. The water was still only waist-high. But when we went around the corner of the sanitation building to cross the street, another wave slammed into us.

At the corner was a red fire pole. We grabbed onto it, all three of us and our two dogs. My daughter tucked the little dog in her shirt, and I had the other poodle. We were holding, holding, and the water was strong. At one point,

Location of garbage truck that Maxmilian Schwarcz climbed on to escape the flood waters.

Pole that the Paraisons held onto.

Location of garbage truck that Paraisons climbed on to escape the flood waters. From there they climbed into the open window to the right of the door.

The NYC Sanitation building where the Paraison's spent the night. Maxmilian Schwarcz was also trapped by the flood waters at this spot.

(ABOVE) Ashleigh, Dom and Robbin Paraison can smile as they are alive by the grace of God. (OPPOSITE, CLOCKWISE FROM TOP LEFT) The entrance into the gated community of Sea Gate, which is at the far western end of Coney Island, surrounded on three sides by the waters of New York Harbor; Sanitation Building where the Paraisons sought refuge; One of the three "Paraison Angels", a red Fire Department post on the corner of Neptune Ave and W 21st St.

my daughter went under and Dominique grabbed her and pulled her. The waves took Ashleigh's boots – she had on knee-high boots! Dominique had on sweatpants with his wallet and keys, and the force of the water took his pants – he was stripped naked. Our legs were up, near the top of the water, it came high and so fast.

Dominique was using all his strength to hold us. I could tell he was losing strength, so I grabbed him and put his shirt in my teeth. That's when the dog slipped out of my arms, along with my pocketbook and everything.

Three gentlemen in a regular truck saw us and were trying to throw us a rope, but it wouldn't reach us. I don't know where they went to; I heard some people swam up Neptune St. I know these gentlemen started as three and at the end of it, there was only one.

We were holding on, and by the grace of God, the wave pushed us – kind of threw us – toward a garbage truck. We climbed atop it, and Dominique wanted to go back for Ashleigh. I told him "No" because he had no pants. I had a neck scarf, so I scaled the sanitation building where the wave wasn't pushing and I went back toward the red pole. By throwing the scarf at my daughter, I was able to get her back to the garbage truck. We knew we had to get into the building because the water was covering the garbage truck. That's 11, 12, 13 feet high. We noticed an open window at the mezzanine level of the sanitation building. Using cables and stuff on the wall, all three of us climbed in.

Survival mode kicked in. Everyone was cold. I started opening boxes and found a bunch of mops. I made blan-

> *"I looked at him. I could tell he was losing strength at this moment, so then I tried to grab him and put his shirt in my teeth, and then the dog slipped out of my arms along with my pocketbook and everything."*

kets out of them. I made coats and a loincloth.

We're watching the water rise – thank God we were on the mezzanine level – and Dominique had a plan to break the skylight if we had to get to the roof.

Transformers were exploding all around us. We were terribly frightened not knowing what was in the building that could explode!

Every time I heard something I climbed back down the wall and onto the sanitation truck. I was screaming and screaming. We were in the building from about 7 p.m. to about 4 in the morning – it was a long night.

Early in the morning I saw a car on Neptune. The waters had subsided a bit – the surge was over. I jumped on the truck and started screaming, and the man actually stopped. I said, "My family is in the building – can you wait?" Thank God for him. He said he couldn't come down the street because the water was still too high. He waited about forty minutes for us to make our way to him.

We climbed out the window, down the truck, right through the water, back to the corner of Neptune, and he let us in. He took us to a newsstand on Cropsy Avenue, where the water was down. We knocked on the newsstand – remember, we had no clothes on – and asked to be let in. The guy wouldn't let us in! So my daughter, thank God, remembered that a friend of her cousin lived on one of those blocks. We knocked on their door at 5 in the morning. They let us in, gave us clothes, and let us stay until about 8. They tried to take us home but couldn't because the blocks were still flooded, but we got to the

phone company building. I'm a manager, so I spoke to the boss and let him know who I was, and they immediately got in a truck and drove us home. They were going to wait to take us back out, but we said, "No, we need to see the damage."

It's a journey, it's an experience, and it's a challenge. My only instinct was to save the lives of my family. Even though the people at 911 said we should have evacuated, we are people, humans. I respect the government for everything they do in extreme weather, but I would never leave anyone behind. "We were advised by the mayor to not rescue anyone, because they had told everyone to evacuate well before the storm." But it's human nature to rescue people.

It's Christmas and the only thing that we put up here is a little light. A lot of our gifts are going to be for the angels – the man in the truck, the family who let us into their house, the food and clothes that we got, and the sanitation building. If we have to get a gift for everybody in that building, that's exactly what we're going to do. I call them the three pillars – the trucks, that pole, and the building.

We lost the chocolate poodle, but the little Bichon survived. We lost our belongings, our cars, keys, wallets, everything. The flood gutted our basement – everything is torn out. Yes, we did get help; FEMA and our insurance companies were great to us, and we were well cared for. No matter how much you lose in life, you can always get the material things back, but what is most precious is you, the fact that you're living. So here we are, able to tell the stories, and that makes us a lot stronger! ●

A stately beach front home in Sea Gate is obliterated by Sandy's unstoppable storm surge. The Verazzano Bridge can be seen in the distance.

(LEFT) Maxmilian Schwarcz holds up his coat, covered in sand, which was left in his minivan when he had to abandon it due to rising floodwaters.

They were screaming "God help us! Someone help us!" I called out to them to come over to where I was but then, all of a sudden, I couldn't hear them scream anymore.

SURVIVAL STORY BROOKLYN

MAXMILIAN SCHWARCZ

Maxmilian's harrowing experience during the storm strengthened his faith in God

I left my home in Sea Gate on the evening of Hurricane Sandy with only a small suitcase with essentials. As I was driving, the floodwaters surrounded my van and when I got out of the car, the water was up to my knees and flowing with such force that I was thrown down. I carried only my tallith (a Jewish shawl) and cell phone out of the car with me.

The water was picking me up off my feet, forcing me to swim, although I'm not a swimmer. This was a matter of life and death and it's amazing what you are able to do when you're trying to save yourself. The tremendous force of the water pushed me over to a nearby garbage truck, by which time the water had risen to the level of my hips. I was sitting at the back of the garbage truck with my feet dangling when I started to feel the water coming up my legs.

To avoid the rapidly rising water, I clasped the cables and hoisted myself higher up into the truck like a monkey. I climbed all the way up and stood a step away from the roof, but didn't go on it, as I was fearful that

the wind might knock me down. The truck shook a few times, and I was afraid it was going to turn over.

It was in the high 50s that night, but I only had my vest and shirt on; I didn't have my coat, and I started to shiver. My teeth were knocking together and I thought I was falling into hypothermia. I called my son and told him a few things to prepare in case they found me dead. At that point, my family told me to put on the tallith and pray!

Shortly after, I saw a couple and their daughter nearby struggling to hold on to an alarm box pole. They were screaming "God help us! Someone help us!" I called out to them to come over to where I was but then, all of a sudden, I couldn't hear them scream anymore. I thought the worst, but was happy to discover that they had actually climbed onto a truck, and then into the sanitation building and were saved!

Meanwhile, I was screaming on top of the garbage truck for help. I was really scared out there, God knows. I was constantly on my cell phone so that my friends and family knew where I was. Finally, one of my brothers who owns a bus company, came in a school bus to rescue me. He tried Ocean Parkway and Avenue W to get through, but the water was too high, so he went around to West 8th, and got to Neptune, where I was. Three of my neph-

Damage caused in Sea Gate, New York, by Sandy's storm surge.

After Maxmilian Schwarcz was rescued by the tractor, he was brought to a medical services unit to be checked out, where he was given a blanket and a cigarette. This photo appeared on the front page of a local Jewish newspaper.

ews got off the bus with a baby swimming pool they had brought along, hoping to use it as a boat. But as they stepped in, they tore a hole in it, so wading in the chest-deep water was their only option. At one point, my brother came across a fire truck and begged the firefighters to help me. "He has a heart condition," my brother explained to them. "He's a sick man, please send somebody." And they did. They sent over a bulldozer tractor.

As I was waiting for them, the water began to subside and I decided to climb down off the truck. It was about 12:15am when the bulldozer got to me, and the water was only to the middle of the tires now. The tractor took me and two others down to the Pathmark parking lot where I met my son who had come from Borough Park to get me. We stopped at the Jewish ambulance service where they checked out my health, and gave me a blanket to keep warm and something hot to drink. I was in good condition so I could go. I was left with just the tallith that saved me.

We say in Psalms, every step is calculated by God. (Psalm 37:23: The steps of a man are ordered by Jehovah.) If I had left my house a minute before or a minute after, I might not have been around to recount this story.

One of my sons made an attempt to come and rescue me, but he never made it. He got stuck in Sea Gate by the gate and was unable to continue his journey. He slept over at one of his neighbor's homes; the neighbor happens to be a friend of the family that I had seen calling for help that night. As the family recounted their story to them, they told of an "elderly Jewish man on the back of a garbage truck telling us to come over to where he was. But we couldn't make it because it would mean walking against the tide." My son exclaimed: "That was my father!"

God knows everything. There's a reason why this experience happened to me. Now, I'm willing to go around—even to churches—to tell my story. I want everyone to know there is a God in the world. I've already given some talks, most recently in Spring Valley, in Rockland County, New York.

There is a verse in Psalms where David says "I won't die, but I'll live and I'll tell God's work." (Psalm 118:17: I shall not die, but live, and declare the works of Jah.) The way I explained that phrase to one man at a church was that it's not that I want to live; I want to make someone else live. How? If I tell him God's ways and God's works, then I bring up his hopes, and he has faith in God. As I was thinking about it, I told him, "Now I see that God wants me to tell the word." ●

Kobe Robertson with mother Faye in a happier moment!

SURVIVAL STORY BROOKLYN

Kobe Robertson's Story

A 10-year-old vividly describes his experience of Hurricane Sandy

On October 29, 2012, in the blazing winds were screams of terror at night. It's coming. It's coming. People saw sea water rushing across the street to our building. The town houses on the ground floor were flooded with sea water. Me and my mom stayed inside on the fourth floor. We didn't evacuate. My mom told me to go to sleep in her bed, because she didn't want me to see what was happening outside.

I went to bed and on the next day my mom took me outside. There were fallen trees, sand, debris, cars flipped over. Destruction and sorrow were everywhere. People were sad and looked depressed. It was terrible. I picked up some souvenirs while we were walking to remind me of Hurricane Sandy.

We stayed in the dark and cold apartment for fourteen days, but after that it started getting better day by day. I am blessed to have my mom. She took care of me, but I will never forget Hurricane Sandy.

_ Kobe Robertson,
10 years old

A truck drives by a flooded gas station in the Gowanus section of Brooklyn as Superstorm Sandy floods the area.

October 29, 2012 Dwight Street in the Red Hook neighborhood of Brooklyn, in Hurricane Zone A, is flooded to 5-6 feet of water at 9:30 PM. The water started rising at approximately 7 PM. Note the completely submerged parked car. The lights of Manhattan, soon to go out, can be seen in the distance.

(OPPOSITE, TOP TO BOTTOM) A beachfront home in Sea Gate is boarded up after being destroyed by Sandy's storm surge. (MIDDLE) Resting among debris from Sandy in a Brooklyn neighborhood. (BOTTOM) The debris-strewn beach shows the power of Sandy at a beach in Brooklyn.

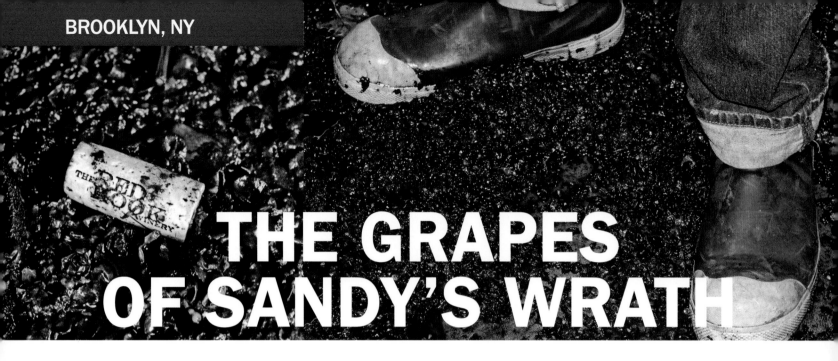

THE GRAPES OF SANDY'S WRATH

Red Hook Winery in Red Hook, New York was a new and bustling business on the harbor's edge opposite Manhattan. That was until Superstorm Sandy swept through and changed things—significantly. Owner Mark Snyder tells his story:

My winery has always been active and bright. People came here to taste wine and have a good time together. Then Superstorm Sandy blew in at the end of October, 2012. After that, we were left with nothing—no equipment, no water to clean the glasses, our wine barrels had tipped over, we even had an organ that used to serenade our customers, and that was destroyed, too. Basically, we were dead in the water.

Before opening the winery, I was in the music business for many years, having worked with Billy Joel, Bon Jovi, Bruce Springsteen and other top-name performers. Then in 2008, some friends and I got together and started the Red Hook Winery. It began as an experiment, to showcase New York's amazing grapes.

Before Sandy hit, we spent three days preparing at our two locations. We lifted everything three feet off the floor. We had pallets of sandbags, and stacked them in double layers, five-feet high around our wineries. We thought we were in pretty good shape.

Turns out, we weren't. Hurricane Sandy brought an unprecedented tidal surge. The ocean came rushing in bringing lots of debris with it. The ocean rushed back and forth, either totally destroying the barrels of grapes or washing them out to sea.

After the storm, the winery was in a state of utter destruction. The first thing I noticed was a barrel rail.

(TOP) A close up of the grapey muck that Sandy left behind.
(LEFT) Workers pose by the winery, taking a break from the seemingly endless clean up.

(OPPOSITE, CLOCKWISE FROM TOP) The winery's steel curtain and double doors are left blown open by debris brought by Sandy's storm surge; Assorted debris washed up against the front entrance of the winery; Men dispose of shopping carts full of food damaged by Storm Sandy at the Fairway supermarket in the Red Hook section of Brooklyn in New York. The food was contaminated by flood waters that rose to approximately four feet in the store during the storm.

(OPPOSITE, BOTTOM LEFT) AP/Seth Wenig

(LEFT TO RIGHT) Grape slurry mixed with debris cover the floor of the winery.
Mark Snyder on top of barrels. All the wine was destroyed as a result of the storm.

A feeling of dread washed over me; the rail was supposed to be located in a different room with hundreds of barrels stored on it. Since over 200 barrels had fallen, I knew we had major issues. Upon entering the storage room, we saw that everything had been washed away. A large pile of broken wood was on the floor, and precious grapes were strewn all over.

When Sandy hit, we were in the middle of a harvest. For a month and a half before the storm, we had been receiving grapes. The storm destroyed an entire vintage; it literally had to be thrown out. The cycle to release the wine takes three years. We had just begun to release the wine we harvested in 2008. This would have been our fifth vintage. Ninety-five percent of our 2012 vintage and 80 percent of our 2010 and 2011 vintages were destroyed. We are in the process of creating wine now that cannot be released to market until 2015.

The people who built this winery—the craftsmen, electrician, the plumber, and construction team—are all from Rockaway and Gerritsen Beach. They all lost their homes so, naturally, the winery was not their first order of business. I was faced with the decision of bringing in new contractors or waiting for the original team who knew the building to make the repairs.

The grapes may have been washed out to sea but the bills for them found their way to me regardless. I received bills for shipments of hundreds of thousands of dollars worth of grapes—grapes that were now floating around in the Atlantic Ocean!

The winery needed help and help came in December, in the form of an organization called Restore Red Hook. It was established by a number of smart business people in the area who set up the charity to aid in the Superstorm Sandy recovery efforts. They actually made a direct impact that was amazing. I received a check of $4,000, and although it's not nearly enough, their generosity was overwhelming.

Another local organization developed was the Red Hook Initiative, which literally saved us. Keep in mind that we were crippled in every way—mentally, physically, and emotionally. The seemingly insurmountable task before us was daunting. Then one day, out of the clear blue sky, I received a general e-mail from the Red Hook Initiative saying that we were registered for assistance. I knew nothing about it, I quickly responded: "This is Mark from Red Hook Winery and I am never one to ask for assistance but we are wrecked!"

Within five minutes, I received a call from a woman named Jill from the Red Hook Initiative. I explained to her my situation and she said that what I needed were volunteers.

"How about we send between 20 and 30?" Jill said. "I will send them there every day until you tell me to stop." And so she did. Twenty to 40 volunteers showed up at the winery each day for three weeks. It literally got to the point where we were sending people away; we could not even organize the next stages quickly enough!

The volunteers came from all over the county and the majority of them were not even Red Hook residents. Everyone in Red Hook was affected by the storm, so the support that came in from outside areas was truly amazing. They performed horrific jobs for no remuneration.

There is a large knick on the winery's music room door to remind us of the ordeal we endured. We call it the "Storm Scar." The scars from Superstorm Sandy will remain for a long time to come. ●

For weeks after Sandy struck, Red Hook Winery was in cleanup phase. Workers here worked tirelessly to get the winery dry and ready for reconstruction. The barrels and containers had to be drained of salt water, and water had to be removed from the wooden floors.

QUEENS

Queens gets blasted like never before. Businesses freeze and beach homes crumble. What follows are gripping stories of survival and rebuilding.

October 31, 2012
Damage is viewed in Rockaway, where the historic boardwalk was washed away during Superstorm Sandy in the Queens borough of New York City.

Spencer Platt/Getty Images

The borough of Queens is home to a number of famous attractions, including Shea Stadium, National Tennis Center, and the Queens Botanical Gardens. Named after the wife of Charles II of England, Queen Catherine of Braganza, Queens became a borough in 1898, resulting in rapid growth economically and physically. When Sandy arrived on October 29, 2012, the highly industrialized borough was slammed by a record 12-foot-high storm surge coupled with forceful winds. Flooding was widespread, halting business for a number of days and brought the runways of two major airports to a halt. Southern Queens is home to beautiful beach towns like Breezy Point and the Rockaways, and hundreds of these coastal homes were reduced to rubble.

SURVIVAL AND RESCUE STORY BREEZY POINT

Chief Richard Colleran of Roxbury Fire Department

Richard Colleran, Chief of Roxbury Fire Department, describes the most frightening experience of his 40-year career.

O**ur firehouse in Roxbury** is on a peninsula separating the Atlantic Ocean from an inlet to Jamaica Bay. No one knew exactly how devastating Sandy was going to be, but with water a quarter mile away to the north and south of us, it only made sense to take preventative measures.

On Monday, October 29 when Sandy came thundering in, the most frightening experience of my career began to unfold. At 6:25pm, a deluge of seawater pushed through the front door of the firehouse. Within five minutes, the water was up to our knees! The ten of us in the firehouse retreated to a little room upstairs. When the ocean met the bay that evening, it was very clear that any feeble storm preparations were well worthwhile.

Upstairs we waited helplessly, with our attention focused on the rising water and the forceful howls of the wind. A little over an hour passed when suddenly a little glow was observed to the west in the Breezy Point area. Right away we knew it was a fire—it just kept on getting bigger and bigger as time went on. Then there were sporadic explosions—big white flashes in the middle of all the orange. Kenny, the city dispatcher, was trying to get through on the radios and phones, but nothing was working because the cell towers were all out. My son, Michael, had a phone, so Kenny told him the number to text, and finally he got through to one of the dispatchers. It turned out that he was the only one able to get a text out. The City Fire Department was at last alerted of the fire at 8:30pm.

Our guys wanted to go, but how could we possibly? The water was waist-deep inside and eight to 12 feet high outside. It came up over the doorknob—and that was upstairs! We kept saying that Breezy was burning, but we couldn't go anywhere. We had lost our electricity, so periodically one of us would walk around with a flashlight, checking on the water levels. Around 11pm, it receded to our

October 30, 2012 Massive fires destroyed 110 homes in Breezy Point, Queens, one of the most devastating fires as a result of Superstorm Sandy. Pictures taken during height of fire storm at about 1 a.m.

(LEFT) Richard Colleran, Chief of the Roxbury Fire Department.

"Upstairs we waited helplessly, with our attention focused on the rising water and the forceful howls of the wind. A little over an hour passed when suddenly a little glow was observed to the west in the Breezy Point area."

— RICHARD COLLERAN

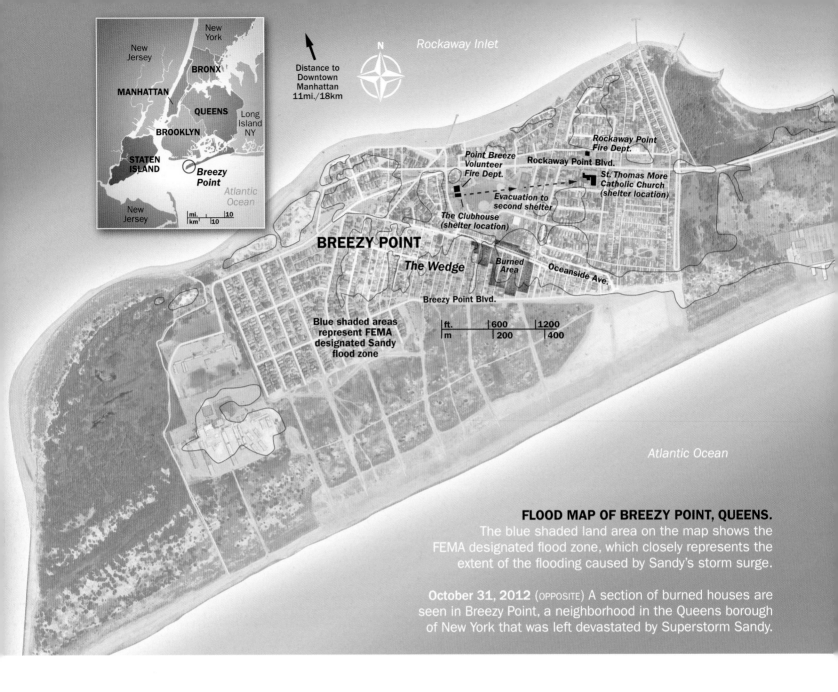

In the map image the following labels appear:

New York, New Jersey, New Jersey, BRONX, MANHATTAN, QUEENS, BROOKLYN, Long Island NY, STATEN ISLAND, Breezy Point, Atlantic Ocean, mi. km 10, 10

Distance to Downtown Manhattan 11mi./18km

N

Rockaway Inlet

Rockaway Point Fire Dept.

Point Breeze Volunteer Fire Dept.

Rockaway Point Blvd.

St. Thomas More Catholic Church (shelter location)

Evacuation to second shelter

The Clubhouse (shelter location)

BREEZY POINT

The Wedge

Burned Area

Oceanside Ave.

Breezy Point Blvd.

Blue shaded areas represent FEMA designated Sandy flood zone

ft. 600 1200
m 200 400

Atlantic Ocean

FLOOD MAP OF BREEZY POINT, QUEENS.
The blue shaded land area on the map shows the FEMA designated flood zone, which closely represents the extent of the flooding caused by Sandy's storm surge.

October 31, 2012 (OPPOSITE) A section of burned houses are seen in Breezy Point, a neighborhood in the Queens borough of New York that was left devastated by Superstorm Sandy.

knee level, so we made an attempt to head out and tend to the fire. With luck and some prayers, we managed to get the engine started.

The truck went at a snail's pace—through three feet of water. Upon reaching Ocean Avenue, the northeastern edge of the fire, we stopped. We stretched our hose down the desolate street, where many houses had already been burnt to mere piles of rubble. There were a couple of other trucks there already, but no water had been put on the fire yet. I saw a Breezy Point truck and asked, "How come you guys aren't doing anything? Draft the water!" We soon realized that all the NYC hydrants had no pressure and no water! When we got there at 11:30pm, we drafted it from the three-foot storm water around us. Basically, the ocean was arresting the fire.

The City Fire Department had arrived and set up a couple of tower ladders, and they drafted water too, just a little east of us. Our crew worked at pumping water for a couple of hours along with members of Rockaway

Point. They stretched another line off our truck but it was a bigger hose; there was too much hose to draft. So I sent a couple of their guys up to another hydrant 200 feet away and said, "If it's good water, shine a flashlight to let me know, and we'll take the line from your truck. Have your truck go hook up to the hydrant and feed us water to our truck." They did just that, but there was very little water—it was not enough.

I knew there were two mains coming down the road, and I was telling other officers, "I don't know which one it is, but it's got to be working." Finally someone came up with the idea of hooking up to a main outside of the city. It was a quarter mile away, but they got the equipment there and got the water out. That is how they finally got water at hydrant pressure on the fire. After two-and-a-half hours of fighting the rampant fire, our fire truck started to break down on us. So I told the Breezy Point members to disconnect from ours and hook up to their truck instead. The fire needed constant water on it.

Flood Map By Steve Walkowiak/swmaps.com, Imagery © 2013 Bluesky, Digital Globe, Landsat, Sanborn, USDA Farm Service Agency via Google

Reuters/Adrees Latif

*"I had **burn marks on my neck** from the embers—the wind just kept **changing directions**. You think you're in a good spot, and the wind's blowing that way, and all of a sudden **it turns around**."*

— MICHAEL COLLERAN

During all this, we had four guys taking turns at the nozzle—Billie Harman (the Lieutenant with the City Fire Department), Louis Satchiano (my deputy chief), my son Michael Colleran, and Peter Morgan, a member here. As if it wasn't tiring enough dragging the hose through debris, they were working amid exploding propane tanks and transformers. My son recalls, "I had burn marks on my neck from the embers—the wind just kept changing directions. You think you're in a good spot, and the wind's blowing that way, and all of a sudden it turns around. There were a couple of times where you just couldn't even breathe. Every once in a while the smoke would change and the three of us would huddle up and wait for it to clear. It was just scary. When we jumped off the truck it was probably waist deep."

The first house would go, then they'd try to save the next one, and finally that house would be gone too. Mike said, "We put one out and then the fire would jump to the next house. (Continued on pg. 212)

October 30, 2012 In the early hours of the morning, firefighters battle flames consuming one of the 110 homes in Breezy Point, Queens that were destroyed during Superstorm Sandy.

Todd Maisel/NY Daily News/Getty Images, (OPPOSITE, TOP) Reuters/Shannon Stapleton, (OPPOSITE, BOTTOM) © FDNY

October 30 2012 Leaving a trail of destruction in its wake, Superstorm Sandy left many homes and neighborhoods in tatters—including in Breezy Point (above) and the Rockaways (below), both in Queens, New York.

(Continued from pg. 209)

There was nothing we could do…the wind was so strong that it was just blowing the flames 20 feet across the street to the other house. It was amazing! The houses that weren't close together, it jumped right over. We would be right in front of a house, about four feet away, putting a fire out. Then the one behind us started on fire! The flames actually went over our heads and landed 15 to 20 feet away on another house."

That was what FDNY Lieutenant Biela was worried about—that we were going to get trapped, surrounded by the fire. He was on the radio and saying, "Tell Harman to move two houses back. They're in a danger zone." Meanwhile, I was trying to alert the City guys that the fire was headed in the direction of Breezy Point Cooperative's fuel tanks, which contain a couple of thousand gallons of gas and diesel. It was a great concern; we didn't know how far the fire would go.

One house started lighting up inside before the outside burned. The radiant heat from the blaze was so intense that the curtains inside caught fire. Billy Harman said to my son, "Get something to break the window!" Michael picked up a big, 70-pound flowerpot—and threw it at the window. The flowerpot just shattered and the window

remained intact! A city fireman had a Halloran tool and he swung at it about five times before the window finally broke. They did what they could to save the house at the time, and at the end, it was the only one left standing.

When we had left the firehouse to fight the fires in Breezy Point that night, a few remained in the firehouse including my wife—who sat in the immobilized ambulance. She said: "I just prayed, all night, because my husband, son and best friends were in that rig. I just prayed they got home. It was the best feeling when I saw the truck coming back to the firehouse. God was good; we had the fire, nobody was killed. We are blessed!" ●

October 31, 2012 A girl cries after looking through the wreckage of homes devastated by fire and the effects of Superstorm Sandy in the Breezy Point section of Queens. (BELOW) Destruction after the fires in Breezy Point.

Left to right; Police Officer Tim O'Brien, Retired Police Officer Tim O'Brien, Sr, Police Officer Sebastian Danese, and Fire Chief Marty Ingram rescued Breezy Point residents who were at risk during Superstorm Sandy.

SURVIVAL AND RESCUE STORY BREEZY POINT

Chief Marty Ingram of Point Breeze Fire Department

Marty Ingram is Chief of Point Breeze Fire Department, headquartered just a few feet from the largest residential fire in New York City's history.

Point Breeze Fire Chief Marty Ingram certainly proved the power of prayer during Superstorm Sandy. He spent the night of October 29, 2012 in Breezy Point where 126 homes burned to the ground, while floodwaters rushed over the peninsula. "I used it (prayer) as a tool—one of the most important tools in the toolbox," said Ingram, his voice still raspy from smoke inhalation. Marty led prayer huddles on several occasions. Each time, there was a positive outcome afterwards.

Before the storm, Chief Ingram had his team prepare for the worst. They loaded up the trucks, gathered the equipment, charged batteries, and brought in food and supplies. As night approached they began cooking supper, but never got to eat it.

As high tide approached, floodwaters came rushing into the firehouse. Marty made the decision to abandon quarters and move to the clubhouse next door, which was on slightly higher ground. The water kept rising, and soon the clubhouse flooded as well. By that time, survivors from around town had come to the clubhouse, which was a public shelter location. Said Marty: "I seriously considered abandoning the clubhouse. But with no way to safely get these people to higher ground, my team had everyone crowd up onto the stage inside the clubhouse, which was the highest part of the building." Floodwaters continued to rise until the stage itself was underwater. There was three feet of water inside the clubhouse, and five feet outside.

Jeff Bachner/NY Daily News/Getty Images

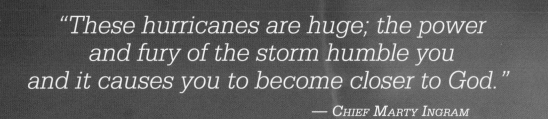

*"These hurricanes are huge; the power
and fury of the storm humble you
and it causes you to become closer to God."*

— Chief Marty Ingram

October 30, 2012
Firefighters stand by in the
floodwaters as fierce fires
destroy homes in Breezy
Point, Queens. This photo
was taken during height of
fire storm at about 1 a.m.

"It was like a blowtorch. At one point we were in a 'cave' of fire!

Then the fire started—just a few hundred feet away. "This was the beginning of the biggest fire in New York City, with 126 residential homes burned to the ground and many more substantially damaged," said the Chief.

At this point, the water was reaching eight to 12 feet deep in some parts. Marty's team was stranded, helpless to respond as the flames increased. Streets had become raging rivers. The ocean met the bay, the water table rose, and the whole peninsula was in the sea. Marty led the survivors in prayer.

In answer to that prayer, Rockaway Point FD, another local volunteer fire department, arrived at the clubhouse with a Zodiac boat and a four-man team. They began to rescue residents in danger and transfer them to the clubhouse. They unloaded survivors through the window, now level with the boat. "They did a great job," said Marty. "They were very courageous, but they probably shouldn't have been out in the Zodiac with a five horsepower motor on it. The water was that outrageous."

High tide on the 29th was at 8:51pm. But that was three hours early and Marty's fear was it would stay three hours later. He again led the group in the clubhouse—now numbering about 40 survivors and 20 firefighters—in prayer. Shortly after, and just barely after moon high tide, Marty noticed the tide miraculously starting to go out. "If the tide had stayed three hours later the whole community would have been lost. We would have lost a couple of thousand homes because the wind was just driving it like a blowtorch," Marty later said. "That was a positive sign."

As Sandy passed through, the winds changed direc-

tion; Breezy Point was now at the back end of the storm with winds coming from the southeast. Initially, Marty thought it was a good thing that the wind direction changed. Then he realized they were now directly in the path of the massive fire. The whole clubhouse filled with smoke. Persons began choking and gagging. Embers the size of softballs were flying overhead, hitting the water and popping. One ember traveled over a half mile and lit up a house on the other side of town. "It was like a meteor storm!" Marty recalled.

After a while, he alerted the survivors that they were going to have to evacuate but there was no viable plan. He knew his fire trucks were dead—their engines covered with four feet of brackish water. Marty led the group in another urgent prayer. After a short while, he dispatched his men to the firehouse in an attempt to get the fire trucks running.

"The miracle that night was the trucks started," Marty recalled. "Not only did they start but they ran continuously in four feet of water. The neighboring fire department, Rockaway Point, never got their trucks started."

They now had a plan. The firefighters transferred the survivors from the clubhouse through the floods and into the firehouse. They loaded them up onto the trucks and began making trips to St. Thomas More, another public sheltering location across town and out of the fire's path. "We had to rescue not only the people in the shelters, but ourselves too. Some people were rescued twice the same night, if you can imagine. Once, they were picked up by boat and brought to the clubhouse. Then they were rescued again out of the clubhouse to the next

November 4, 2012 The aftermath of Hurricane Sandy on Breezy Point, New York. Panoramic view of the fire's aftermath.

The wind was pushing the heat, smoke and embers away from us."

sheltering location," said Marty.

As Fire Chief, Marty ensured he was the last one to leave the clubhouse. With himself and the survivors safely away, he then got to call a rescue someone at the north end of the peninsula. "En route, we immediately saw that the house that was hit by one of the embers was on fire. We left the survivors in the back and worked to extinguish the flames," he said. After dropping the survivors off at a shelter, he and his men turned their attention to the massive main fire.

Marty recalls the scene: "It was like a blowtorch. At one point we were in a 'cave' of fire! The wind was pushing the heat, smoke and embers away from us. All the houses were on fire and it was just a matter of which houses we needed to tend to first. Everybody had a gas grill with a propane tank, and those things were blowing out; the power transformers were blowing out; there were cars parked right near the houses, and their gas tanks were blowing up. It was like a combat operation— explosions going off embers popping everywhere."

By five o'clock they were all exhausted and Marty ordered his guys out. The fire was still going but it was under control for the most part. They took a quick rest and slept only three hours. Then they were up and out again, responding to more calls for evacuation help and false alarms about power generators going on fire.

It wasn't until later in the day that Marty went to check on his own house. "We didn't know if our houses were still standing when we left here that night," he said. The fire had stopped just 200 yards from his house, but it was filled with smoke. With his asthma, Marty couldn't even stay in his own house.

Marty's team immediately went into recovery. They requested assistance from other volunteer fire departments and formed a crew called 'Gut and Pump.' Together they gutted and cleaned 700 homes —close to 25 percent of the town. They also maintained 24/7 watch over the deserted town.

"It has been adventure ever since," relates Marty. "We've been involved in a lot of different things. We had become the universal firehouse. Firemen from all over the country came in to assist—from Chicago, Pennsylvania, Miami. They helped us clean up and move forward." Acts of kindness started coming in from the unlikeliest of places, Marty noted. For example, "A man in Minnesota saw one of my guys on Good Morning America talking about a lamp that was destroyed, and he felt compelled to do something. So he flew out 200 lamps! We have had so many examples of that. I like to think that we're getting 'swamped by the angels.'"

Amazingly, nobody died in Breezy Point that night. Marty attributes this to the commitment and bravery of his men. "I think that is why you didn't see any people die, because of what my guys did that night. We're trained to put water on fires and put them out, but nobody is trained to hunker down in the face of an atom bomb.

"These hurricanes are huge; the power and fury of the storm humble you and it causes you to become closer to God. A lot of these guys are rough-and-ready types, but the power of prayer really worked for us throughout this ordeal. I think our collective faith gave us the strength to carry on. ●

Photograph by Bobby Plasencia

God Bless my
Breezy Point Family
Looking forward to
opening my door
again soon.
Frances A.

SURVIVAL STORY BREEZY POINT

Frances Abbracciamento

The oldest person living in devastated Breezy Point conveys her thoughts on the harm left by Sandy

I will be 100 years old this year—and Breezy Point has been my home for the last 50 of them. For me, it is a community filled with love, dedication, friendship, character and, most of all, a true spirit of good intent for one another.

This seaside community has weathered many storms, so when the mandatory evacuation for Sandy was issued, many residents listened to the warnings with a cavalier attitude, but I decided to heed the warnings and leave my home. I took a small overnight bag, with just the necessities of spending one night away. Who knew this would turn into the most life altering experiences I would ever have encountered?

After Sandy passed, what I came back to changed my life forever. My journals that recounted all my life's adventures, joys, and sorrows were gone. My bedroom set that I bought 74 years ago with my beloved husband had to be trashed. My photos, my angel collection, my treasured cards and words that I so tenderly shared with my loved ones had all washed away. I had no chance to decide what to keep and what to let go. Essentially, all the things that meant the most to me were indiscriminately destroyed.

I am most grateful for the fact that I am here to tell the story, but my heart is broken for all my dear friends who have lost their homes and everything they held most dear. My family has given me the support that I have cherished throughout my lifetime. Events like Sandy make you stop and ask a question: "What really matters?" What matters are sacrifices you have made in a lifetime to your family, to your friends, and to those less fortunate than you who are struggling through sorrows. What matters is what you have done to help those who have lost family and those caring for the terminally ill.

I will finish my years in Breezy Point, and I can only hope that I do it with all my loved ones standing right next to me. ●

(OPPOSITE, LEFT) A printed picture of Frances Abbracciamento, almost 100, looking out her front door in Breezy Point. Muddy waters flow through the streets of Breezy Point and were used to fight fires. (BOTTOM, LEFT) A National Guard truck heads down a flooded Breezy Point street. (BELOW) Firefighters look at flood waters left from Superstorm Sandy at the Breezy Point section of Queens, New York.

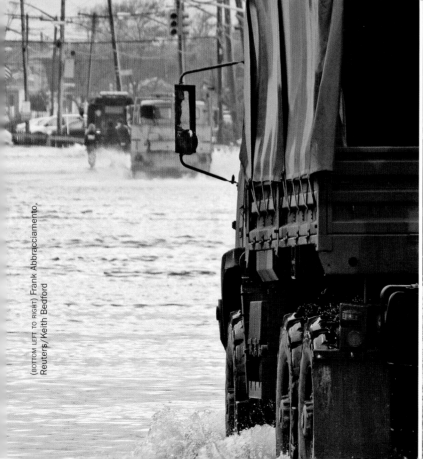

*Before I knew it, the business on the corner of my block, **Harbor Light Pub, was ablaze!** My house was just seven homes away, and seeing the flames, my husband knew **it was time to evacuate.** I can no longer walk due to Multiple Sclerosis, so my **husband knew we needed help.***

— *MARY ELLEN OLSEN*

Monday, November 5, 2012
In the path of Superstorm Sandy is a destroyed residence
entangled with a car alongside the Belle Harbor section
of Rockaway Beach in Queens, New York. Tens of thousands were
without electricity along the coasts of the tri-state metropolitan
area of New York and with the temperatures approaching
freezing, many needed to find a place to stay.

Firefighters work to extinguish a fire in the Rockaway section of New York.

(BELOW, LEFT TO RIGHT) The charred brick is all that is left of the Olsen's home. A torched chair is somewhat recognizable after the blaze in the Olsen's home. The Olsen's appreciative family includes Mary Ellen, husband Donald, and the two boys Michael and Ryan.

SURVIVAL STORY BELLE HARBOR, ROCKAWAYS

MARY ELLEN OLSEN

Mary Ellen Olsen, immobilized from MS, tells the story of her evacuation to escape a raging fire.

I will never forget the night of Monday October 29, 2012. Superstorm Sandy was about to strike and Rockaway was supposed to evacuate. We had survived Hurricane Irene in August 2011 without evacuating, so I decided to weather Sandy as well. I am much more comfortable in my home because it is handicapped accessible.

As the hurricane drew closer, we lost power and realized our finished basement and both brand new cars (one, a handicapped-accessible vehicle) the other a minivan, were flooded and ruined. As the water came into the house and filled the basement, it sounded like a waterfall. I constantly asked my husband Donald (FDNY,

ret.) if we were going to be safe in our home. He assured me and my two teenage boys, Michael (17) and Ryan (14), that we would all be fine.

I'm still unsure if it took minutes or hours for the basement to fill with water, stopping at our first floor. Still, we were okay. We could surely replace our basement and cars, although it wouldn't be easy. I was still able to use my custom wheelchair and bathroom, and stay in my home for the time being.

My next memory is of my husband yelling with some other firemen outside. On our block live four retired FDNY firefighters and one active FDNY Lt.; men that know how to fight fires! They were discussing fires that were two blocks away. Before I knew it, the business on the corner of my block, Harbor Light Pub owned by two firefighter brothers and their father, was ablaze! My house was just seven homes away and seeing the flames, my husband knew it was time to evacuate. I can no longer walk due to Multiple Sclerosis, so my husband

November 1, 2012 Harbor Light Pub, a popular restaurant in Belle Harbor, was reduced to rubble after a raging fire during the storm.

knew we needed help.

Taking one small essentials bag for the four of us, I was carried onto a surfboard and began our journey in waist high, smoke and ember filled, freezing cold water. Along the way, we stopped at a neighbor's home where many other neighbors had gathered, but soon, the fires were getting close again, so we made the decision to leave. I was then placed onto a kayak, and with my dog in the front, we were pushed along the water five blocks to our neighbor's brothers' home where we stayed until the morning.

At that home, there were approximately 25 people, four dogs, and a pet bird—and no heat. All of us, with the exception of the homeowners, lost their homes that night. Fifteen homes and the Harbor Light Pub burned down to the ground on the 400 block of Beach 130th Street in Belle Harbor, Rockaway.

In the early morning, I was again evacuated with the help of the FDNY, to my sister's home three blocks away. She, like everyone else in Rockaway, lost power and had a completely flooded basement, but her home was standing. We stayed at my sister's for three days, until we were able to find a rental home in Brooklyn.

That night will be etched in my mind forever. I will always be thankful to our neighbors, my amazing husband, our very brave boys, and the FDNY. I feel most sad for my kids. They left the comfort of their home, their room, and everything they had known. This is just one of several tragedies they have faced in their young life. On 9/11 we lost many friends from both the FDNY and in the neighborhood. Two months later, an AA587 plane crashed into our neighborhood and onto my sister's home, killing her and my nephew. Now this.

Ryan asked at dinner one night "Why do so many bad things happen to our family?" How do you answer such a question? I told him, "It makes us stronger, Ryan!"

In the months since Sandy, we have been shown incredible acts of humanity. The kindness of strangers who just want to help, has reached our door. Our friends and family have picked us up and will not let us go! This latest obstacle did indeed make us stronger. ●

– Donald, Mary Ellen, Michael and Ryan Olsen

October 31, 2012
An aerial photo of people strolling by a ruined section of the historic boardwalk in the Rockaway section of Queens, New York. Much of the boardwalk was washed away during Superstorm Sandy.

LONG ISLAND

It was Mother Nature at its worst—bringing floods, fires and winds to wreak havoc across the region. But in the wake of Superstorm Sandy, we saw many examples of goodwill, charity and brotherhood—Human nature at its best.

A **venerable seaside community,** Long Beach lies just to the south of Long Island and rolls out the welcome mat for residents seeking a quiet refuge from New York City, and for visitors looking to experience the seaside at its best. Once dubbed "The Riviera of the East" by former State Senator and real estate developer, William Reynolds, Long Beach was anything but in the wake of Superstorm Sandy. In addition to the destruction of many homes and businesses, Long Beach's iconic boardwalk suffered the same fate. A major tourist attraction for decades was felled in one 24-hour period.

October 28, 2012 Heavy surf from Superstorm Sandy pounds the shoreline in Point Lookout, Long Beach, New York.

Wreckage of the Long Beach boardwalk the morning after Superstorm Sandy came through. The water was still flowing under the boardwalk and into the streets. Pieces of the boardwalk were found for days afterwards.

NEW YORK

CONNECTICUT

Long Island Sound

Montauk

LONG ISLAND

Southampton

Atlantic Ocean

NYC

Freeport
Baldwin
Bellmore
Lindenhurst
South Oyster Bay
Long Beach

N

mi. | 5 | 10
km | 10 | 20

Photograph by Christina Tisi-Kramer

Adam and Robin Dodge and sons, Sam and Flynn

SURVIVAL STORY LONG BEACH

Adam Dodge
AIG Senior Underwriter

Despite water everywhere, Long Beach residents battled a fiery nightmare that claimed eight houses during Hurricane Sandy.

Adam Dodge, a senior underwriter at AIG, chose to live in Long Beach because surfing was his hobby. He and his family love the beaches and the boardwalks. On the night of Superstorm Sandy, he decided to stay in his home with his wife Robin, and their 2-1/2 year old twin sons, Sam and Fynn.

Adam and his neighbors watched the weather reports about Sandy but they didn't expect the storm to create much of a surge. After all, he reasoned, Hurricane Irene a year earlier proved to be a lot of false hype. Many Long Beach residents evacuated their homes but in the end, not much happened. So here was Hurricane Sandy looming. Considering the past, many residents decided to stay. That turned out to be the wrong decision.

At 5.30pm, the flooding started in the streets of Long Beach. Says Adam: "My wife and I watched the water rise, first in the streets, then into the house. By 7pm, the water was ankle deep and we went to the second level of the house." At 8pm they lost power.

"Suddenly, I heard 'FIRE, FIRE!' This was the last and worst thing I could think of happening in a storm surge. It was my neighbor, Jimmy Jones. A Toyota Highlander parked in a narrow driveway between two houses on the next block had shorted out and caught fire!" exclaimed Adam.

There was no way fire trucks could get through their neighborhood in the five feet of water. Adam threw on his wet suit and waded out into the street to help douse

*Suddenly, Adam heard "FIRE, FIRE!".
It was his neighbor, Jimmy Jones.
"This is the last and worst thing
I could think of happening in a storm
surge," exclaimed Adam.*

the flames. Grabbing a floating garbage can, he hopped the fence, and ran to meet eight other neighbors at the scene. Using salt water from the street they doused the Toyota with water. The car fire was under control, but the flames had now spread to the side of the house. Quickly, they put the house fire out. "It looked to the naked eye like everything was out," says Adam.

They went home feeling like heroes, having accomplished something monumental, but just 30 minutes later, he heard his neighbor yelling 'Fire!' again. Adam was stunned: "When I looked out the window this time, I saw the house in flames with 60-80 mph winds whipping them around."

He and his neighbors soon realized the fire was too far gone to fight on their own. Knowing that fire trucks couldn't come and that their houses were in the fire's path, they quickly decided to evacuate their families to their neighbor Caroline's house—five houses south of where the fire started. Her house soon became a haven for the neighbors that night.

(OPPOSITE PAGE, TOP RIGHT) A charred car sits amidst the rubble at 44 Barnes Street in Long Beach directly across from Adam Dodge's home. (ABOVE) East Broadway, Long Beach: This photo, taken the night of the storm using a tripod and a long exposure, shows a car shorting out as a result of floodwaters, lighting up the night sky.

With his family safe at Caroline's, Adam returned to his house to get his important belongings—Blackberry, passports, and checkbook. He also rescued Fifi, the family dog, who swam for the first time, alongside him.

Neighbors stood helplessly on the front porch of Caroline's and watched through the night as the fire spread to eight of their houses. Then the wind switched direction and put Adam's house right in the line of the fire. "As the fire got closer to my house," said Adam, "I started losing hope."

All at once, the wind switched direction and the water began to subside. This allowed the firefighters to come in and deal with the burning fires, which were brought under control in the nick of time, and Adam's house was saved.

"It was a traumatizing night. We lost both cars and the entire first floor of the house was ruined, but we're all thankful that no one got hurt during the experience," said Adam. He's also thankful that they had other family members to lean on throughout the rebuilding process.

Adam credits the Long Beach Fire Department and the width of Barnes Street as the reasons his house still stands today. "It's just surreal, it was an act of God," he said, adding, "and it could easily happen again." ●

George and Deb Trepp

Deb Trepp

The storm's dark hours led to a bright spot in its aftermath, as family and friends rallied around the Trepps.

My husband, George, and I have had the pleasure of living in Long Beach for most of the 35 years that George has been Library Director. The community has gone through its ups and downs but emerged in recent years more vital than ever—with a beautiful beach and boardwalk, jazz and other music festivals, and many individuals committed to a wide variety of causes. When I retired in 2010, George and I decided to renovate our house and we were thrilled to create a home where we could welcome our friends and have them delight in the beautiful resources the seaside offered.

While we have always evacuated for big storms in the past, we stayed home this time—my choice, not George's—and given ours is a two-story, newly renovated house with attic, I thought we would be safe where we were. We did everything we could to prepare, moving most of our belongings to the second floor. But our house is only one house off the bay, perhaps some 50 feet, so we knew we were really vulnerable. Sunday was windy and wild but nothing out of the ordinary given our prior experience with Nor'easters.

Monday morning, however, high tide came in quickly and the water rose to the first outside step of the house and some three feet around it. That's not unusual for a Nor'easter, but unlike prior tides, it did not recede for some six hours. We became increasingly concerned as projected tide heights scaled to to 11 feet. We had sandbagged the front, rear, and electric room, and we watched with great concern as evening tide (due at 7:30-8pm) began rushing in at 4pm. It was immediately clear that we would be in trouble. The only question was how much trouble. By 6pm the water was level with our porch, about four feet high, and five feet around the house. Water continued to rise and at about 7pm,

it began to leak in through the front and rear doors just as the power went out. Using flashlights and towels, we attempted to stem the tide, but the water was now nearly six feet around the house and poured in through our air conditioner. In five minutes we were ankle deep. We gave up and went upstairs to dry off and to sleep, knowing there was nothing else to be done. The water apparently kept rising, eventually reaching about three feet on the first floor. By midnight it had mostly seeped through the floorboards leaving us with mud striped floors throughout.

We awoke to a different world. Our woodpile, neatly stacked eight rows high, was gone. We found some of it eight blocks away. Our shed was upside down on our front lawn. Not a fence on the block remained standing. Garage doors were bent in and opened from the force of the waves. Belongings were strewn everywhere. Our cars, and the cars of everyone we knew, were fishbowls. Around the corner eight houses burned down at the height of the storm when two cars exploded and the fire department couldn't get through the shoulder-deep water. The Library's first floor sustained major damage. Long

(ABOVE) Christina Tisi-Kramer

(ABOVE) Long Beach's boardwalk couldn't withstand Sandy's heavy battering. (ABOVE, RIGHT) **November 1, 2012** A boat upended from the powerful winds of Superstorm Sandy.

Beach's water plant failed and the sewage plant was swept away entirely. Parts of the boardwalk were all over town and our beautiful beach was gone. Many of our friends lost everything, although thankfully nobody died.

I spent Tuesday cleaning my wood floors in a totally useless attempt to exercise some sense of control. I heated water in a fondue pot with a candle and devised some "creative" restroom solutions, but it was clear we had to evacuate. Though we had several offers of places to stay, we had no means of reaching anyone or getting anywhere but to a shelter. A mandatory evacuation was issued, due to rapidly developing public health concerns. Our son, Alex, who was studying in Boston, was unable to reach us. He had friends from all over visiting us to determine if we were alright. As we contemplated moving to the shelter on Tuesday night, I discovered around 1am that I could receive texts. The first one I received was from Alex, who wrote that he had rented a car and would arrive the next morning to take us wherever we wanted to go and help us clean up. He showed

up shortly with food, hand sanitizers, water and other things. Within the hour we left what remained of Long Beach—no easy task given the absence of any traffic lights between our house and the highway!

In the months that followed, we resided in a hotel in Cambridge, and spent many hours in conversation with insurance agents and FEMA. George began his work locating staff and arranging restoration of the Long Beach Library. We had no idea at the time how long it would take to get everything back to normal, but we kept at it.

Although we were sad and tired, on a misery scale of 1-10, we were perhaps a 3. So many people in single-floor houses lost everything and had to flee with the clothes on their back. We had each other, the means to rebuild, and an amazing demonstration of love and care from Alex throughout the ordeal. We even formed new friendships with neighbors we didn't even know. Most of all, our family and our Library family have rushed to our aid with abundant offers of housing and help. For this, we extend our deepest gratitude and heartfelt thanks. ●

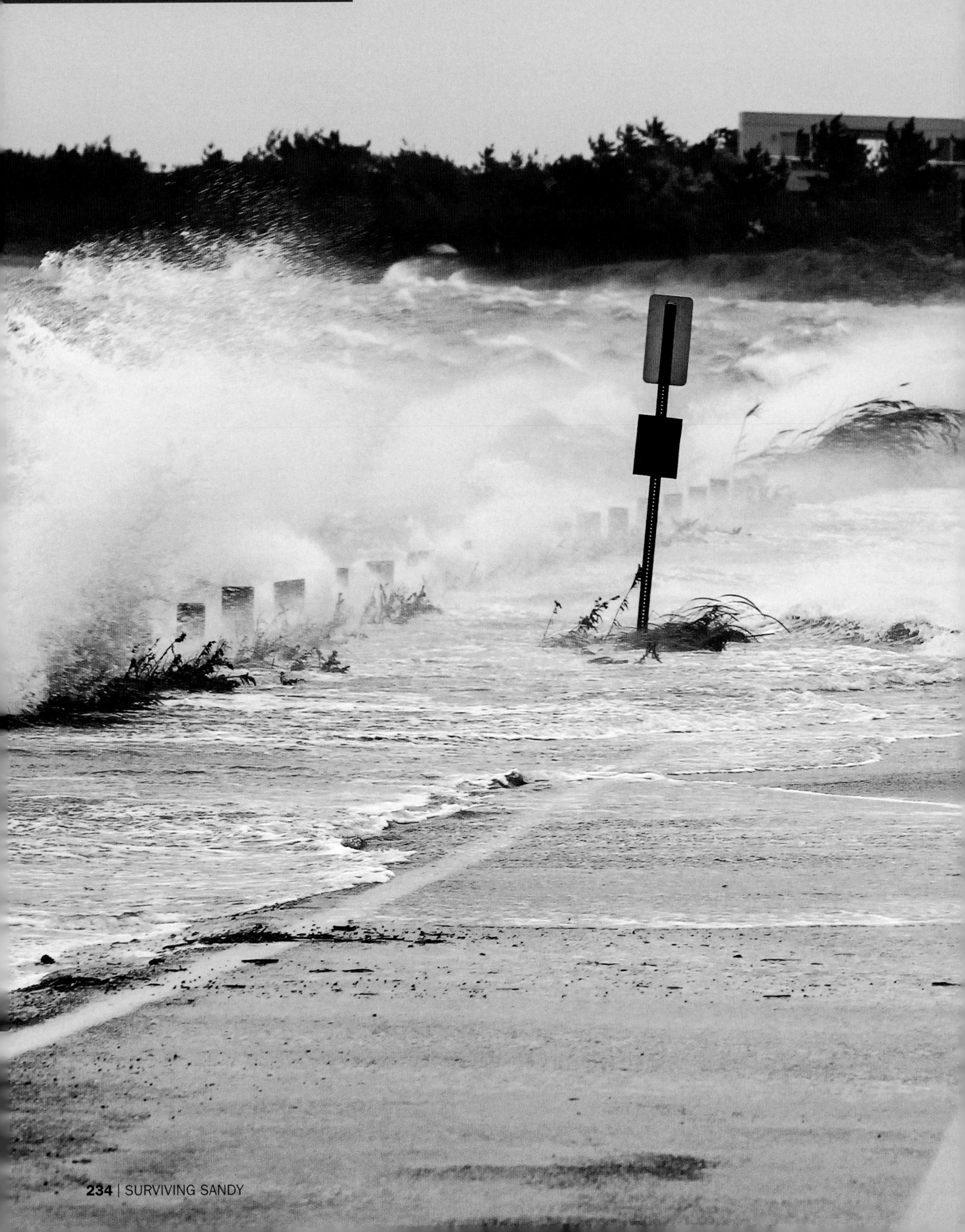

October 29, 2012 A truck drives through water pushed over a road by Superstorm Sandy in Southampton, New York.

James and Margaret Gallo

SURVIVOR STORY BALDWIN

James Gallo

Refusing to be intimidated by Sandy, James Gallo soon realized that this was a storm like none other.

"**I have experienced every hurricane** since 1943 and Hurricane Sandy was the worst," said Baldwin resident, James Gallo. "We have been through Hurricanes Donna, Gloria and Irene and we never had any problems. The highest the water had ever come up was to the garage door. But Sandy? That was another story altogether!" he exclaimed.

James Gallo, a retired plumber, has lived in the Baldwin, New York area all of his life. His house backed onto an inlet of Baldwin Bay, so he was preparing for Hurricane Sandy. The weekend before, he secured the outside furniture, got his boat out of the water, turned over the picnic tables, took the flags down, and got the generator ready for a power outage. By Monday, the 29th, the Gallo's were all ready for the big storm to hit."I sat down to do my crossword puzzle," Gallo recalled. "All of the sudden there was a BAM, and I said 'Oh, that's it!'" A nearby transformer had blown and the power went out. James dragged his generator onto the porch to restore power as they had done during previous storms.

By 5pm, it was raining hard and the wind was increasing. Realizing that the water was going to continue to rise in the street, James moved his car to Atlantic Avenue, which was on higher ground. All the while, he told his wife that they would be fine, assuring her that the water would not reach the house.

His daughter called quite distraught telling him that water was in her house, and she needed help. Still trying to play down the seriousness of the situation, James lightheartedly told her to stay on top of her bed. He felt

October 29, 2012 Jerry Smith of South Long Beach Avenue watches his dogs take a dip in the flooded street in front of his home as high tide and winds from Superstorm Sandy combine to flood the area in Freeport, NY.

bad later when he discovered she ended up leaving her house during the storm, and had to swim with her three cats to higher ground.

Like Hurricane Irene, the water got to the first step of the house. James continued to calm his wife's anxieties: "It will never come up here," he said. But the water continued to rise, and James had to put the generator up on a table. He was beginning to accept that this storm was not like any he had ever experienced before. James went down to the basement and he suddenly heard a loud rushing sound—water was gushing into an opening in the foundation. He eventually worked to stop the water by filling the hole

"I don't know what time it was, but the water was rising very quickly. We were rushing around trying to save as many household belongings as possible and all of a sudden, I felt something next to me—my refrigerator was floating!" said James with astonishment. It tipped,

"All of the sudden there was a BAM, and I said 'Oh, that's it!'"
A nearby transformer had blown and the power went out.

(ABOVE) Bruce Bennett/Getty Images

(ABOVE) Betsy and Steve Froehling outside their home on Grant Street with the piles of possessions that were ruined by the floods of Superstorm Sandy in Freeport, NY. (RIGHT) **October 29, 2012** Residents of Freeport make their way up through flooded streets.

brushing his shoulder and flopped onto its side. Fortunately, it didn't take James with it! Eventually, Gallo made his way upstairs. The water was at the top step of the basement stairs. With water coming in the fireplace, through the French doors, and up through the bedroom floorboards, there was not much they could do to save anything else.

James told a neighbor to bring his boat to his floating dock to salvage it. A little while later, James looked out his back window to discover the boats were torn away from the dock and were up against his window! He noticed his neighbor's boat was resting on the railing of the bridge – still tied to the dock. "I called my neighbor and said, 'We have got to save Billy's boat,'" James said. "As the tide started to recede, my neighbor and I went out together and made our way through three feet of water to the boat. We were very lucky—we were able to untie the boat and attach it to my dock," said James.

The next day, everyone was utterly devastated; Sandy had changed life forever. The Gallo's daughter moved in with her pets because she had lost her entire house. With the basement completely submerged, James used a huge gasoline pump to clear it out—a process that took all day. They lost 40 years of belongings from their basement including family pictures, business records, Christmas items, James's puppets, two exquisite dollhouses and two refrigerators stocked with food. "Everything was wrecked and had to be put out to the curb," said James. "Two dumpsters full of destroyed belongings were hauled away the next day."

The losses the Gallo's endured could not be tagged with a price but, like the rest of the community, they continue to recover. ●

Stuart Chase and friend Geri with their two dogs.

SURVIVAL STORY LONG BEACH

Stuart Chase

Stuart Chase resided at 54 Tennessee Avenue in Long Beach until the day Hurricane Sandy abruptly changed that.

Stuart Chase of Long Beach, New York, had heard the warnings in 2011. A mandatory evacuation was issued for Hurricane Irene. Most everyone in the community heeded the warning, including Stuart and his girlfriend, Geri. They packed up their three dogs and went to live with a relative in New York City, returning to their home after that storm to find very little damage.

A year later, in 2012, Mother Nature conjured up Hurricane Sandy for the East Coast. Again a mandatory evacuation was ordered, but remembering the minimal impact Hurricane Irene had, many residents decided to weather the storm and stay put.

At around 7:30pm on Monday, October 29, Sandy arrived. Stuart and Geri were eating dinner and watching TV when there was a loud knock at the door. Their neighbor, Mike, was there, and when they looked past him, their mouths dropped. "The water was waist high and flowing down the street!" recalled Stuart. "Mike's wife was carrying their two-year-old across the street to a friend's apartment on higher ground."

The Chases didn't know what to do. They had already placed hundreds of sandbags in front of the garage and front door, so their next decision was to put towels down to help stop any water from gushing in if it came higher. With their house six feet above the ground, they felt safe—until around 8:30pm—when they discovered water on the first floor. "It didn't take long for us to realize that water was seeping into the house through all the walls, not to mention that the electricity had gone out

October 30, 2012 This aerial photo taken by the U.S. Coast Guard shows flooding in the coastal neighborhoods on Long Island, New York. As Hurricane Sandy struck the U.S. Northeast, many businesses and airports were forced to close. Millions of people were affected by widespread power and transportation outages, which caused difficulties in carrying on with ordinary life in the days following the storm.

too. We were left with Yortzeit candles for light, which would only last 24 hours," said Stuart.

Panic ensued when the water rose to the level of the stairs leading to the second floor. They had no way to contact the outside world for help—their phones were ruined and reception was gone. For the first time, Stuart and Geri began to wonder if they would even make it through the storm.

Around 9pm, the water started to recede. "It began rushing out of the house faster than we had ever seen, and it left a disaster in its wake—with the entire first floor ruined," recalled Stuart. "We were sick, but went to bed knowing there was nothing we could do."

In the morning, Stuart and Geri awoke to a scene of utter devastation. Their garage door was wide open, and the contents were strewn about. Their new car of seven months had been under water, like most of the other cars on Long Beach, and was destroyed. Said Stuart: "The 'Long Beach' we knew and loved was gone—and we were left with an overwhelming mess!"

> *Panic ensued when the water rose to the level of the stairs leading to the second floor. They had no way to contact the outside world for help...*

The community was in shock, and stood around in stunned silence, trying to comprehend the scope of the devastation. How would they recover? Could this ever be normal again? Sand, sewage, and garbage were scattered everywhere, creating an awful odor. The seawater had risen to a little over seven feet, leaving many residents homeless. Homeland Security and the National Guard transported homeless people to shelters. An older man was dazed and walking in circles. Stuart approached him to hear that his wife, 75 years old, was incapacitated on the second floor and he didn't know what to do. They called in the National Guard trucks to make the rescue.

As they had done during Hurricane Irene, Stuart and Geri packed up their two dogs, and went to New York City to stay with Geri's sister. A few days later, they moved to another friend's home to stay before settling in a rented home, where they set up Stuart's office. Life was beginning to feel like normal again.

They lost everything on their first floor: living room, kitchen appliances, dining room furniture, and, most of all, the very things that told the story of their lives. "The entire experience was like a nightmare," Stuart recalled, "But Long Beach will recover, and become the welcoming place it always has been in the years gone by." ●

SURVIVOR STORY SOUTH OYSTER BAY

Joe Kamel

Despite great loss of property and possessions, Joe Kamel and his family emerge with renewed strength to start again.

What we saw was truly unbelievable: the usually calm inlet behind our home had joined with the raging Atlantic Ocean.

Like so many coastal areas in the New York metropolitan region, mandatory evacuations were issued in the days leading up to Hurricane Sandy. My town was no exception. There was a lot of hype around the storm, with weather reports becoming increasingly more ominous. As Sandy closed in, it was easy to see that all that hype was not hype at all. It was completely justified!

The time had come for my family and me to leave our beautiful home that backed on to the picturesque inlet of the South Oyster Bay. The home that was my pride and joy. The home into which I had poured my life savings. All we could do was pray for a happy ending.

Days had passed before we were able to return home in Sandy's wake. What we saw was truly unbelievable: the usually calm inlet behind our home had joined with the raging Atlantic Ocean. Waves had been crashing against our house and eventually gushed inside. The surge had

brought debris with it including three boat docks—one of which destroyed our house, landing in the living room. The water level reached almost six feet inside our first floor during the height of the storm. Our barbecue area was destroyed, not to mention all of our landscaping.

One of our most sentimental possessions was a 200-year-old chess table. It proved too difficult to haul it up to the second floor, so we decided to keep it on the first floor. We put it on top of the dining room table—a good 30 inches from the floor. It was destroyed as well.

Our life will never be the same. Our family has lived with a feeling of sadness ever since that October day. Things that we treasured were now gone, some of which can never be replaced. Besides our antique chess table, we lost family photos and a greatly valued Bible from Italy. At the outset of this storm, we prayed for a happy ending. In retrospect, it was, considering we all emerged together and unhurt—and ready to start again. ●

(CLOCKWISE FROM OPPOSITE LEFT)
This boat dock was a missile of destruction, piercing through a back wall of the Kamel's home. Another look from further away - our first thought was, "Where do you begin?" Debris from boat docks is strewn through the Kamel's living quarters. This dock was an uninvited guest, which smashed into the house.

SURVIVOR STORY LINDENHURST

Dyana Grenke

*How the support of a close-knit family helped
Dyana and her husband weather the storm.*

(ABOVE) Army trucks were a welcomed sight with the insurmountable task of clean-up ahead of us.

(BELOW) Storm waters rush through the streets of Lindenhurst.

Mike and I always go to Lancaster County, Pennsylvania for the annual Mud Sales held all over the County at local fire departments. This was the last one for the year. My young son Matthew wanted to stay with his Aunt Kee-Kee and her twins for the weekend.

On Saturday I remember getting a call from her saying that Hurricane Sandy was going to be a bad storm and they were already starting to evacuate Fire Island. After the auction, we ran to a local store and stocked up on candles, lighters, batteries, water—the essentials that would be hard to find once getting back to the Island. We left about 5am for the three-hour drive home.

I remember looking at the sky when we were merging from the Pennsylvania Turnpike to the New Jersey Turnpike. I had never seen a red sky like that before. Mike reminded me of the old adage: "Red sky at night sailors delight; red sky in the morning, sailor take warning." Little did we know what was brewing out in the ocean! We did know that a lot of work would be ahead of us, so the quicker we could pick up Matt and head home, the better. When we got home, the first thing we did was lift the appliances off the ground. We even lifted our 1970 Corvette onto blocks in the garage, and cleaned up the yard so if it became flooded, nothing would float away.

The Copiague Fire Dept. drove around the neighborhood a few times informing us that there was a manda-

(ABOVE) Time for a break during the devastating and exhausting clean-up after Sandy.

tory evacuation, and it was possible they wouldn't be able to reach us if needed. I turned and said to Matt, who was starting to become frightened: "We are leaving to go back to grandma's house in Levittown."

After a few hours securing the house as best we could, Matthew, Buddy (our dog) and I headed inland. My husband needed to work the next morning, but he promised that if it got too bad, he would leave. Once the water started coming in through the back of the house, he knew it was time to go! The water was more than halfway up the driveway, he said, and in the street it was up to his shoulders. Mike waded through the water to a friend's house, which was not in much better condition than ours.

After the storm, we could not return home because of the water, downed trees and debris everywhere. We lived with my parents for two weeks and I thank God for them. During that time, I went to Wal-Mart with Matt to buy some supplies for their house. I told my son that since he was such an awesome kid during this whole

ordeal, he could pick out a toy. As we were passing the card section he asked me "Mom what is Grandpa's favorite thing?" I said, "Matt, don't worry. It's not his birthday, let's go get your toy." On the way back to the register we passed the card section again, and Matt pulled me over to a card that had a dog on it. When I asked him why he wanted that card, he responded: "To thank Grandpa for letting us live with him because of the storm." It's a good thing we were in public, because if ever there was a time I wanted to burst into tears, that was it. (I held it together until later that night when he was asleep.)

Speaking of emotions, my husband is not the type of person to show his. On one occasion, he had come back to my parent's house after working all day, and then going to Lindenhurst to check on our house. He walked in the front door, shook his head, walked to my mom and hugged her, and started to cry. I stood there in shock. Maybe this was as good a time as any to tell him about the card our son got for his Grandpa. ●

Thomas Stoerger

SURVIVAL STORY BELLMORE

Thomas Stoerger,
Bellmore Fire Department Captain

Stoerger and his team fight Sandy through the long hours of darkness.

October 30, 2012 An emergency vehicle inspects the streets covered by beach sand in Long Beach, NY.

In the days leading up to Superstorm Sandy, firefighters, police and first responders began preparing for the arrival of the storm. But all the pre-planning in the world would not be a match for the worst weather disaster to strike Bellmore, Long Island or the tri-state area since 1938.

Bellmore is located on the south shore of Long Island, approximately 25 miles east of Manhattan. It is easily accessible by the Long Island Railroad, and John F. Kennedy International Airport is less than 15 miles away. Sandy shut all of that down.

I had prepared my family and home for the approaching storm. We live north of Sunrise Highway so I wasn't concerned about flooding. The wind is what worried me. As it turns out, it was the water I should have been most concerned about.

I took a ride around Bellmore in the harbor areas on Monday—before the storm made landfall. To my surprise, the tides were already rising above the bulkheads. I thought to myself: "This is only the beginning and it's still a full tide cycle away!"

By late afternoon, the phones started ringing at the firehouse. Most were about downed wires and power outages. However, as wind gusts increased to near hurricane force, things took a turn for the worse. Large trees that stood for centuries started toppling down—onto roofs, cars, garages, you name it. Then came the darkness.

As the sun started to set, the darkness brought winds, high tide and a full moon. Water ran down the streets and through people's homes at an incredible rate. Those who failed to evacuate earlier were trapped, and in complete darkness.

The Bellmore Fire Department was becoming overwhelmed. There were house fires, transformer explosions, live wires down, and trees had trapped people in homes and cars. It became difficult prioritizing which emergency to respond to first. They were all disasters.

We set up our own Communications Center because radio communication became impossible with the number of alarms being generated around the area. We also were forced to become self-sufficient because every other police and fire department was facing similar circumstances.

Early in the evening, we were dispatched to a call about a house on fire on Dock Road and Hewlett Lane. A pole had severed the transformer and caused an explosion. Several units were dispatched but we couldn't get to the fire because of the still-rising water and the danger of being electrocuted.

Soon after, I noticed a strange occurrence: the water was receding ever so slightly although it was high tide. Then, water began to rise rapidly. Was it a tsunami? We never figured out what happened but the local paper, Newsday, reported that others had experienced the same phenomenon.

As power went out across the Southern peninsula,

(TOP LEFT) Bill Kelly, (ABOVE) Mike Stobe/Getty Images

The docks and backyard swimming pools were destroyed all along Jason CT. in Bellmore, NY.

there was nearly total darkness. We drove around town and couldn't see anything, but there was plenty to hear—car alarms were sounding off everywhere.

The fire department has an army surplus truck that turned out to be our most powerful tool in fighting Sandy. The water was so high it was rising over the headlights and into the cab! When we got to the intersection of Anthony and Bedell Streets, we couldn't believe our eyes. The water was at the top of the "Stop" signs, there were white caps on the street, and a boat was floating upside down. People who needed to be rescued flagged us down by flashlights and we put them in the back of the truck. After dozens of rescues, I thought the worst was over but conditions deteriorated even further.

As we crossed Centre Avenue, I looked to the south and saw a large glow in the sky—another fire. The water was so high, getting the truck in was impossible, so we had to go by boat and by foot. Firefighters James McCarthy, Mike Boettcher, Will Colon and I proceeded ever so cautiously. We had to walk nearly half a mile through the water. At one point, we were concerned about floating sewer caps and other debris so we used a paddleboat to get to the fire.

The house was fully engulfed from bottom to top. Adding to the difficulty was that the fire was being fanned by the hurricane force winds and threatening other homes. We decided to conduct a search of all homes and evacuate those that were in danger of flying embers.

We took hoses and a small floating pump from Engine 2 and loaded them onto small boats and brought them to the scene. Our battle lasted five hours. Because of the flooding, pumpers could not access the location and the only water source was obtained by connecting to hydrants across the street and pulling hoses through rear yards. It was odd because we were standing in three feet of water! During this time, our Communication Center called and reported smoke in another home. This time the address was mine—a firefighter's worst nightmare. My wife and son were home, I thought. Thankfully, it turned out to be smoke that drifted in from another fire.

The Mineola Fire Department brought some backup support so we were finally able to pack up. Our team worked 24/7 without sleep or food and responded to more than 75 alarms, but the worst was still yet to come. Many of the members of our department who served so valiantly had to return to their own homes only to find them damaged or destroyed.

Despite the devastation and heartbreak, Sandy brought out the best side of Bellmore's residents. In the days and weeks that followed, firefighters worked with the Ladies' Auxiliary to collect food and clothes even as they fought to save their own homes. Despite the darkness Sandy brought, she also shed some light. We saw neighbors helping neighbors and families come together to help others in need. Sandy was a "Superstorm" but she also gave many of us "Superpowers." ●

ROCKLAND COUNTY

*Located 15 miles northwest of Manhattan, Rockland County
borders the Hudson River. As with oceanfront communities, Superstorm Sandy
brought its fair share of devastation to many historic rivertowns.*

MOLLY B

Photograph by Jaime Martorano/ARTSWESTCHESTER

October 29, 2012 Boats washed ashore, lumped together in random piles, were just some of the surreal sights at the Tarrytown Marina (across the river from Rockland County) the morning after the storm.

(ABOVE) The Village of Piermont already saw flooded streets on the Monday morning before the storm. (BELOW) The entrance to Washington Irving Boat Club is blocked by an assortment of boats that were washed up during the storm.

WASHINGTON IRVING BOAT CLUB

Photograph by Jaime Martorano/ARTSWESTCHESTER

(ABOVE) Superstorm Sandy inflicted hundreds of thousands of dollars worth of damage to boats moored on the Hudson. (BELOW) The rising Hudson tide gave an ominous warning to onlookers at Nyack Memorial Park on the Monday morning before the storm.

A river runs through it: The mighty Hudson is 315 miles long and flows north to south in New York State.

WESTCHESTER
NEW YORK

ROCKLAND

Hudson River

NEW YORK
NEW JERSEY

● Nyack

Tappan Zee
Bridge

● Tarrytown

● Piermont

N

| mi. | 2 | 4 |
| km 2 | 4 | 6 |

(TOP BOAT IMAGE) Photograph by Tom Van Buren/ARTSWESTCHESTER

Bill Herguth in front of Paradise Boats

(LEFT) Bill Herguth stands ready for a canoe ride at his boat rental facility in Piermont, New York. (ABOVE) Bill Herguth's house, on Paradise Avenue, backs up on a creek that snakes its way through marshland and empties out into the Hudson River.

SURVIVAL STORY PIEDMONT

Bill Herguth

In just 7 hours, some residents along the banks of the Hudson River lost everything. Bill Herguth shares his experiences of riding out Supersorm Sandy in his riverfront home.

My mother always said, "If you're having a bad day, just start over." But bad days were few and far between back when I was a kid. I used to float down the Hudson River on pieces of ice and wave to her. A love of the water was in my blood, having a family with long and established roots in Piermont, a small riverside town in Rockland County, New York since 1620.

My home has endured both the floods of 1928 and 1950. In 1950 when I was three years old, there was water everywhere and my sister and I played in it until we were forced to evacuate. When I gained ownership of the building in 1984, water would come in during every high tide so I jacked the entire building up 3 feet and drilled holes in the sill plate so that water would drain off. However, Hurricane Sandy was unlike anything I had ever experienced, and far beyond anything I could have expected. My property suffered extensive damage and I lost 5 cars after the entire area was submerged.

We remained inside the house throughout the storm. We moved everything from the bottom shelves up to the table. Once we realized the water was going to be so high, we started moving everything again. We lost our couch but managed to save the television and even the cable box, although it did fall in the water. Eventually I had to stop walking in the water. I knew my electrical meter was going to go under, and there would be 240 volts running through the water. I told my girlfriend I didn't want to take a chance on being electrocuted so we took refuge upstairs. On the first floor, the water was 6 inches above the dining room table! Water was pouring in the windows. My neighbor's garbage and his boats floated over my 6 foot fence and into my yard. The force of the water was amazing. Cars were sinking and their alarms were going off until they finally submerged. Outside, all I could see were waves coming across the water. That was scary. The wind was horrendous. I feared that the roof was going to lift off and I'd be looking up at the stars.

When the water finally receded, I couldn't get out the front door because a boat had jammed up against it. Muddy sewage was left behind throughout the house. There was so much damage on the ground that I didn't realize until a few days later that the roof had been damaged. When it began raining, the roof started leaking all

(LEFT) Looking out over the creek behind Bill's house.
(ABOVE) A view of Bill's yard, which was totally submerged with water from the storm surge.

My mother always said 'If you're having a bad day, start over' and that is exactly what I am doing.

over the living room causing even more damage.

Six people came to help on the first couple of days following the storm and everything was thrown away. I kept running out to the garbage to get things back that weren't even damaged. My daughter and her boyfriend also came over for 2 days to help. They mopped the floor 20 times to get rid of the muddy sewerage. We couldn't use a vacuum because we had no electricity. Everything had to be done manually. We took advantage of the daylight in order to get a lot done, and used candles when it was dark.

The only vehicle that I could get running after the flood was my truck. A huge branch had landed on the hood but luckily the windshield was not broken - yet. The young fellows from the volunteer fire department came over to help remove the branch, and when they cut it, it fell back onto the windshield and broke it! What could I say? I could not yell at someone who was trying to help me.

We also lost one of our four cats during the storm. We did not know where it had gone until Thanksgiving when it started stinking. It had gone under the house where it thought it would be safe, and drowned. Every day I would go underneath the house and try to find it, but the smell was so strong I could not tell where it was coming from.

I received $9,000 from the Homeowner's Policy to use towards repairs on the damaged roof. Instead of replacing it, I patched it, and used the money to get a new hot water heater and boiler installed. We were then able to take hot baths within a week. That kept us sane. Fortunately, we were also able to keep our gas on.

As we worked through the cleanup, I just went day by day. I hated it, because I wanted to get a move on. I don't like being a victim. I hate being a victim; with my training in Special Ed, I am always the guy that helps people. Every day somebody would show up offering assistance. I was amazed; there are a lot of kind people out there. Six teachers from Clarkstown had no school and came down to help. My girlfriend went into town and came back with two hearty sandwiches. Somebody had recognized her and said, "This is for you and Bill." This helped us through a difficult day! People came from Buffalo, NY to take away the ruined cars. They said they had to pick up 22,000 or more cars! The man who appraised the damage on my house came from Mississippi.

Defending my house was a real issue. I've been through floods before, but not like this one. Then I remembered what my mother always said: "If you're having a bad day, start over." And that's exactly what I've been doing – each and every day since the storm. ●

CONNECTICUT

THE CONSTITUTION STATE RACKED UP MILLIONS OF DOLLARS IN EXPENSES
AFTER HURRICANE SANDY LEFT HER MARK—DESTROYING HOMES, BUSINESSES,
TOWNS AND ROADWAYS. STATE OFFICIALS NOW WRESTLE WITH THE QUESTION
OF WHETHER THEY CAN PREVENT SIMILAR STORM DAMAGE IN THE FUTURE.

*"We need the public
to take this storm seriously."*

— Connecticut Governor Daniel P. Malloy

AP/Jessica Hill

October 29, 2012
Storm surge hits a small tree as winds from Superstorm Sandy reached Seaside Park in Bridgeport. Water from Long Island Sound spilled onto roadways and towns along the Connecticut shoreline, the first signs of flooding from a storm that delivered a devastating surge of seawater.

CONNECTICUT

MASSACHUSETTS

NEW YORK

RHODE ISLAND

CONNECTICUT

● Hartford

● New Haven
● East Haven
● Milford
● Bridgeport
Westport ● ● Fairfield
● Stamford

Long Island Sound

Long Island, NY

Atlantic Ocean

NYC

N

mi. | 10
km | 10 | 20

October 30, 2012 (ABOVE) Milford Fire Department Captain Christopher Waiksnoris checks for residents during the evacuation due to high tide in Milford. (BELOW) People stand next to a house that collapsed from Superstorm Sandy in East Haven.

October 29, 2012 (ABOVE) Ken Esposito, left, helps neighbor and homeowner Rob Hoxie, sandbag his beachfront home before high tide in Milford. **October 29, 2012** High tide begins to flood a street on the shoreline area of Milford, as Hurricane Sandy approaches.

Photograph by Victoria Godfred/ARTSWESTCHESTER

October 30, 2012 (LEFT) A home is nearly washed away on Fairfield Beach Road, Lantern Point.

(RIGHT) U.S. Coast Guard image shows an aerial view of the storm damage to parts of New Haven. (RIGHT, MIDDLE) U.S. Homeland Security Secretary Janet Napolitano, right, speaks at a news conference on Thursday, **November 1, 2012**, in Bridgeport, after touring storm-damaged areas with Connecticut officials. From left to right are U.S. Rep. Rosa DeLauro, U.S. Rep. Jim Himes, U.S. Sen. Joe Lieberman, Napolitano, Connecticut Gov. Daniel P. Malloy and Lt. Gov. Nancy Wyman.

November 14, 2012 Engineers stand next to the destroyed home of Benjamin Baron as they assess damage to the neighboring homes along Fairfield Beach Road.

SHE'S

"The devastation on the Jersey Shore is some of the worst we've ever seen.
The cost of the storm is incalculable at this point."
— *New Jersey Governor Chris Christie*

"The ocean is in the road, there are trees down everywhere.
I've never seen it this bad."
— *Long Branch, New Jersey resident David Arnold*

"You want to talk about a situation that gets old very quickly. You are sitting
in a house with no power and you can't open the refrigerator."
— *New York Governor Andrew Cuomo*

"It's 3 feet of heavy snow. It's like concrete."
— *West Virginia meteorologist Reed Timmer*

GONE
AND LEFT US WITH DEVASTATION

"The Hudson River came in and filled half of Hoboken like a bathtub."
— Hoboken, New Jersey Mayor Dawn Zimmer

"The New York City subway system is 108 years old, but it has never faced a disaster as devastating as what we experienced last night."
— MTA Chairman Joseph Lhota

"This is the largest storm-related outage in history."
— Con Edison spokeswoman Sara Banda

"Clearly the challenges our city faces in the coming days are enormous."
— New York City Mayor Michael Bloomberg

October 30, 2012 View of Sandy from the rear, as she leaves Roanoke Valley, Virginia.
Photograph by Kurt Konrad

When Sandy shut down New York, it paralyzed the economic center of America. But when the storm passed, New Yorkers were ready to get back to work—and they needed the Metropolitan Transportation Authority to get them there. The transit agency had moved equipment out of harm's way and did not lose a single subway car, and positioned its people so they could immediately begin recovery work as soon as it was safe.

The first buses began running just seven hours after the storm ended; the first commuter trains within 24 hours, and limited subway service within 36 hours. Crews cleared hundreds of trees (and dozens of boats) from subway and railroad tracks, pumped millions of gallons of water, and repaired miles of tracks, third rails, power lines and signal systems.

Diesel trains were pressed into serving areas with no electric power. A "bus bridge" shuttle used 330 buses to move commuters between Brooklyn and Manhattan while the subway tunnels beneath were pumped dry. Subways moved on manual controls while signals were repaired. Five days after the storm, Governor Cuomo was able to announce that the busiest subway lines in America had been pumped dry and returned to service faster than anyone had imagined – getting New York moving again.

Yet long-term challenges remain. Returning the MTA network to the condition it was in before Sandy struck will cost an estimated $4.755 billion in insurance proceeds and federal funds. Rebuilding stronger to protect against future storms and make the network more resilient will cost billions more. That effort will require years of work and some inconvenience to MTA customers – but the MTA has committed that those customers will not have to pay for it with any increased fares.

(ABOVE) **November 5, 2012** MTA employees worked around the clock for more than a week to pump water out of the L train's 14th Street tunnel under the East River, after it was flooded for more than 3,000 feet with seawater. After pump trains emptied the tube, crews inspected and repaired tracks, signals, switches, electrical and power components to restore service within 10 days of the storm.

October 30, 2012 The MTA suspended all bus service during Sandy, but began restoring it the next afternoon – seven hours after the storm departed.

(ABOVE) **October 30, 2012** When the storm cleared, MTA Metro-North Railroad found a boat had floated from the Hudson River onto the nearby Hudson Line train tracks at Ossining. Railroad employees needed a crane to remove the boat, and were confronted elsewhere by downed trees and power lines.

(BELOW LEFT) **November 3, 2012** Crews begin assessing damage to the A train bridge to the Rockaways. Restoring service to the destroyed line took seven months. (BELOW RIGHT) **November 5, 2012** The Long Island Rail Road restored limited service on all branches except the Long Beach Branch in time for the Monday morning commute.

October 29, 2012 Water from New York Harbor rushes into the Hugh L. Carey Tunnel (previously the Brooklyn-Battery Tunnel) as Sandy's surge swamps Lower Manhattan. An estimated 60 million gallons of water flooded both tubes of the tunnel, forcing crews to work around the clock to reopen it for limited traffic two weeks later.

The **Hugh L. Carey Tunnel**, the longest underwater vehicular tunnel in North America, became a giant drain for lower Manhattan when Sandy surged through the streets. An estimated 60 million gallons of water rushed down the entrance ramps of the four-lane tunnel, filling both tubes from floor to ceiling. More than a mile of the 9,117-foot tunnel connecting Brooklyn to Manhattan was swamped with water, posing an unprecedented challenge for the Metropolitan Transportation Authority.

Saltwater penetrated critical systems from above the ceiling to below the floor, destroying communications, power, safety, ventilation and surveillance equipment – even ceiling tiles, wall finishes and air ducts. Crews attacked the problem from both ends and from a ventilation building on Governors Island in the middle – pumping out oily water, inspecting the damage, cleaning surfaces and putting temporary repairs into place.

The damage rendered a vital connection for 50,000 vehicles a day, and led to emergency round-the-clock work by MTA crews and contractors. Two weeks after the storm hit, the tunnel reopened to buses during rush hours, and to general car traffic one week later. While long-term repairs will require many months of overnight lane closures, the reopened tunnel was an important step forward in New York's recovery.

November 2, 2102
The Battery Park Underpass, which carries traffic to and from the tunnel at the tip of Manhattan, was also clogged with water and debris.

(RIGHT) **October 30, 2102** When the storm cleared, both tubes of the tunnel were filled with corrosive, oily water that reached to the ceiling, creating an eerie reflection as they met. Under the surface, everything made of metal was destroyed.

(RIGHT, BOTTOM) MTA Bridges and Tunnels employees removed 2,300 lighting fixtures from the tunnel to salvage enough parts to put some of them back in service. Here, maintainer Caesar Laterza shows how he bandaged his fingers after suffering cuts from handling the metal parts.

(BELOW) **November 1, 2012** Homeland Security Secretary Janet Napolitano, U.S. Senators Charles Schumer and Kirsten Gillibrand, Gov. Andrew Cuomo, Mayor Michael Bloomberg, U.S. Rep. Jerrold Nadler, Assembly Speaker Sheldon Silver and MTA Chairman and CEO Joe Lhota toured the flooded tunnel and updated New Yorkers on efforts to reopen transportation after Sandy.

October 30, 2012 (ABOVE) Storm surge flowed down the stairs into the South Ferry subway station, along with a pile of timbers that came to rest by the turnstiles. Salty, oily water filled the station 80 feet deep.

When the Metropolitan Transportation Authority opened the new South Ferry subway station for the No. 1 train in 2009, it marked a huge improvement over the curved and cramped loop station that had served the southern tip of Manhattan for a century, but when Sandy's surge poured down the stairs and into the new terminal, it swamped the complex in 80 feet of salt water.

The water ruined everything customers saw – escalators, turnstiles, lights and walls – as well as behind-the-scenes gear-like power equipment, a computer-filled control room and hundreds of electrical relays that oper-

ate the circuits that keep trains running safely, switching smoothly and properly spaced on the correct track.

Rebuilding the ruined station will be a years-long process. So to serve more than 10,000 daily riders at the closest station to the Staten Island Ferry terminal, the MTA put the old South Ferry loop station back in service. While the old station can hold only the first five cars of a 10-car train, and requires special plates to bridge the wide gap between the cars and the curved platform, the reopened station is a temporary measure that marked another step forward in New York's recovering transportation network.

Photos Courtesy of MTA

November 5, 2012 (ABOVE) With the water finally pumped out, the scope of devastation became clear – everything from ceilings and walls to escalators and electronics was ruined.

April 4, 2013 (RIGHT) Customers return to the old South Ferry loop station. The MTA put it back in service as a temporary station for lower Manhattan while the new station is rebuilt.

January 17, 2013 (BELOW) MTA New York City Transit Chief Electrical Officer Wynton Habersham surveys the damage in the South Ferry dispatch room, which was flooded and ruined by the storm.

LIBERTY ISLAND

**Lady Liberty stood proud and tall
as Sandy's winds and storm surge came roaring in.**

In the middle of New York Harbor not far from Manhattan lies a small 12 acre island that is home to the iconic Statue of Liberty, the symbol of America's freedom. On October 28, 2012, this island, known as Liberty Island, was in the direct path of Superstorm Sandy's devastating storm surge. Across the harbor, in Battery Park itself, water soared over 13 feet high, which meant that almost 75% of Liberty Island was under water.

The strength of the 126-year-old iron framework allowed the Statue to withstand the brutal storm winds, but the rest of the island did not fare as well. The island's utilities, backup generator and power systems were all destroyed. Additionally, there was severe damage done to the passenger and auxiliary docks. Some of the brick pathways around the island were also uprooted by the storm.

In just a few weeks after the storm, on November 9, 2012, the Statue of Liberty was shining brightly across the bay as a beacon of hope to the storm devastated inhabitants of New York and New Jersey.

Due to the strong iconic bearing the Statue of Liberty has on the residents of New York and New Jersey, and on Americans as a whole, it was stated that repairs to the Statue and the island would be done as soon as possible. It was estimated that repairs to both Liberty Island and Ellis Island would cost as much as $59 million.

On July 4th, 2013, less than one year after Sandy tore through the region, the Statue of Liberty and Liberty Island reopened to the public.

November 30, 2012 Parts of the brick pathway that surround Liberty Island–which were torn up by Superstorm Sandy's brutal winds–are shown during a tour of the Island. The Statue of Liberty remained closed to the public after Superstorm Sandy but reopened on July 4th, 2013. At the same time, Statue Cruises resumed their ferry passage to Liberty Island from Lower Manhattan.

(OPPOSITE) Looking across the storm-damaged auxiliary docks of Liberty Island, Manhattan is visible. The Statue survived Superstorm Sandy, but the Island did not fare so well. Buildings and the Island's power and heating systems were damaged, which will keep the island closed until the repairs are completed.

November 2, 2012
People wait in line to buy gas for cars and generators in Asbury Park, New Jersey in the aftermath of Superstorm Sandy.

GASOLINE FRENZY

Sandy severely disrupted the gasoline supply chain, resulting in long tiresome lines at the pump and 1970's era gas rationing.

Sandy brought a lot of sights that no one ever expected to see including mile long lines at the gas stations. It became so serious that police officers had to keep law and order in New York, New Jersey and Connecticut as motorists exchanged words – and even shoves and punches – as they faced days of stressful lines at stations that still had both electricity and supplies after the storm.

Far from a mere inconvenience, the shortage of fuel made recovering from Sandy far more difficult. Businesses couldn't operate. Relief efforts were hampered; Construction crews couldn't travel. The lack of fuel also spread fear.

In Union Beach, New Jersey – one of the hardest hit towns in the Garden State- one father ran up and down the line of hundreds of people begging for gas for his generator. He offered all his money for five gallons of gas. The desperate man had three young children at home, including a 9-day old newborn at home, and a sick wife. There were tears in his eyes as he dropped to his knees and sobbed. As the crowd watched and heard his story, several sympathetic people walked over and filled his red canister. Who would have thought Sandy would bring a scene like this?

For days, motorists looked like refugees as they sought to satisfy their thirsty vehicles. Some people walked for miles for gas. Others slept overnight in their cars with blankets waiting for fuel trucks. In an effort to boost supplies and turn the pumps back on, officials got involved.

New Jersey's Governor Chris Christie announced odd/even days to ease the long lines. License plate numbers became the key as to what day you could purchase fuel. Christie also directed Treasury officials to waive licensing requirements so merchants could buy fuel from out-of-state supplies. He even called President Obama on his cell phone. According to several news stories, Christie told a crowd at the New Jersey Hospital Association in Princeton that Obama had given him his number and told him to call any time. And he did.

Bloomberg News outlined Christie's conversation with the President:

"I said, 'I need gas.' He said, 'OK. How much do you need?' 'So at this point, I did what any person who has no idea what they're talking about does when asked a question like that over a cell phone with the President of the United States. I was standing in front of my Cabinet, who knew I was on the phone with the President, and I said, 'Uh, uh, sorry sir. You're breaking up. Did you ask how much gas I need?' I then desperately began looking

Reporting by Reuters bureaus throughout the U.S. Northeast; Writing by Daniel Trotta and Michelle Nichols; Editing by Mohammad Zargham and Jim Loney

Reuters/Tom Mihalek

at someone in my Cabinet to give me an answer."

The news reports say it was Bob Martin, Commissioner of Environmental Protection, who whispered, "12 million gallons." So Governor Christie requested 12 million gallons from the President. The President called Defense Secretary Leon Panetta and a few moments later, Christie was told, "Gas is on the way."

But it would still take nearly one week before New Jersey drivers were able to say, "Fill her up."

Meanwhile, in New York City, officials required all motorists entering Manhattan to have at least three passengers. Police set up a checkpoint outside the Lincoln tunnel to check cars before entering. The checkpoint caused miles of traffic jams and delays that lasted hours.

On Thursday, Sen. Chuck Schumer (D-N.Y.), urged the Coast Guard to clear the way for barges carrying fuel to enter the Port of New York bringing millions of gallons of gas. And the Environmental Protection Agency temporarily waived clean-fuel requirements for 17 eastern states. Nevertheless – the fuel shortage crippled the tri-state area for days.

By Friday, a fleet of New Jersey Transit buses resumed service to the cheers of commuters and New York City started to hum again. It took still several more days before the tri-state was operating normally but hope had been restored.

Reuters/Mike Segar

November 1, 2012 Cars wait in long lines at a Sunoco gas station on the Garden State Parkway in Montvale, New Jersey. Lines formed at gas stations amid fuel shortages around the U.S. Northeast and emergency utility crews struggled to reach the worst hit areas and restore power to millions of people affected by Hurricane Sandy.

A truck sits at the back of the gas line almost a quarter mile away from the station on Myrtle Street in Cranford, New Jersey.

LIGHTS OUT

As the storm made its way across the heavily populated East Coast, the night sky was lit up with exploding transformers and then...darkness.

After surviving the terrifying winds and rain, millions awoke Tuesday, October 30 and the lights were out. Even though "Sandy" was stripped of her hurricane status, the Superstorm continued packing a stiff punch on the electrical grid, cutting service to more than 8.2 million homes and businesses from the Carolinas to Canada and as far west as Chicago.

The combination of wind, rain, and heavy flooding created unprecedented outages the nation had never seen. Sandy knocked down trees and power lines in 21 states and left millions in the dark in the nation's largest cities. She caused scares at three nuclear power plants and stopped the presidential campaign cold.

New York was among the hardest hit, with its financial heart shut down for two days after seawater gushed into Lower Manhattan, inundating tunnels, subway stations and the electrical system that powers Wall Street. For many, it was eerily quiet as Ground Zero was in the dark once again.

And then came the linemen. Utility companies from Oklahoma – and as far away as California – were brought in to help. Crews worked sixteen hour days. By Thursday, November 1, the number of outages was cut nearly in half to 4.5 million. But that still provided little solace for those in the dark or still living under the sound of gas generators. One week after the storm, there were still more than half a million people without power in New Jersey. It would take days and even weeks before all the region's residents could turn their lights on. With standard avenues of communication shut down, local township officials were challenged with how to effectively communicate with residents. Some townships handed out leaflets with updates as to power restoration or arranged town wide conference calls.

The historic levels of power outages contributed heavily to the costs that Sandy brought: More than 50 billion dollars in damage.

October 29, 2012 A general view of submerged cars on Ave. C and 7th St, after severe flooding caused by Superstorm Sandy, in Manhattan, New York.

(OPPOSITE) Roxanne Boothe uses a flashlight as she walks a hallway in Sam Burt Houses, where she is president of the tenants' association, on Saturday, **Nov. 3, 2012** in Coney Island, N.Y. The complex, which had been without power since Monday, flooded during Superstorm Sandy and a 90-year-old woman who had lived there for more than 40 years drowned on the first floor. "We have no heat, no water, no electricity, it's dark in the whole building," said Boothe, frustrated that the Red Cross or FEMA assistance had not reached her neighborhood.

LIGHTS OUT

Westover C-5B and crew participate in round-the-clock relief ops. In response to President Obama's call for the government to support Hurricane Sandy relief efforts, a Westover C-5B flew to March Air Reserve Base, Calif., picked up 73 electrical workers and two utility trucks, and dropped them off at Stewart Air National Guard Base, East Windsor, N.Y. hours later. The workers and equipment augmented relief efforts in New York and New Jersey.

U.S. Air Force/SrA. Kelly Galloway

8.2 MILLION WITHOUT POWER

This graph shows the extensive number of power outages as recorded by the Department of Energy per state and by day. On November 6, over a week after the storm hit, there were still almost 1 million customers without power.

State	PM Outage Reports								
	29-Oct	30-Oct	31-Oct	1-Nov	2-Nov	3-Nov	4-Nov	5-Nov	6-Nov
Connecticut	2,073	626,559	502,465	348,294	232,142	132,805	64,955	30,608	7,371
Delaware	2,406	18,611	2,757						
District of Columbia		3,010							
Illinois		1,149							
Indiana		9,224							
Kentucky		8,379	2,941						
Maine		72,049	9,145						
Maryland	20,199	253,315	103,997	40,760	17,803	12,064	7,198	4,155	1,666
Massachusetts	30,413	256,039	82,809	12,883	2,248				
Michigan		69,006	35,422	10,004	10,020				
New Hampshire	18,190	136,565	55,809	8,324					
New Jersey	87,649	2,615,291	2,052,724	1,733,202	1,491,529	1,241,763	999,927	756,774	537,089
New York	105,089	2,097,933	1,948,282	1,525,969	1,269,392	871,161	654,623	492,575	348,985
North Carolina	15,466	1,998							
Ohio		267,353	162,637	96,880	60,273	25,244	10,007	2,589	
Pennsylvania	12,944	1,221,536	800,745	509,839	304,094	153,695	77,630	31,114	10,074
Rhode Island	11,009	116,592	50,468	21,376	5,962				
Tennessee		2,120							
Vermont		8,104							
Virginia	11,125	147,622	33,385	7,538	2,176				
West Virginia		271,765	218,490	139,581	95,956	60,689	41,618	33,868	25,598
TOTAL	**316,563**	**8,204,220**	**6,062,076**	**4,454,650**	**3,491,595**	**2,497,421**	**1,855,958**	**1,351,683**	**930,783**

Source: U.S. Department of Energy Office of Electricity Delivery & Energy Reliability

November 8, 2012 Con Edison workers work to restore power to Manhattan Beach, Brooklyn, NY after Superstorm Sandy.

iStock/Samaro

FALLEN

A car cannot stand up to the weight of fallen trees at Mamaroneck Ave. and Crossway in Scarsdale, NY.

GIANTS

The Northeast Woodlands has beautiful trees – the mighty oak, the colorful maples, and other majestic hardwoods that take years to grow to their full height of sometimes 100 feet plus. These giants were no match with Sandy's hurricane force winds and fell by the 1000's, like soldiers in the midst of a battle of giants. Nearly 10,000 trees fell in New York City alone, with 1000's more across the Eastern Seaboard. As they fell, many of them became Sandy's agents, administering devastating blows to houses, cars, and even lives. In Mendham Township, New Jersey, a falling tree struck the car of Richard Everett and his wife Elizabeth, killing both him and his wife, while sparing the lives of two sons in the back seat.

October 30, 2012
A large uprooted tree lies on a house following a night of high winds and rain from Hurricane Sandy in Bethesda, Maryland. (BELOW) A tall one lands on the backyard shed in Pleasantville, NY.

Photograph by Brian Turner/ARTSWESTCHESTER

(ABOVE) Reuters/Gary Cameron

October 30, 2012 A huge tree split apart and fell over the front yard and fence of a home on Carpenter Avenue in the aftermath of Superstorm Sandy, in Sea Cliff, N.Y. (BELOW) Two fallen giants, look like best friends, laying side by side on Ardmore Road, Scarsdale, N.Y.

Photography by Raphael Abada/ARTSWESTCHESTER

SCARSDALE, NEW YORK

White Plains
USE BY-PASS
1/2 MILE AHEAD

CONEWAGO TOWNSHIP, YORK COUNTY, PENNSYLVANIA

REDDING, CONNECTICUT

ALEXANDRIA, VIRGINIA

BROOKLYN, NEW YORK

HOBOKEN, NEW JERSEY

A DEVASTATED FISHERMAN

"Sometimes the water gives, and sometimes it takes... it can take away in one minute what it took a lifetime to build"

JAMES "FRANK THE FISH" CULLETON

Fishing is the last thing on the minds of many folks who bore the brunt of Hurricane Sandy. As the dust settled months later, it became clear the fishing and boating industries took multi-million dollar hits. The economic loss is massive.

Not only did Sandy end the 2012 season early but she also wiped out the availability of fresh fish to local markets and restaurants that did survive the storm.

For James Culleton, a commercial fisherman and charter boat captain, Sandy has brought more devastation to the East Coast than any other storm he has ever seen Culleton has been fishing Jamaica Bay for nearly half a century.

"I thought the night of the storm was the hardest thing I would ever experience but getting my life back together has been far more difficult," Culleton says.

On October 29, Culleton was in his Rockaway home. He thought he was safe and had taken all necessary precautions. But at 8pm, water started pouring into his house. Minutes later – his 30 foot Grady White crashed through the front door. Fearing for his life, he got in his car and drove down the street. The water was inching up higher so he drove onto the front lawn of his friend's home and ran inside.

James Culleton stands out on a lonely pier looking at the ocean, which provides him with his livelihood. Sandy dealt him a devastating blow financially, however James confidently states, "The water will give what it took, back to me..."

Photographs by Jonah Markowitz

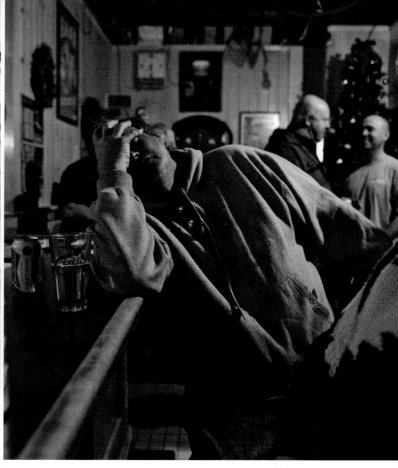

(ABOVE) Culleton's boats can be seen in the yard, lodged up against his house by the force of the storm surge. (RIGHT) One of Culleton's many moments of utter desperation as he tries to cope with everyday life after Sandy.

"There were gas explosions under the water and we thought the flames were going to reach the house. I remembered the photos of people in Hurricane Katrina standing on their roofs. I thought that's what we were going to have to do – go through the roof to escape the rising water," he says.

Like many people who feared for their life that night, help never came. Police and fire departments were so inundated with calls that many went unanswered.

"I knew we were on our own and I was scared," Culleton says. That fear hasn't left Culleton and he wonders if it ever will.

After Sandy left the East Coast, Culleton discovered he had lost his house, two boats, and three vans he used to deliver fish. Most of his customers had lost their restaurants and his marina was gone. What was worse…. Culleton was not insured. He had paid off the mortgage of his home only months ago and thought he was still insured. He wasn't. He estimates he lost more than $250,000 to Sandy – his entire life savings.

"The hardest thing has been not knowing what to do. I'm told to go to this agency or see this person but nothing happens," he says.

When spring finally came, Culleton says the season brought more despair but some hope, too. Many of his customers weren't sure if they wanted to go back into the water. Culleton says the 2013 boating season will be a loss because no one really knows what lurks underneath. There are tales of lost debris, beach sand, and sunken ships and there's enough worry to keep boaters away.

Culleton says that Sandy continues to wreak havoc and she likely will for several years to come.

"Buildings were knocked off their foundations and carried into the water. It has affected tide levels on many waterways which will remain higher for the coming years, so when it rains, flooding is a regular occurrence. I don't know when that will change," he says.

"I've heard of boaters being stuck at their own docks because houses are blocking them in," Culleton explains.

While water conditions might scare off pleasure boaters, fishermen are having a good 2013 season. Culleton attributes some of the excitement to post-Sandy recovery. Fishing provides a bit of relief to those problems.

Plus – he says – the fishing is better this year oddly. The cold winter brought in a lot of fish in the spring. He also says the storm affected the currents and that sand bars are more pronounced.

"It has helped us bring in some good fish," he says.

Culleton remains buried in debt. He is now on food stamps and sleeps on his friends' couches in between rooms that FEMA has provided. He wonders when he will get his life back together. Still – there is hope.

"If you're a fisherman, you're always hopeful," he says. "You may not have a bite for weeks but you never know when you put your lure in the water what the sea will bring, but you hope. That's all I can do right now."

Culleton says Sandy brought devastation but also brought people together. He says, maybe it's a good lesson in life. Maybe I had it too easy for too long. Sandy has humbled me. ●

LENDING A HELPING HAND

The First Response Team of America brings much needed assistance to a stranded community.

Tad Agoglia (left front) works with Emergency Management to develop a plan to combat Sandy.

ASSISTANCE LONG ISLAND, NEW YORK

THE FIRST RESPONSE TEAM OF AMERICA

Aid came to flooded neighborhoods, blocked roads and powerless residents stranded in the storm's wake.

Arriving on Long Island, NY 24 hours before Sandy struck the East Coast, the First Response Team of America immediately got to work. Led by Tad Agoglia, the Team worked alongside the emergency services departments in Huntington, Melville, Northport and Asharoken, pre-positioning their equipment and supplies.

As Sandy approached, the town of Northport lost power. Tad and his team assisted by setting up lights downtown so that residents could easily see any rising water. The powerful winds, which reached 93 mph in this area of Long Island, pushed down huge trees, bringing down power lines and blocking roads. This prevented emergency vehicles from responding to distress calls. In one incident, an ambulance was needed to get to a woman in labor. Tad told his team, "Every time this ambulance hits a roadblock, we're going to pull our saws out and cut a way through." Although it was a risky task carving through trees entangled with power cables, the determined team enabled that woman to get to the hospital.

As all communication was cut off, Tab feared that many people were stuck in their homes with no way to call for help. The team climbed into an old army truck and began searching.

Tad's tireless efforts didn't stop when the sun came up the next morning. With their track loader, they cleared three feet of sand off the road connecting Asharoken with

One of the First Response Team's large pieces of equipment helps clear a road. (TOP LEFT) One of the First Response Team members on the lookout for those needing to be evacuated. (TOP RIGHT) Clearing the roadway to Asharoken with the track loader the day after the storm.

Long Island to enable emergency vehicles to access the island. They brought in their generator strong enough to power the entire Huntington Town Hall, so the emergency management center could get back to business again. Eight days later, power was restored to the building, but the First Response Team stayed to continue clearing roads and helping the Long Island communities recover.

First Response Team of America is a nonprofit organization that responds to communities with highly specialized trucks and equipment in the immediate wake of disasters. Too often, communities must fend for themselves because the resources for rescue and recovery are either damaged, inaccessible or unavailable. The First Response Team fills the gap between the onset of a disaster and the arrival of traditional relief agencies, reducing the time it takes to reach those in need and joining local first responders in saving lives and restoring hope. ●

First Response Team's large trailer generator pulls up to hook up the Huntington Town Hall.

(LEFT) The Lane twins watching a young volunteer. (RIGHT) Joe Lane's house in Queens was the first project for New York Says Thank You. They have committed to rebuilding 200 homes of firefighters, police and first responders. "If they aren't safe in their homes, no one is protecting us," says NYSTY Founder Jeff Parness.

ASSISTANCE BROAD CHANNEL, QUEENS, NEW YORK
NEW YORK SAYS THANK YOU

The Foundation helps one of New York's finest get back on his feet after a devastating blow from Sandy.

Joe Lane has been a New York City police officer since 1995. As a detective with the homicide unit in Queens, he's protected city streets for eighteen years and seen his share of horror. But when Sandy hit, he never expected "he" would become a victim.

On the days leading up to the storm, Lane did what most homeowners did who live near the water. He taped up his windows, secured his belongings, and stocked up on bottled water, but because of how serious the threat had become, Lane and his family had no choice but to pack up and leave their home. Despite the elevated threats, Lane says he never imagined the horror he would witness in the coming days.

On October 29, 2012, Sandy struck the East Coast with such devastating force, she pummeled

entire neighborhoods to the ground. In Lane's Broad Channel neighborhood, front porches floated out to sea, roofs collapsed, and roads became impassable.

When Lane finally returned two days later to survey the damage, his worst fear was confirmed.

"Our entire first floor was destroyed. Everything was gone," he says.

Lane says it was the first time he was afraid. He and his wife Jennifer spent their entire life savings on their new home and their twin daughters were less than one-year old. There was a harsh reality: His family was now homeless.

"I couldn't bring my family back here. I was afraid they would get sick with the mold so I packed what I could and left," he says. "I had no idea where we would go or where we would live."

As a victim, new father and working cop, the fear of finding housing was also daunting.

"I saw so many others in need including fellow police officers," Land said. "I didn't know where to turn."

According to the New York City Police Department, there were more than 2,000 police officers whose homes were damaged or

> *He and his wife, Jennifer, spent their entire life savings on their new home and their twin daughters were less than one-year old. There was a harsh reality: His family was now homeless.*

Photos by Mia Toschi

(ABOVE) Firefighter Hutch Ryder (left front row) poses with college students from the University of North Carolina Western campus. The students traveled hundreds of miles to help Ryder rebuild his Staten Island home and were organized by New York Says Thank You.

destroyed by Sandy, and like so many officers of the law, Joe Lane was too humble to ask for help. Although he wears a badge of honor, he says he wouldn't consider it honorable to ask for help.

Without asking for assistance, help arrived on the Lane's doorstep in less than 48 hours. People whom he had never met asked, "What can we do for you?"

The volunteers who came knocking are part of an organization called the New York Says Thank You Foundation. And in less than three weeks, these volunteers whom the Lanes call "angels" rebuilt a walkway, rewired electrical outlets, took out moldy insulation, and built new walls. The house was even painted.

New York Says Thank You was formed in the aftermath of September 11th and since 2003, the nonprofit group has rebuilt communities around the country in the wake of disaster. They have helped wildfire victims in California, tornado victims in Indiana and Kansas, and hurricane victims in New Orleans, but this was the first time they rebuilt in their own backyard.

New York Says Thank You founder Jeff Parness explains, "This is our New York family. These are the people who protect us. If they're not in their homes, they can't do their jobs."

Police officer Joe Lane's house in Queens was the first

to be rebuilt. Firefighter Kinga Mielnik's house in Brooklyn marks the 26th. Firefighter Hutch Ryder's house in Staten Island marked the 48th. And that's not all. The organization has committed to rebuilding 200 homes of tfirst responders, firefighters and police officers. September 5–8, 2013, volunteers nationwide came to New York to finish the efforts.

New York Says Thank You brought much of the nation together with their rebuilding efforts. Colleges nationwide sent volunteers – from West Carolina State to University of West Virginia to Lasell College. Corporations like KPMG donated resources and manpower. Jet Blue and Hawaiian Airlines flew volunteers to New York for free. The National Association of Women in Construction was there to help, and firefighters from Louisiana and as far away as Hawaii worked alongside victims. And there were donations from BASF, AirSeals, Newell Rubbermaid, Home Depot and Lowes.

"I am truly humbled and so thankful," says Lane.

Parness says the "Pay It Forward" movement philosophy that has become the motto of the foundation is simple: What we do is about 9/12. September 12th was the first day the world came together to help New York heal. October 30th was the second. It has been inspiring to say the least." ●

Mia Toschi

STARS OF HOPE

Students from across the country painted "stars of hope"... wooden stars with inspirational messages which were hung by volunteers in Staten Isand, Queens and the Jersey shore. Stars of Hope is a non-profit organization which sends "stars" to areas hit by disaster. They have been sent to Japan after the tsunami and numerous places in the U.S.

Photos By Mia Toschi

KINGA MIELNIK

Firefighter Kinga gives birth during Sandy and has her home rebuilt by complete strangers.

October 29 was a night Kinga Mielnik will never forget. Hurricane Sandy destroyed her home and in the midst of howling winds and complete darkness, the nine-year veteran of the New York City Fire Department also gave birth to her third son.

And while Sandy has left some sadness in these flooded neighborhoods, it has mostly receded and turned to gratitude for Mielnik.

On one chilly Saturday in early March, Mielnik's home was filled with complete strangers putting up walls, sheetrocking, painting and much more.

"I ask myself "why?" "Why was I so lucky?" she says.

Lenoble Lumber donated materials and volunteers poured in including the National Association of Women in Construction.

"When we heard there was a female firefighter who needed help, our group sent out emails to volunteers and here came the ladies,"says Saadia Walters from Local 157.

With a new kitchen floor, ceiling, walls and newly painted rooms, Aidan "Storm" and all the Mielniks will have a new beginning filled with gratitude thanks to these volunteers.

Kinga Mielnik poses with her son, Aidan Storm, as volunteers repair her damaged home. Mielnik is a nine-year veteran of the New York City Fire Department and gave birth to her third son, Aidan Storm, the night that Hurricane Sandy destroyed her Brooklyn home.

Students at the temporary Lavellette School are thrilled to receive a "Book and a Blanket" from Hugo's Hero's who experienced the loss of their schools and homes in 1989. Linda Rumph, of South Carolina, lost her home and remembered her children receiving "Books and Blankets" so she drove to New Jersey to organize the ribbon-wrapped packages for distribution.

HUGO'S HEROES

New Jersey Governor Chris Christie called relief organizations in Charleston, North Carolina to say "thanks." Some of the heroes included victims of Hurricane Hugo. One of Hugo's Heroes included Chris Donavan who teamed up retirement community Bishop with Holy Cross Episcopal Church to send 300 sets of household appliances to victims of Superstorm Sandy (each included washer/dryer, stove, microwave, dish washer and refrigerator). The local football team from Wando High School loaded up the trucks and Kenmar Express Incorporated donated their delivery truck and driver for free.

As Donavan says, "We were once homeless and people came to help us. Now it's our turn."

(CLOCKWISE FROM TOP LEFT) Makeshift administration room for animal and owner's records; Feline dormitory, Forlorn animal gets all the love it needs and a new home if needed; The larger dog dormitory in the gym; Jo Ellen Cimmino in front of her own camper brought to the site for Volunteer's respite; Smaller dog area in the gym with quarantined compound behind the blue tarps for sick dogs.

BEVERLY POPPELL VICE PRESIDENT OF PET SAFE

Finding Shelter from the Storm

Volunteers at the American Disaster Relief and PET SAFE go many extra miles and hours to help Sandys' animal victims.

After a crisis, such as Superstorm Sandy, the question inevitably arises about the fate of the animals that have been displaced. The Pet Safe Coalition, based in Wantagh, New York, was called upon by Nassau County to manage and staff the Nassau County Emergency Pet Shelter, located in the former Navy Athletic Complex at Mitchel Field.

Initially, it was intended that the Pet Safe Coalition would provide emergency shelter services for 515 pets, enabling pet owners who were forced to evacuate, to find safe housing for themselves without the temptation to stay behind with their pets, which were not permitted in temporary "people shelters."

"Team Pet Safe is comprised of an all-volunteer staff that provided free, round-the-clock care, boarding, medical services, and ultimately relocation services for pet owners who were not able to be reunited with their pets after the immediate aftermath of the storm," said Beverly Poppell, Vice President of Pet Safe.

Volunteers came from a variety of disciplines, all work-ing to ensure that each pet was well cared for. They included veterinarians, vet technicians, doctors, nurses, lawyers, construction workers, professional photographers, business administration professionals, teachers, real estate brokers, operating engineers, religious leaders, and law enforcement and animal control personnel.

There were almost 100 volunteers who were actively involved over the course of five months—from October 27, 2012, until the end of March 2013.

"This ultimately became one of the longest animal disaster response deployments in the history of the nation," says Beverly. "Throughout the deployment, there were no serious injuries to people or animals, nor were any animals lost or left unaccounted for."

Pet Safe volunteers were able to find homes and fostering arrangements for all the animals whose owners decided to give up their animals for adoption. What that means, says Beverly, is that "no animal that stayed at the emergency shelter had to be moved to another shelter situation where she/he had to live in a cage." Besides dogs and cats, other pets included bunnies, birds, turtles, ferrets, fish and guinea pigs.

Since their super-long Superstorm Sandy deployment, Pet Safe has returned to their former offices at Bidawee in Wantagh, New York. They're busy taking inventory and readying themselves for the next emergency that requires "Team Pet Safe" to respond. ●

(TOP RIGHT, DOG) IStock/NYPhotoboy

(LEFT) In his office, Bob Dennis logs in donations that the church has received. Saint Margaret Mary's Church (ABOVE) where Bob is the caretaker.

Bob Dennis

Caretaker of Saint Margaret Mary's Church knows the meaning of 'Love thy neighbor.'

Like so many residents in the tri-state area, Bob Dennis had his fair share of personal hardships during Hurricane Sandy—including a flooded home and lots of property damaged. But it was overwhelming acts of charity that most impressed Bob in the days following the storm. He saw many of them at his own Saint Margaret Mary's Church, where he was caretaker.

"I went down to the Church and donations started coming in. The Cardinal sent his representative from Catholic Charities with gift cards amounting to $145,000. Then we received about $23,000, which we dispersed to people in need," said Bob. "Shortly after, we received a couple of very large gifts, which swelled the Church's fund to about $246,000." The money was used to buy building materials for residents to repair their damaged homes, and the Church then applied to the Robin Hood Foundation for funding to purchase appliances—washers, dryers, refrigerators, etc.

At one point, a group of policemen and firemen got together and set up a barbeque, cooking food for whoever needed it. They called it the "Comfort Grill" and they continued this for several days. "As the days went on, the number of hungry people went from a few dozen at the start to over 700," said Bob.

The goodwill kept on coming: A sports player who just signed a sponsorship deal with Nike donated 400 pairs of sneakers; someone brought a refrigerated trailer loaded with ice to the work site.

One Good Samaritan volunteered to have a pre-Thanksgiving meal catered at the Church Hall the day before Thanksgiving. Another matched that offering by having a meal catered on Thanksgiving Day itself. "The number of persons wanting to have a Thanksgiving meal got so large," recalled Bob, "that we ended up having Thanksgiving on Friday as well—so we had a three-day Thanksgiving meal with all the trimmings," recalls Bob.

Several days later, a group of volunteers from the "Occupy Wall Street" movement came to help with repairs, supplying much-needed tools. "Almost immediately, UPS was delivering here all day long," said Bob.

Selfless acts defined the post-Sandy days and weeks at St. Margaret Mary's Church: people coming together to give of their time, money and effort to help out those in need. A classic example of "Loving thy neighbor." ●

The goodwill kept on coming: A sports player who just signed a sponsorship deal with Nike donated 400 pairs of sneakers; someone brought a refrigerated trailer loaded with ice to the work site.

Runners line up at the starting line at the Tunnel to Towers Run/Walk in New York City in September 2012.

TUNNEL TO TOWERS

Photos Courtesy Tunnel to Towers

ASSISTANCE STATEN ISLAND, NY

The Stephen Siller Foundation

Selfless Devotion To Help Others In Need Provides Help for Sandy's Victims.

On September 11, 2001, firefighter Stephen Siller had just finished the late shift at Squad 1 in Brooklyn. He heard on the scanner that a plane had crashed into the World Trade Center. He grabbed his gear, jumped in his truck and headed for the Battery Tunnel. When he got to the tunnel, he found it blocked. So – he picked up his 70 pounds of apparatus and ran through the tunnel. There were dozens of people who witnessed this heroic act and thousands who continue to honor his actions each year.

Stephen Siller was killed when the World Trade Center towers fell. He left behind five children – 9 months old to 9-years old.

After he died, Siller's siblings and wife decided to create the "Stephen Siller Foundation" and arrange an annual fundraising 5K run to "Follow in Siller's footsteps." This became known as the Tunnel to the Towers Run and every year on the last Sunday in September, the Brooklyn Battery Tunnel is shut down for thousands of runners.

"The first year we had 2,500 people. In 2012, we had more than 30,000," says Anthony Navarino, Director of Event Planning for Tunnel to the Towers.

According to Navarino, the Siller family was exceptionally close. Stephen Siller was orphaned at 10-years old and was cared for by his older brother and his wife. He worked for another brother and later married his childhood sweetheart, Sally. His death shattered the family. Instead of grieving, the family decide to celebrate Stephen's life by creating the Siller Foundation with the motto, "Let us Do Good."

Since 2001, the foundation has done a lot of good. In the early years, the funds raised were donated to special

(ABOVE, LEFT TO RIGHT) Tony Navarino, Joe Cardinale, Frankie Malerba Jr., Frank Malerba Sr and wife Jean Malerba pose for the camera at the Hurricane Relief Center in Staten Island. (ABOVE, RIGHT) The Stephen Siller Hurricane Relief Center at 2145 Hylan Boulevard in Staten Island, New York. In the days immediately after the storm, vehicles of all sorts lined Hylan Blvd to unload donated goods. A man all the way from Pennsylvania showed up with a truckload of diapers, wipes, and formula.

needs such as the burn center, scholarships, and orphanages. There is even a home on Staten Island called "Stephen's House" which houses many orphans. But after the military became involved in Afghanistan and Iraq, the foundation also became involved in helping amputees.

When Sandy hit, Frank Siller spoke to honorary chairman, ex-mayor Rudy Giuliani. Frank asked him "What do we do for these poor people." The Stephen Siller Foundation met with residents of Staten Island where 80,000 people were affected and said "We're going to help." Millions of dollars have been raised, dozens of homes have been rebuilt, and lives have been changed.

Frank Malerba is one of the ongoing volunteers with the Stephen Siller Foundation. "I was a rescue worker at Ground Zero so I had seen devastation. When I saw how much Tunnel to Towers was doing, I felt it was my calling to come here as a volunteer."

According to Joe Cardinale who also works for the foundation, the Sandy relief began with donations from people nationwide. "We have passed out millions of dollars' worth of products. We have received items from every state including Hawaii and Alaska," he said.

Navarino adds, "Sandy victims were just so happy we were helping them. We even sent families into New York City to eat at places like the Four Roses Restaurant."

The Siller family says they will keep rebuilding until everyone is back in their homes – even if it takes years.

> *Cardinale added, "The President shook the boy's hand and said he was sorry he had lost all his toys. The boy said, "Mr. President, you don't have to worry about my toys. Tunnel to the Towers gave me my favorite toy, a Matchbox set."*

Their focus continues to be the "Tunnel to the Towers" run so that it becomes bigger and better each year. There is also a renewed focus on making sure it is safe in the wake of the Boston bombing tragedy.

Still – the Siller family says it is the work of volunteers that keep this foundation "running."

"We couldn't help so many people without the help from others," Navarino says. "From individual volunteers to corporations like Gap, Vanderbilt, Home Depot and Baxter Baseball Bats. All the donations – large and small – make a difference."

Cardinale recalls one particular incident where a small donation made a huge difference. "There was a mother and her five-year old son who we met during the holidays. We had received truckloads of toy donations so I went and got a Matchbox set. The little boy's face lit up and his mother told me that was his favorite toy."

After that, this mother and son were one of the Sandy families who were handpicked to go and meet with President Obama in the White House.

Cardinale added, "The President shook the boy's hand and said he was sorry he had lost all his toys. The boy said, "Mr. President, you don't have to worry about my toys. Tunnel to the Towers gave me my favorite toy, a Matchbox set."

Tunnel to the Towers and the Siller family have made differences big and small and will continue to do so for many years to come. ●

Gerritsen Beach Cares

Passionate and driven, Mike Taylor works to help Hurricane Sandy victims regain their lives—losing 40 pounds along the way.

For Mike Taylor of Gerritsen Beach Cares, a non-profit group established to aid residents in need, the situation was dire for quite a while after Hurricane Sandy hit the area. "It was very, very bad," says Mike. "People had the impression that things were okay, but in actuality, there was a percentage of the population that is never going to recover." The big concern in Sandy's aftermath was the serious mold problem that set in—a problem that put at risk the health and well-being of hundreds in the area.

"People don't realize the severity of mold, but there were cases fairly early on after the storm where 25 percent of the local school was sick—with headaches, flus and coughs all as a result of—or exacerbated by—the mold growing in their homes," says Mike.

That problem was just the tip of the iceberg for Gerristen Beach Cares, which continued to make every effort to help residents in need. Says Mike: "We've been fortunate because in addition to our established volunteers, others stepped up to help. As a result, we've been able to service about 2,200 homes in our area that were affected."

In one instance, 1,800 homes were left in the dark for over two weeks, until Mike's group of volunteers, along with other concerned residents, held a community meeting and demanded to know what the electrical delay was and a plan for restoration. "The next thing we knew, Con Ed came in the following day and within the week, lights started coming on."

Mike personally had his own hardships to bear, with floods and damage to his property, particularly the basement apartment he lived in at his mother's house. The clean-up process involved a lot of time, effort and resources—removing everything, washing everything down, cleaning everything with bleach and water and then getting it dry. "At least the boiler was running so there was heat. I had to worry about the pipes freezing because as the winter set in, that was going to be the next big problem." It's something he worried about for many homes in the community.

The Sunday after the storm, Councilman Lou Fiddler organized a tractor trailer filled with supplies. A local organization called the Core Club donated their space and Mike and his team got to work disinfecting, cleaning and washing everything down twice in preparation for its arrival. The community was also contributing all kinds of resources including clothes, a commodity that is one of the most important, according to Mike.

"The supplies that came in were able to be distributed through the community. I had megaphones and would call out: "If you need cleaning supplies, food, wave to the car!" People would wave, and come over to the car, and we would give them what they needed. We were able to deliver the supplies to the 2,000 homes down here," he explained.

In the end, they distributed about 20 tractor trailers of supplies, with another seven diverted to other neighborhoods—such as Rockaway, and Coney Island. People's lives were at stake, and Mike and his group made it a point not to discriminate: "I don't care where you live, I don't care where you're from, I don't care what color you are, I don't care what religion you are. If you come to us and you need help, we will help you!" It's a philosophy that is not necessarily shared by other organizations that, according to Mike, "are worried only about the people within their organization's boundaries. With us, none of that matters."

Mike is proud of his "no discrimination" mentality but confesses that even under the best of circumstances, the injustices he sees can get to him. "There are people who are going to just take new stuff; maybe sell it or something. My focus is on the people who are sick and in need of help. I lost 40 pounds before the storm (I was on a diet) and then lost another 40 pounds since the storm…let me tell you this 'Hurricane Diet' is awesome. All you have to do is know that people are cold and sick and potentially going to die, and you don't have an appetite."

Despite the difficulties, there was a silver lining in the weeks and months following Hurricane Sandy—the overwhelming show of good works by so many caring individuals. Says Mike: "We've been visited by angels." ●

Mike Taylor

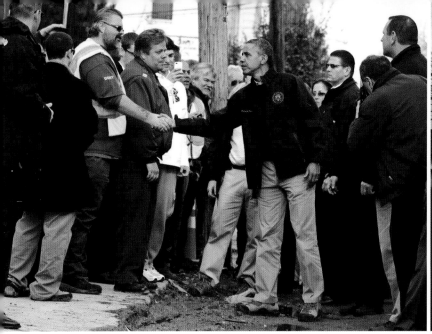

November 15, 2012 U.S. President Barack Obama (C) shakes hands with weary residents and workers along a street that was hard hit by Superstorm Sandy in Staten Island, NY.

January 17, 2013 Tony Murray and a group of volunteer carpenters from Dublin, Ireland help renovate a private residence flooded and damaged during Hurricane Sandy in the Rockaways, Queens, NY.

November 22, 2012 Volunteers at Saint Charles Church prepare Thanksgiving meals to be delivered to the victims of Superstorm in the Staten Island borough of New York City.

November 13 2012 New York Mayor Michael Bloomberg (C) stands outside after launching NYC Restore, a new initiative to assist those in areas hard hit in Far Rockaway, Queens, NYC.

To help her community, eleven-year-old Lucy Walkowiak hosted an internet cafe and charging station at her home in Hoboken, NJ. In the process she also raised over $2,000 for the American Red Cross.

November 10, 2012 Volunteers for New York City Mayor Michael Bloomberg's NYC Service initiative clean sand off the Coney Island boardwalk in New York.

March 21, 2013 Workers rebuild a boardwalk destroyed by Superstorm Sandy nearly five months ago, in Bay Head, New Jersey. The Jersey shore, a 127-mile stretch of beaches, small communities and famous icons, remains largely in shambles, with the traditional Memorial Day start to the summer season a mere two months away.

Reuters/Lucas Jackson

RISING FROM THE RUIN

"Restore the Shore" is the battle-cry of the Jersey oceanfront.

Daily life became uncertain and unpredictable for millions of people in the aftermath of SuperstormSandy. While the Seaside Heights rollercoaster – the "Jet Star" became the iconic image of the storm, it was the rollercoaster of emotions that families, first responders, business owners and families experienced that became the real story. The ups and downs eventually gave ways to a deeper resilience to fight back after Sandy. "Rising from the Ruin" became an inspiration to the rest of the world.

Bruce Springsteen's songs usually fill the summer air on New Jersey's boardwalks. In the summer of 2013, people now sang "Stronger than the Storm" – a commercial to entice tourists back to the beaches. "Restore the Shore" t-shirts could be seen everywhere. And volunteers – from as far away as Saudi Arabia – made Sandy-affected areas their destination of choice as they donated time and money to displaced victims.

It hasn't been easy. Rebuilding has been a messy and sometimes cold reality for many. While sorting through the FEMA red tape and countless hours talking with insurance agents, there remained as much uncertainty as there were still half-empty houses in the summer of 2013. But through the anger, sadness, and dismay, many say there were key elements that carried them through and made the impossible seem possible.

Says one Ortley, New Jersey homeowner Bob Depietri, "It's the simple acts of kindness that have helped me," he says. The New York ironworker adds, "As tragic as the September 11th attacks were, the world came together on "9/12. That's what we saw post-Sandy. There was a group from South Carolina who gave me a new set of kitchen appliances. They didn't even know my name."

Others have relied on their faith saying "faith is the one component that neither the flood nor the authorities could take away." And many say that rebuilding a more environmentally-friendly coastline that will be able to bear the brunt of another Sandy has given them strength. Says Katrina Wilson of Staten Island, New York: "I am heartbroken for what I have lost but I will raise the house and make the coastline safer. I feel like we're leaving the world a better place for future generations."

While Sandy shattered homes, she didn't shatter the human spirit.

January 7, 2013 (ABOVE) A bulldozer pushes sand near a boardwalk that was destroyed by Hurricane Sandy, in Ortley Beach, New Jersey. The sand was trucked in from as far away as 100 miles to rebuild the dunes that were destroyed by the Superstorm.

March 22, 2013 (LEFT) A heavy machinery moves large rocks to build a new sea wall, nearly five months after the landfall of Superstorm Sandy, in Bay Head, New Jersey. The Jersey shore, a 127-mile stretch of beaches, small communities and famous icons, remains largely in shambles, with the traditional Memorial Day start to the summer season a mere two months away.

January 7, 2013 (BELOW) Dump trucks unload screened sand for a bulldozer to push, as crews work to restore a beach that was heavily damaged by Superstorm Sandy, in Ortley Beach, New Jersey.

Spikes Seafood & Restaurant

For eighty-seven years Jakeabob's has been a gathering place of celebrities and ball players.

There is little left of nearly 72,000 New Jersey homes and businesses obliterated by Superstorm Sandy, but some popular eateries have vowed to rebuild so the throngs of summer vacationers who visit the Jersey Shore will have a place to go and see familiar faces.

Spikes Seafood & Restaurant in Point Pleasant was the first restaurant to open at the "shore" after nearly everything was destroyed. The fish market opened its doors in 1926 and was originally owned by Spike Stengel, brother of Yankee great Casey Stengel. The restaurant is known as much for its fresh seafood as for the famous faces who still frequent here. It's not unusual to sit next to a celebrity or ball player here.

But it wasn't just the owner, Steve Weinstein, who "pitched" in to rebuild but also the customers. With appliances destroyed, floors ruined and 50-foot boats pushed up to the back door, the impossible became the possible.

Weinstein says, "We opened two weeks after the storm and I was so proud to be the first restaurant to open its doors. I might own Spikes but she belongs to New Jersey and I'm just so grateful to everyone who helped."

Meantime, in Union Beach, Jakeabobs also reopened its doors five months after the storm. While there is little left of the homes, many of the front doors were saved and have now been converted into tables at the local restaurant.

Among the front doors now decorating Jakeabobs is one from the 150-year old house that was so badly damaged that it was featured on the cover of *Newsweek*.

Ironically, the owner of Jakeabob's is named "Dorr".... Angelita Liaguno-Dorr. Angelita says she was searching for a way to keep the spirit of Union Beach alive in the newly located restaurant so she thought of the doors to keep the town and its heartbroken residents "connected."

Dozens of newly painted doors now serve as tables and walls in the 70-seat restaurant. The simple doors from modest homes are poignant reminders of the terror from Sandy but also now serve as "doorways" to hope. ●

(ABOVE) **History comes alone.** One of New Jersey's oldest and most famous establishments reopens two weeks after Sandy with the help of patrons who volunteered hours to repair Spikes Seafood Restaurant. Spikes "served" more than food in the months after the storm. The Point Pleasant restaurant became a hub for victims to meet, get information and share a hug.

(RIGHT) **Doorways to Hope** Jakeabob's owner, Angelita-Liaguno-Dohr reopens her Union Beach, New Jersey restaurant using the front doors of damaged homes.

1. **March 7, 2013** Union Beach, N.J., New framing is in place on a home that is being elevated after having been damaged by Superstorm Sandy in late October. Photo by FEMA/Sharon Karr

2. **March 22, 2013** Belle Harbor, N.Y., U.S. Army Corps of Engineers continues to work with local communities to remove debris from houses destroyed by Superstorm Sandy. More than 5.5 million cubic yards of debris have been removed so far. Photo by FEMA/K.C.Wilsey

3. **June 4, 2013** Ortley Beach, N.J., Seven months after Superstorm Sandy touched down on the East Coast last fall, Ortley Beach can finally begin to rebuild their boardwalk, which was demolished by the storm. Photo by FEMA/Rosanna Arias

4. **June 21, 2013** Seaside Heights, N.J., New Jersey's First Lady, Mary Pat Christie, hammers the last nail into the new Seaside Heights boardwalk to mark its completion after Superstorm Sandy destroyed most of it last fall. FEMA contributed funding to the rebuilding efforts. Photo by FEMA/Rosanna Arias

5. **February 6, 2013** – The boardwalk, in Asbury Park, N.J., was destroyed during Superstorm Sandy. One hundred days after the storm, it is now being rebuilt. The historic Convention Hall lies at the other end of the boardwalk, which was also damaged by the storm. Photo by FEMA/Liz Roll

6. **Januray 17, 2013** Rockaways, Queens, New York. A FEMA representative surveys Lori Faillaci, left, about heat and power availability in a neighborhood damaged during Superstorm Sandy. Photo by Robert Nickelsberg/Getty Images

7. **February 20, 2013** Atlantic Beach, N.Y. At The Sands Atlantic Beach, workers continue to rebuild despite the cold temperatures. 130 cabanas were destroyed during Superstorm Sandy. They are aiming to reopen by the Memorial Day weekend. Photo by FEMA/K.C.Wilsey

8. **March 22, 2013** Residents of this Breezy Point, Queens, N.Y. neighborhood are rebuilding their homes damaged by Superstorm Sandy. Contractors are installing flood vents under this house to create permanent openings in the foundation walls that will allow water to move through the foundation of the house freely, thereby reducing water pressure applied to the structure. Photo by FEMA/K.C.Wilsey

9. **Feb. 15, 2013** Atlantic Beach, N.Y. At The Ocean Club, steel reinforced concrete pilings replace the old wood pilings that could not withstand the force of Superstorm Sandy. The new pilings are being placed 8 feet down and will raise the new structure above the flood level. Photo by FEMA/K.C.Wilsey

Waves from Hurricane Sandy slam into a Scituate, Massachusetts's seawall during mid-morning.

ACKNOWLEDGEMENTS

THE STUDENTS at Sterling East-Pascack Valley Learning Center in Airmont, NY had the longing to help the victims of Hurricane Sandy. They arranged a clothing drive and conducted a bake sale, which was a huge success. A truck full of clothing and $2,800 in profits was donated to charity. This pushed them to do more. This book is a result of that desire, and the students would like to express their appreciation to all those who helped make that vision a reality. This book was not completed by one individual or by a group of persons, but by a community of selfless volunteers. It is a combination of first-hand accounts, photos, desperate incidents and reminiscences of that day on the 29th of October, 2012. The coordination of a team was the only way this was accomplished.

Genuine thankfulness is extended to everyone who was willing to contribute information and donate material for this book. Thank you for sharing in the healing and rebuilding process.

Abbracciamento, Frances
Argentina, Joe
Barker, Wayne
Bowker, Eileen
Boyd, Tommy
Chase, Stuart
Cirigliano, Lou
Connors, Bill
Culleton, James
D'Antonio, Frank
Dennis, Bob
Dodge, Adam
Forster, Ronald
Gallo, James
Gillis, Katie
Harrigan, Ellen
Herguth, Bill
Grenke, Dyana and Michael
Joyce, Kim
Kamel, Joe
Kelly, Matt
Laberta, Robert

Ludomirsky, Achiau
Magovern, Brian
Magovern, Patrick
Nelson, Larry
Niebling, Chris
Olsen, Mary Ellen
Oppegaard, Michael
Paraison, Dominique & Robbin
Robertson, Kobe & Fay Robinson
Rose, Leon
Schoener, Abe
Schwarcz, Maxmilian
Snyder, Mark
Stoerger, Thomas
Taylor, Mike
Todd, Daniel
Trepp, Debra
Vanzant, Donna
Wagner, Pat
Zolatares, Mark

SCIENCE AND RESEARCH
AccuWeather

FDNY
Cassano, Salvatore
Herlocker, Tim
LaRocco, Robert
Lane, Joe
Mielnik, Kinga

US COAST GUARD
Gera, Nick
Henry, Chris
Todd, Daniel
Ustler, Katherine
Wishnoff, Dan

MTA
Lisberg, Adam

NYC OEM
Bruno, Joseph F.

NON-PROFIT ORGANIZATIONS
ArtsWestchester
First Response Team of America
Gerritsen Beach Cares
Hugo's Heroes
NY Says Thank You
Pet Safe
Stars of Hope
Tunnel to Towers

PHOTOGRAPHERS
Many thanks to all of the photographers and photo agencies who contributed their work to the pages of this book.

TRIBUTE

N JUNE 2013, nearly eight months after Sandy made landfall, the 44th victim in New York City was positively identified. Keith Lancaster was discovered inside a trailer on a junk-filled lot in Rockaway, Queens. Lancaster was using the trailer as his home when Sandy sent 5 feet of water churning through the neighborhood. When he was finally found, he was discovered lying next to a calendar marked October 29, 2012.

The death of Keith Lancaster marks Sandy's final victim. Altogether—she claimed 285 lives from the Caribbean to the United States. Everyone was a hero to someone.

Sandy not only shattered the lives of the families who lost loved ones, but she has forever changed the way millions close to the water's edge will live their lives in the years to come. She brought a newfound respect for the ocean after years of warnings went ignored. And she came with a costly pricetag: 63 billion dollars in damage was reported.

Sandy also stole precious memories. As Colleen Verile wrote about her family's home in Lavallette, New Jersey: "We celebrated 46 birthdays, 19 anniversaries, 8 graduations, and 23 Labor Day celebrations in our home. This is where we welcomed the golden days of summer and said goodbye to the season of boardwalk rides, sunsets and the hot, salty air. We lost our home but we will forever cherish our memories."

Like September 11, 2001, the world had changed for millions of people on October 29, 2012.

This book honors all the victims, their families, as well as the people who lost homes, businesses, and treasures. We also thank the heroes who saved lives and helped others rebuild in the months after Sandy hit. A portion of the proceeds from this book will be donated to several charities which will need continued financial assistance as the rebuilding continues for many years to come.

The week of October 23-30, 2012, was tragic for millions. But Sandy also brought some unlikely people together. One story is particularly poignant.

In the Long Island village of Patchogue, Sandy joined an entire community together including a grieving mother and a Parks Department employee. Brian Waldron has worked for the village of Patchogue for 23 years. While cleaning up debris from the storm, he found a message in a bottle.

The message was written on a scrap of paper and placed into a ginger ale bottle by a 10-year old girl. The child who cast that bottle into the bay is dead. Sidonie Fery died in a fall in Switzerland at the age of 18. She was Mimi Fery's only child.

The bottle only traveled a mile or two westward from where it was deposited and was found tangled in broken docks, boating gear and a spectrum of sea trash. But inside was a treasure.

The note had a message, "Be excellent to yourself, dude."

It was a quote from Sidonie's favorite movie, "Bill and Ted's Excellent Adventure." But the note also had a phone number so what otherwise would have been a worthless piece of trash became a priceless memento to Sidonie's mother. The Patchogue workers called the number and returned it to Mimi Fery.

In July 2013, hundreds from the seaside village honored the memory of Sidonie and all the victims of Sandy. A plaque was placed near the bridge at Patchogue, Long Island Beach Club, where the bottle was discovered.

It reads: "Be excellent to yourself, dude."

The plaque also reads: "I learned that even though someone is very small they may have a big heart."

And so – to all those whose hearts were broken by Sandy, we dedicate this book to you. And for those who gave their hearts to rebuild and help others, we thank you.

— Mia Toschi

New Dorp Beach neighborhood of Staten Island, New York.

Sunrise the morning after Sandy,
Long Beach, Long Island, New York

Photograph by Christina Tisi-Kramer